# The Role of the Professional Football Manager

Considering the celebrity-like status of the professional football manager, surprisingly little is known about their role. This book provides an unprecedented insight into the chronically insecure and vulnerable world of the contemporary professional football manager. Drawing on original research, it explores the complex challenges and skills of the football manager in an increasingly cut-throat, ruthless and results-based industry.

Written by a former professional footballer, the book examines how personal contact, networks and the social mobility of different actors within the industry influence various elements of the manager's role. Beginning with an overview of literature on football management, its subsequent chapters each examine a key aspect of a manager's work, such as:

- managerial recruitment and appointment;
- the role of previous playing experience and formal education;
- the assessment and recruitment of players;
- maintaining discipline and control;
- maintaining successful working relationships with players, coaches, agents, club directors and owners.

Shedding light on the inner workings of the football industry, this book is fascinating reading for any serious football fan and an essential resource for any student or scholar researching football, sport management or sport business.

**Seamus Kelly** is a Lecturer in, and the Director of, the Centre for Sport Studies at University College Dublin, Ireland. He previously played professional football in the English Football League (Cardiff City) and the League of Ireland (Bohemians, Longford Town, St Patrick's Athletic, UCD). His research examines many aspects of professional football.

# Routledge Research in Sport, Culture and Society

**69 Sport, Medicine and Health**
The medicalization of sport?
*Dominic Malcolm*

**70 The International Olympic Committee, Law, and Accountability**
*Ryan Gauthier*

**71 A Genealogy of Male Body Building**
From classical to freaky
*Dimitris Liokaftos*

**72 Sport and Discrimination**
*Edited by Daniel Kilvington and John Price*

**73 Seeking the Senses in Physical Culture**
Sensual scholarship in action
*Edited by Andrew C. Sparkes*

**74 The Role of the Professional Football Manager**
*Seamus Kelly*

**75 The Rugby World in the Professional Era**
*Edited by John Nauright and Tony Collins*

**76 Sport and English National Identity in a 'Disunited Kingdom'**
*Edited by Tom Gibbons and Dominic Malcolm*

**77 Phenomenology and the Extreme Sport Experience**
*Eric Brymer and Robert Schweitzer*

# The Role of the Professional Football Manager

Seamus Kelly

Routledge
Taylor & Francis Group

LONDON AND NEW YORK

First published 2017
by Routledge
2 Park Square, Milton Park, Abingdon, Oxon OX14 4RN

and by Routledge
711 Third Avenue, New York, NY 10017

*Routledge is an imprint of the Taylor & Francis Group, an informa business*

© 2017 Seamus Kelly

The right of Seamus Kelly to be identified as author of this work has been asserted by him in accordance with sections 77 and 78 of the Copyright, Designs and Patents Act 1988.

All rights reserved. No part of this book may be reprinted or reproduced or utilised in any form or by any electronic, mechanical, or other means, now known or hereafter invented, including photocopying and recording, or in any information storage or retrieval system, without permission in writing from the publishers.

*Trademark notice:* Product or corporate names may be trademarks or registered trademarks, and are used only for identification and explanation without intent to infringe.

*British Library Cataloguing-in-Publication Data*
A catalogue record for this book is available from the British Library

*Library of Congress Cataloging in Publication Data*
A catalog record for this book has been requested

ISBN: 978-1-138-69773-7 (hbk)
ISBN: 978-1-315-51817-6 (ebk)

Typeset in Sabon
by Keystroke, Neville Lodge, Tettenhall, Wolverhampton

Printed and bound by CPI Group (UK) Ltd, Croydon, CR0 4YY

# Contents

| | | |
|---|---|---:|
| | Introduction | 1 |
| 1 | The history of the professional football manager | 14 |
| 2 | Managerial recruitment and appointment | 40 |
| 3 | Previous playing experience and formal education | 62 |
| 4 | The assessment and recruitment of players | 79 |
| 5 | Maintaining discipline and control | 99 |
| 6 | Agents | 118 |
| 7 | Directors and owners | 138 |
| | *Conclusion* | 151 |
| | *References* | 156 |
| | *Index* | 176 |

# Introduction

## Introduction

This is the first academic book of its kind that endeavours to provide unprecedented insight into, and a more reality-congruent understanding of, the role of the contemporary professional football manager. This is achieved by incorporating empirical data in what has been a largely ignored context to date. It is surprising, considering their celebrity-like status and their central role in the game, that so little is really understood about football managers and their role (Perry, 2000a). It is certainly the case that, despite a growing body of autobiographical and journalistic literature on football management (Ronay, 2010; Carson, 2013; Bolchever & Brady, 2004; Grant & Robertson, 2011; Calvin, 2015), academic literature on the professional football club manager remains rather limited. Pawson (1973) explored football management and the managers' jobs at club level, and Rogan (1989) focused on managerial 'greats' of the post-war period. Carter (2006) outlined the historical origins of football management, while Bridgewater (2010) examined aspects of football management. Useful though these studies are, none of them have explored the strong persistence of tradition, and the resistance to modernisation, in the role of the professional football manager. Moreover, there are few empirically based academic texts that examine the role of the contemporary professional football manager. Carter (2006) identified one possible reason for this academic neglect, arguing that the difficulties that researchers face in obtaining access to this closed social world concern their outsider status. Specifically, Carter stated that 'in football there is distrust towards the outsider' (Carter, 2006: 23).

Internationally, the English Premier League attracts considerable interest. Professional football in the UK has been the subject of significant transformation and commercialisation and has become an increasingly pressurised financial environment (Morrow & Howieson, 2014) due, in part, to an escalation of revenue from media rights deals. Aided by its commercialisation and media hyperbole, the professional football industry in general and the English Premier League in particular attract global attention whereby its players and managers are viewed as celebrities and cultural icons. More specifically, professional football managers, such as José Mourinho, Arsène Wenger and the recently retired Sir Alex Ferguson, have become pivotal figures at almost all British football clubs (Morrow & Howieson, 2014). The widely held assumption among football fans and the general public is that these managers travel an inevitable path to fame and glory. However, behind the scenes a different picture exists and the path to becoming a professional football manager is rarely so uncomplicated. Professional football management, particularly at the highest levels, is a results-based industry in which chronic insecurity, vulnerability, rejection and a psychological fear of failure are prominent characteristics of managers' daily lives (Carter, 2006). Professional football managers are also the subject of considerable scrutiny from industry stakeholders such as media and fans concerning team selection, style of play and player recruitment strategies in particular. More recently, managers have been faced with a working environment epitomised by interference from owners and directors and are viewed as marketable assets and commodities who are bought, sold and discarded by clubs and their owners once their managerial value dissipates. The overall powers and role of English Premier League managers, in contrast to those of managers at lower-league clubs, have become more narrowly defined, while the growing power of agents has had important implications for both the role and security of the football manager.

## Methodology

Located within the interpretive paradigm, this book utilises semi-structured interviews conducted between 2004 and 2006 with 25 players, 20 managers and five football agents. Further interviews were conducted between 2010 and 2015 with key stakeholders in professional football in the UK. More specifically, in 2011 four interviews were conducted with English Premier League club coaches and in 2014 interviews were conducted with the head of international player recruitment and two academy managers at an English Premier League club. In 2015, semi-structured interviews with four players with experience of the academy structure at English Premier League and Championship clubs were conducted. The careers of those interviewed ranged between the extremes of outstanding professional success and more modest success. For example, some of the interviewees had played or managed in the English Premier League and at senior international level, while others had spent their entire careers in the lower leagues in the UK and Ireland. Attempts to penetrate 'beneath the veil' (Reynolds & Herman, 1994) and provide a rich, thick description of the interview as a lived experience (Gubrium & Holstein, 2002; Geertz, 1997) and interactional encounter (Riesman & Benney, 1956) involved capturing and noting much of the emotional context of the interview, as well as non-verbal and paralinguistic communication such as gestures, facial expressions and hand movements (Denscombe, 1998).

Between 2012 and 2015, a number of participatory action research workshops were conducted. The first workshop involved 12 current and/or former English Premier League players, all of whom possessed considerable senior international experience. The second workshop involved over 40 participants who were coaches and managers currently employed at an English Premier League club. The purpose of these research workshops was to examine aspects of player management, recruitment, assessment and development, and they lasted between 90 and 120 minutes. Two management education workshops, lasting between 120 and 150 minutes, were conducted as part of the UEFA Pro Licence with 17 current football managers. During these workshops, aspects of football management such as player assessment and management, managing conflict and dealing with stakeholders were examined. The final stage of data collection, conducted between 2013 and 2015, involved over 20 action research workshops incorporating over 300 participants. The purpose of these workshops was to critically evaluate how academic literature could assist in the assessment, development and management of players. The participants were coaches, managers and player development officers currently employed within national football associations or within the league structures in the UK or Ireland. The coaching and managerial careers of the participants ranged between the extremes of outstanding professional success and more modest success. More specifically, some of the participants had coaching and managerial experience at English Premier League academies, national football associations and underage international level, while others had spent their entire careers at grassroots or youth level in the lower leagues. The participants possessed various levels of coaching experience and qualifications from the UEFA B Licence up to and including the UEFA Pro Licence. The reliability and trustworthiness of data collected from participatory action research is enhanced when participants are actively involved in the knowledge production process (Bray *et al.*, 2000). More specifically, participants were given individual and group tasks incorporating open-ended unstructured questionnaires, discussion sheets and various task activities which preceded an opportunity to engage in group dialogue, debate and knowledge production within the group (Park, 2001). Because action research is done 'with' research participants rather than being done 'for' or 'to' them (Ristock & Pennell, 1996), all of the research workshops were participatory in nature. These workshops facilitated participants' learning through the process of engaging in practice-based inquiry (Frisby *et al.*, 2005) involving critical evaluation and discussion of their experiential knowledge of this closed social world. Despite the extremely time-consuming and laborious nature of participatory action research, the workshops were enlightening from both researcher and participant perspectives in terms of the open discussion and debate. The key learning processes adopted by the author in the workshops involved observing, listening, questioning, feedback and combining challenge and support within a critical dialogue (Higgs & Titchen, 2000).

Because an efficient and well-structured data management system is critical to tracking, assessing and documenting the data available and the analysis applied to it (Miles & Huberman, 1994), the data analysis procedures adopted in this research were drawn from guidelines developed for inductively analysing semi-structured interviews and open-ended unstructured questionnaire data (Gratton & Jones, 2010; Miles & Huberman, 1994; Moustakas, 1994; Hycner, 1999; Tesch, 1990; Côté *et al.*, 1993). First, interviews were transcribed verbatim and then subjected to a process of inductive content analysis, which organised the data into a number of interpretable and meaningful units of meaning or themes. This involved a 'progressive process of classifying, comparing, grouping and refining groupings of text segments to create and then clarify the definition of categories, themes, codes, labels and tags' (Fossey *et al.*, 2002: 728–9) or units of general meaning. In other words, inductive content analysis organised the raw data into interpretable and meaningful themes and categories that were generated from the data (Miles & Huberman, 1994; Tesch, 1990). Meaning units were then grouped into higher-order categories that naturally clustered together. This involved examining units of relevant meaning and eliminating those that were clearly irrelevant to others previously identified. The next step involved categorising each meaning unit into a lower-order theme based on its content. In this step, meaning units were tagged independently, then similar tags were grouped and labelled with lower-order themes that best described the cluster of tags (Côté *et al.*, 1993). The penultimate step of the data analysis involved identifying the source of each unit of general meaning. In this regard, a number of deviant themes were identified that were unique to individual participants. The identification of deviant cases can not only strengthen the validity of the research (Gratton & Jones, 2010; Silverman, 2005) but, as we shall see in the results section, can also be more enlightening. The final stage of analysing the data involved the selection of appropriate verbatim statements associated with each common theme. These verbatim statements were designed to produce 'a composite description of the essence of the experience' of the participants (Creswell *et al.*, 2007: 252). The data were analysed manually rather than by using computer analysis software such as NVivo.

The sample of interviewees was a convenience sample, based on the personal contacts of the author, and this sample was then expanded on a 'snowball' basis, with interviewees being asked after their interviews if they knew of other players or managers who they thought might be prepared to be interviewed. Because snowball sampling has been criticised as tending to produce a homogeneous sample (Fossey *et al.*, 2002), 'extreme case sampling' was adopted to enhance both the completeness of the information gathered and the credibility of interpretations generated (Crabtree & Miller, 2002). The selection of interviewees based on their considerable experience or knowledge proved useful in the selection of managers and players in particular. Though not always possible, it was decided that the most appropriate players to interview were those with considerable experience of working with professional football managers. In terms of an adequate sample size, the objective was to continue interviewing until 'saturation' occurred (Biddle et al., 2001; Crabtree & Miller, 2002). Formulating an appropriate sample can be problematic (Gilmore, 2001) and, in an attempt to ensure its appropriateness and adequacy (Fossey et al., 2002), it might be argued that the data collected were fairly representative of professional football players, managers and coaches more generally. At the outset of each interview, interviewees were given an assurance of anonymity. This was designed ot reduce interviewees' anxieties about discussing former or current players and/or managers.

The presentation of the data takes the form of narrative analysis in which attempts are made to identify meaning, make sense of interviewees' and workshop participants' lived experiences and experiential knowledge of professional football and communicate this in as objective a manner as possible. It is important to note that, in telling their story, the author's experiential authority and interpretive omnipotence (Smith & Sparkes, 2009) are utilised in communicating interviewees' and workshop participants' embodied lived experiences through the eyes of the objective researcher. Thus, the aim is to interpret the ways in which people – in this case professional football players, managers and coaches – perceive reality and make sense of the world of the professional football manager (Smith & Sparkes, 2009). In addition, throughout the book, numerous references are made to aspects of football management in other countries such as Germany, Holland, Italy, Spain and Portugal. There are two central approaches running throughout the book.

## Research approach

The first approach, which utilises the concepts of Max Weber (1964, 1968), examines traditional aspects of the role of the contemporary football manager. For example, such elements of the football manager's role include the imposition of fines on players, an emphasis on learning on the job, a lack of formal management training and the widespread assumption that previous playing experience is sufficient preparation for entry into football management. In addition, traditional forms of authoritarianism allow football managers an unusually high degree of autonomy in defining their own role and placing few constraints on the appointment of their support staff. Many of Weber's ideas are developed in *Economy and Society* (1968), which is not only a presentation of typologies or models, but is also crammed with historical explanations. Unfinished and fragmented though it may be, *Economy and Society* is 'one of the intellectual foundation stones of the academic discipline of sociology' (Camic *et al.*, 2005: 3). Before examining Weber's concept of domination, there are a number of themes within his work that need to be identified. Weber argued that science concerns 'itself with the interpretive understanding of social action and thereby with a causal explanation of its course and consequences' (Weber, 1968: 4). Central here is Weber's emphasis on 'interpretive understanding' and 'causal explanation', and the connection between the two. What this means is that first we must engage in an interpretive understanding of people's behaviour, and second we must use this understanding in order to provide a causal explanation of an individual's pattern of behaviour. In trying to understand the motives that guide people's behaviour, it is necessary to penetrate the subjective understanding of individuals. Thus, for Weber, 'understanding goes further by asking not only why an action has taken place but also why a certain behaviour pattern continues to be followed' (1962: 16). Weber (1964: 88) proposed '*Verstehen*' as one possible method for achieving this interpretive understanding of the motivations behind people's choice of action. In other words, *Verstehen* allows us to get into the inner sense of how individuals subjectively interpret and choose what they are doing (Allen, 2004). Such *Verstehen* or understanding can be achieved in two ways: direct observational understanding of those individuals whose behaviour is being studied (*Aktuelles Verstehen*) and explanatory understanding (*Erklarendes Verstehen*), which involves trying to grasp the motives and subjective meanings of the various actions (Weber, 1964: 94). Thus, in trying to identify why an action occurred, we place the action in a 'sequence of motivation, the understanding of which can be treated as an explanation of the actual course of behavior' (Weber, 1968: 9). In attempting to trace people's 'sequences of motivation', Weber developed the concept of the 'pure' or 'ideal' type.

Ideal types are conceptual constructs that are ideal in the sense that they are abstractions from, and simplifications of, concrete social reality. Such ideal types are designed to capture the essential characteristics of a particular phenomenon and can be used in objective explanations of social action. For Weber, the ideal type, as a conceptual tool, is to be used as a yardstick to examine empirical cases and to determine the probability that people will follow one course of action and not another. Hence, Weber's ideal types are actually similar to what Menger referred to as 'realistic-empirical types' (Camic *et al.*, 2005: 17), which facilitate determining the causes that lead to differences between the ideal type and empirical reality. As Weber stated:

> whatever the content of the ideal type . . . it has only one function in an empirical investigation. Its function is the comparison with empirical reality in order to establish its divergencies or similarities . . . and to understand and explain them causally.
>
> (Weber, 1949: 43)

Thus, the discrepancies between the ideal type and the actual forms of the behaviour pattern being investigated become the object of theoretical interest. For Weber, the development of social theory should always be subservient to, and propelled by, the construction of causal explanations. While such causal analysis does not produce universal laws of human society, it does however generate statements of tendency regarding the nature, course and consequences of human action. Weber makes it clear that 'an ideal type must be at least in the realm of probability and not merely possible; that is, there must be found somewhere at least a close empirical approximation' (Weber, 1962: 14). In this regard, the construction of an ideal type may also be viewed as a working hypothesis, which, until its realistic worth has been proved by observation, may, like any other hypothesis, be of little analytical value (Weber, 1962). Moreover, the ideal type is purely descriptive and should not be misused to explain the data it reveals. Therefore, the ideal type is an instrument for classification and is useful for the systematic arrangement of several categories in each of which all observations – qualitative – that are covered by its description may be grouped together. In this regard, it is possible to construct ideal types and then classify the data according to their proximity to one of these types rather than to others (Weber, 1962). Thus, the researcher's task concerns determining in each individual case the extent to which the ideal type approximates to or diverges from reality. Thus, what deviates from the ideal type is important because it contributes to our understanding of the adequacy of the ideal type. More specifically, the task at hand is to determine if the contemporary football manager approximates to or diverges from this ideal type. More important, though, is an understanding of *why* a particular ideal type approximates to or diverges from a particular ideal type.

As mentioned, Weber developed typologies to categorise the different forms of social action. One of the most famous of these is the typology of domination, which provides the cornerstone for his celebrated concept of legitimate authority. An intrinsic part of Weber's vision – which drew on the philosophy of Friedrich Nietzsche – was that power and domination were at the heart of all human relations. For Weber, domination, which he saw as a special case of power, was 'the probability that certain specific commands (or all commands) will be obeyed by a given group of persons' (Weber, 1968: 212). Weber's concept of domination deals with legitimation and administration in the triangle of ruler, staff and the population at large (Roth & Schluchter, 1979). Thus, any relationship of domination has three elements: the ruler, the administrative staff and the ruled. However, Weber only focused on the first two: the relationship between the ruler and his or her administrative staff. In addition, Weber paid particular attention to the material interests of the staff, the organisational principles according to which they operate, and their wider relationship to the ruler.

Weber ignored any structures of authority that relied more on coercion than on willing compliance and concentrated solely on the authority of office: the authoritarian power to issue commands. He assumed that all sources of power require a belief in its legitimacy: people obey authority because they view it as legitimate. Thus, if a system of authority has survived for any appreciable length of time, this implies that it has won its legitimacy. Thus, the relationship between ruler and ruled hinges on the belief of both sides in the legitimacy of the authority that exercises domination. What Weber deemed important was that in any given case the particular claim to legitimacy 'is to a significant degree and according to its type treated as valid; that this fact confirms the position of the persons claiming authority and that it helps to determine the choice of means of its existence' (Weber, 1968: 214). Put simply, legitimacy occurs when a subordinate group accepts commands as 'valid norms' out of a genuine belief in the worthiness of those in control. More specifically, orders from a ruler appear to be met with a positive commitment to obey where such obedience is willingly given and is not simply a matter of external appearance. Weber identified three ideal types of legitimate domination: rational, traditional and charismatic. Each system or type of domination attempts to establish and cultivate the belief in its legitimacy. However, as Weber (1964: 325) noted, 'according to the kind of legitimacy which is claimed, the type of obedience, the kind of administrative staff developed to guarantee it, and the mode of exercising authority will all differ dramatically'. Hence, it is useful to classify the types of authority according to the kind of claim to legitimacy typically made by each. Weber's types of domination are, of course, ideal types and, as he (cited in Bendix, 1962: 329) pointed out, all forms of domination occurring empirically are 'combinations, mixtures, adaptations, or modifications' of the charismatic, the traditional and the rational types.

Despite the considerable strengths of Weber's work, some limitations of his writings become clearly visible when one considers an individual's personal contact network. Weber's sociology is characterised as being methodologically individualistic, whereby 'action exists only as the behaviour of one or more' individuals and society is 'never more than the plurality of interactions of individuals within specific social contexts' (Weber, 1968: 13). Thus, for Weber the unit of analysis was the individual and he viewed groups and institutions as merely the outcome of the social action of individuals. He certainly did not ignore collective institutions or groups, but his analysis of these social formations was linked to the behaviour of the individuals within these institutions. Weber recognised that mainstream economics needed to be complemented and not substituted with an institutional analysis (Parsons, 1935). In contrast to the methodological individualism of neoclassical economics, Granovetter's new economic sociology marked a shift in the relationship between economics and sociology. He argued that economic institutions are socially constructed and that economic action is embedded in ongoing networks of social relationships. Therefore, one obvious and fruitful approach to complement the work of Weber would incorporate examining how personal contact networks influence aspects of the manager's role.

Professional football managers are enmeshed within personal contact networks with current/former players, coaches, managers, directors and agents. These networks prove useful in the search for employment and in the recruitment of prospective players and backroom staff. Thus, in developing the argument that mobility in the professional football industry is socially embedded and facilitated through personal contacts, the theoretical frameworks of embeddedness and trust are utilised (Granovetter, 1973). Granovetter (1974) coined the term 'strength of weak ties' to refer to the power of indirect influences outside the immediate circle of family and close friends that serve as an informal employment referral system. Granovetter (1973: 1361) defined the strength of a tie as a 'combination of the amount of time, the emotional intensity, the intimacy (mutual confiding), and the reciprocal services which characterize the tie'. Reciprocity is the giving of benefits and gifts to another in return for benefits received and facilitates the development of bonds of trust (Molm, 2010). Weak ties therefore allow an individual to reach beyond his small, well-defined social circle in order to make connections with parts of the social structure not directly accessible to him. Weak ties also serve as channels through which 'ideas, influences and information socially distant from ego may reach him' (Granovetter, 1973: 1371). Sociologists and economists tend to conceptualise trust as a phenomenon that exists within and among institutions (Lewicki & Wiethoff, 2006). Granovetter's notion of embeddedness has some connection with Anthony Giddens' description of 're-embedding' processes that provide 'encounters and rituals which sustain collegial trustworthiness' (1990: 87). Giddens conceptualised trust as an organising principle, or social mechanism, that coordinates expectations and interaction in relationships between managers and staff within institutions. Thus, trust is not purely viewed as an attitude or state of mind, as micro-level approaches suggest, but instead conceptualised as a decision that embedded social actors make in light of specific institutional arrangements. Institutions are structural arrangements represented by formal and informal rules of behaviour to which individual and collective action is orientated (Giddens, 1984). Therefore, while acknowledging organisational and institutional bases or antecedents of trust (Zucker, 1986), this research focuses on micro-level interpersonal trust mechanisms and processes. This is important because trust is a deeply contextualised phenomenon (Granovetter, 1985). More specifically, one important aspect of examining multi-level approaches to trust concerns utilising qualitative approaches that reveal and assist our understanding of the 'constitutive embeddedness of actors' behaviour in the institutional environment' (Bachmann, 2011: 203) and the micro-level mechanisms, practices and processes that shape an individual's trust intentions (Wang & Gordon, 2011; Fuglsang & Jagd, 2015).

One important issue raised by Granovetter (1973) concerns the temporal and developmental dimension of ties and personal contacts. Moreover,

Granovetter (1973: 1378) correctly argued that 'treating only the strength of ties ignores, for instance, all the important issues involving their content'. This suggests that there are additional concerns regarding the nature and strength of personal ties. For example, we know that developing personal contact networks may be conducive to generalised trust and commitment (Seippel, 2008) and that trust, respect and openness are key aspects in building relationships (Misener & Doherty, 2009, 2013). Moreover, in terms of the developmental sequence of network structures over time, we know that social capital is embedded in social relations and that the development of social norms, networks and trust may be facilitated through social interaction (Granovetter, 1985). Therefore, one distinguishable aspect of the strength of personal ties, which contributes to determining whether they are strong (embedded ties) or weak (arms-length), is trust. Thus, in addition to the strength of the tie, it is important to examine the nature and content of personal contacts in terms of trust. Embedded relationships can produce a number of benefits such as greater knowledge sharing and can be viewed as sources of assistance or guidance that 'are tied, implicitly or explicitly, to the development of trust and affective bonds' (Molm, 2010: 125).

However, once developed, these personal contact networks are not self-sustaining but the 'result of a process of construction and recomposition' (Bidart & Degenne, 2005: 283) that must be maintained over time through reciprocity and the sharing of information. In this regard, considerable academic attention has been focused on the conditions that promote the emergence of 'bases of trust' (Mayer *et al.*, 1995; Lewicki & Bunker, 1995; Miles & Creed, 1995; Zucker, 1986). These bases of trust influence individuals' expectations about other people's trustworthiness and their willingness to engage in trusting behaviour when interacting with them. Rotter (1971, 1980) argued that, in the context of people's general predisposition to trust other people, they extrapolate from their early trust-related experiences to build up general beliefs about other people. So, while 'trust is based on reputation and that reputation has ultimately to be acquired through behaviour over time' (Dasgupta, 1988: 53), trust is also a function of individuals' cumulative interaction concerning information that is useful in assessing other people's dispositions, intentions and motives, by which predictions can be made concerning their future behaviour (Boon & Holmes, 1991; Solomon, 1960). Thus, the emergence of trust concerning people's judgements about other people's trustworthiness is anchored, at least in part, in their prior expectations about other people's behaviour. Such expectations may change in response to the extent to which subsequent experiences either validate or discredit them and can be construed as an important form of knowledge-based or personalised trust in organisations (Lewicki & Bunker, 1995).

It is well known that interpersonal trust develops through repeated interactions with other people and is based on familiarity, interdependence and continuity in relationships (Granovetter, 1985; Shapiro, 1987). More specifically, thick interpersonal trust, also known as 'characteristic-based trust' (Zucker, 1986) and 'particularised trust' (Uslaner, 2002), is embedded in strong emotional relationships and is generally restricted to people from similar backgrounds. This makes the development of trust less risky and produces tight-knit networks that do not link people to members of out-groups (Cook, 2005; Uslaner, 2002). Thin interpersonal trust, on the other hand, involves people whom an individual may not know well or with whom he or she has not had a great amount of interaction or personal dealings and involves trusting members of out-groups. In general, thin interpersonal trust, also known as 'process-based trust' (Zucker, 1986) or 'generalised trust' (Uslaner, 2002), can be viewed as a 'standing decision to give most people, even people you don't know, the benefit of the doubt' (Putnam, 2000: 136). Such trust has to grow and is 'as much the outcome of a relation as the basis for it' (Nooteboom & Six, 2003: 23). As a result, a relationship in which trust is not predetermined requires the relationship to be 'worked upon' by all parties, which involves a 'mutual process of self-disclosure' (Giddens, 1990: 121). What this means is that if trust is evident, it provides the basis for a relationship and it may be deepened to provide the means for further extending the relationship.

Despite a growing body of literature exploring multi-level approaches to organisational trust (Rousseau *et al.*, 1988; Bachmann & Inkpen, 2011; Schoorman *et al.*, 2007; Bachmann & Zaheer, 2006), research perspectives integrating both the institutional bases of trust and interpersonal trust relations tend to be neglected (Fuglsang & Jagd, 2015; Bachmann, 2011; Wang & Gordon, 2011). In response, this book examines how specific social practices facilitate the development of interpersonal trust relations between individual actors in an industry that is characterised by chronic uncertainty, paranoia and distrust. The aim is to provide a better understanding of how trust-building processes can assist in the development of appropriate methods and practically relevant management knowledge in terms of trust-building and trust repair strategies (Bachmann, 2011; Lewicki & Wiethoff, 2006).

## Book structure

Chapter 1 contextualises the role of the football manager by identifying key developments in the history of professional football and how they have impacted on the manager's role. In addition, this chapter serves as a brief overview of the academic literature on football management.

Chapter 2 examines the role of informal personal contact networks in the recruitment and appointment of professional football managers. This chapter also highlights the appointment of backroom staff and the lack of detailed job descriptions in professional football. A recurring theme throughout this chapter is how the authority of the football manager continues to be based on traditional forms of authoritarianism, which allows managers an unusually high degree of autonomy in defining many aspects of their role.

Chapter 3 develops points touched on in the previous chapter and examines the role of previous playing experience and coaching qualifications in the appointment process. In particular, this chapter identifies managers' hostility towards education and coaching qualifications in professional football. The chapter also highlights the lack of formal management training and the widespread assumption within football that previous playing experience is sufficient preparation for entry into management. A picture emerges of an industry managed largely in isolation from external management influences by those who are ill prepared, insular in outlook and drawn from a narrow segment of society.

Chapter 4 examines what is arguably a football manager's most important role: the process of assessing current and prospective players and recruiting reinforcements. This chapter identifies how managers utilise 'gut feeling and instinct' in the assessment and recruitment of players. Related to this is the considerable importance of how a player's attitude and off-field behaviour influences player recruitment and assessment. While the use of formal and informal contact networks are utilised in the recruitment of players, the chapter also sheds light on the investigative and in some cases questionable practices employed by some managers in trying to elicit information concerning a player's background and off-field behaviour.

Chapter 5 examines an issue that is linked to the previous chapter: how football managers manage and maintain control of players. More specifically, this chapter focuses on the ways in which disciplinary codes are established by managers and the sanctions that are imposed on players for breaches of club discipline. The chapter also highlights the arbitrary character of these disciplinary codes and the central part played by intimidation and abuse – both verbal and physical – as aspects of managerial control within football clubs.

Chapter 6 seeks to examine an issue that naturally emerges from the previous chapter: the central role that agents play in the contract negotiation process and the unethical side of their behaviour. The central issue at the heart of this chapter concerns the recent shift of power from clubs to players and their agents and how this shift impacts on the role of the contemporary football manager.

Chapter 7 explores the working relationship between managers and club directors and owners. A key issue at the heart of this chapter concerns the recent shift in balances of power between managers and directors/owners. Related to this is the influx of foreign owners and its impact on the role of the contemporary football manager. The chapter examines the perceived motives of owners and directors and their interference in issues traditionally seen as falling within the manager's role.

The conclusion draws together the key academic ideas and themes examined in the above-mentioned chapters. In addition to reviewing the main themes previously presented, the chapter identifies the key findings of this study and provides recommendations for further research.

## Conclusion

I bring to this academic research the context of my experience as a former elite professional football player, having played in the English Football League (Cardiff City) and in the League of Ireland (Bohemians, Longford Town, St Patrick's Athletic, UCD). It is argued that this combination of academic excellence in research and the reality of my experience as an elite athlete leaves me uniquely placed to publish an insightful academic text on the notoriously closed world of the professional football manager. Sociological research is 'about making visible that which is invisible' (Liston, 2004: 7) and 'mak[ing] known something previously unknown' (Elias & Dunning, 1986: 20). Sociological research is not so much about discovering 'absolute' or 'law-like' explanations as an attempt to develop an understanding of people's behaviour and the difficulties they face in their everyday lives. Therefore, in attempting to achieve *Verstehen* (Weber, 1964) regarding the role of the contemporary football manager, the author avoided 'going native' (Denzin & Lincoln, 1998) by adopting an appropriate balance between involvement and detachment (Elias, 1987) throughout the research process. Insightful advice from an academic mentor and colleague drew my attention to the dangers that the 'emotional reactivity that comes with involvement poses the biggest threat to developing a reality-congruent view of the social world, because it lessens the likelihood of researchers being able to bring their critical intellectual faculties under control' (Waddington, 2000: 4). It is hoped that this research has successfully achieved an appropriate balance between involvement and detachment and presented a sufficiently detached and reality-congruent understanding of the role of the contemporary football manager.

# Chapter 1
# The history of the professional football manager

**Introduction**

This chapter chronologically traces the development of the role of the professional football manager since the game's professionalisation in 1885. More specifically, the chapter consists of different sections examining key developments in the game's history that have impacted on the role of the manager. In tracing the development of the role of the football manager, the chapter examines the academic literature on professional football in general and football management in particular. Because 'British football has a powerful sense of its own history' and 'the culture of the game is replete with reminders of the past' (M. Taylor, 2008: 1), it is necessary to examine the origins of football management for, as with social phenomena more generally, it is not possible to adequately understand contemporary structures without reference to the ways in which those structures have developed (Elias, 1987).

**1885–1920**

Prior to the 1880s, football was viewed by many as a casual pastime for 'schoolboys and wealthy sportsmen' (Tischler, 1981: 31). However, this was to change dramatically with the advent of professional football in 1885 (Tischler, 1981). Considerable controversy accompanied the transition from amateurism to professionalism in football, much of which was social rather than economic (Vamplew, 1988). Specifically, this was a period of great status anxiety and deepening social division in British society (Carter, 2006; Vamplew, 1988; Mason, 1989; Tischler, 1981), and football was not impervious to the wider class confrontations in society. Considerable tension existed between players and club owners (Mason, 1989), as many owners regarded professionalism as a necessary evil. During this period, the vast majority of club owners and directors regarded players as socially inferior and treated them with disdain, and the notion of 'masters' (club owners and directors) and 'servants' (players) was particularly evident (Carter, 2006). As a result, many club directors and owners were reluctant to have any direct dealings with players and utilised intermediaries (club secretaries) when dealing with players. As we shall see, these club secretaries began to assume an increasing number of responsibilities, particularly in the recruitment and development of players.

## The professionalisation and unionisation of football

Between 1880 and 1920, football experienced unprecedented rationalisation and bureaucratisation (Mason, 1989). In 1863, the English Football Association (FA) was formed and assumed responsibility for the game's governance, administration and organisation (Mason, 1989). In 1871, the English FA established the FA Cup competition, which was subsequently imitated elsewhere by the Welsh FA in 1877, the Scottish FA in 1874 and the Irish FA in 1881 (Garnham, 2002; Mason, 1989). Then, in 1880, the English FA developed a universally accepted and recognised – by both players and clubs – set of laws that governed all aspects of the game (Mason, 1989). In 1887, the English FA created a new competition, the Football League, and by 1924 there were four divisions, each comprising 22 clubs (Mason, 1989). However, the overwhelming concern of the English FA between 1880 and 1885 was the notion of professionalism. In 1885, the English FA agreed, subject to strict labour market controls, to legalise professionalism (Crolley & Hand, 2006; Mason, 1989). As a result, three different types of labour market controls existed: restrictions on the recruitment of players, limitations on the movement of players between clubs, and the maximum wage (Dabscheck, 2000; Cairns *et al.*, 1986).

In terms of player mobility, the retain-and-transfer system governed the movement of players between clubs (Sloane, 1969; Dabscheck, 1986; Stewart, 1986; Stewart & Sutherland, 1996) and remained in many respects a powerful symbol of clubs' control over professional players (Mason, 1989; Sloane, 1969; Maguire, 1999; Horne *et al.*, 1999).[1] The English FA formally introduced benefit payments and signing-on fees while the maximum wage, £4 per week, came into effect for the 1901/02 season (Dabscheck, 2000; Taylor, 2001; Mason, 1989). The principle objectives of the maximum wage were to reduce wage bills and, in tandem with the existing retain-and-transfer system, encourage equality of competition by preventing 'a small number of rich clubs monopolising all the talent' (Mason, 1989: 160). Both the retain-and-transfer system and the maximum wage severely limited the economic freedom and income of players (Dabscheck, 1986) and became a key feature of the industrial relations of football and the battleground for numerous disputes between football's governing bodies and the Players' Union, which was established in 1907 (Taylor, 2001; Dabscheck, 2000).

## The ownership and structure of Football League clubs

During the 1880s, the majority of professional football clubs were managed by committees and boards of elected directors consisting of individuals from the local business community (Mason, 1980; Tischler, 1981). These committees and boards of directors who managed Football League clubs, in addition to running their own businesses, had a number of responsibilities such as the finance and administration of the club, player recruitment and team selection. In short, their work encompassed a number of duties that are nowadays associated with the role of the contemporary football manager. Following professionalisation in 1885, a number of England's leading football clubs converted to limited liability companies (Garnham & Jackson, 2003) and, by 1914, the majority of football clubs had adopted this structure (Tischler, 1981).

Because many club owners and directors were unable to combine the demands of managing a club and running their own businesses, they began delegating responsibilities to secretary-managers, match secretaries and financial secretaries. The early 1900s witnessed the emergence of the secretary-manager, with John Cameron employed as the player/secretary-manager of Tottenham Hotspur in 1899. It is difficult to define what, or more importantly who, constituted a manager and the title of secretary-manager had a number of different meanings. Regardless of the different job titles, these secretary-managers were responsible for administrative duties, salary negotiations and the assessment and recruitment of players. Thus, the role of the secretary-manager developed in a kind of piecemeal fashion and responsibilities and roles associated with the position varied considerably between clubs. The secretary-manager figures of the early 1900s all had a variety of backgrounds; some were qualified accountants and others possessed teaching experience, while Derby County and Tottenham Hotspur both employed secretary-managers who possessed formal management training. However, in general the educational levels of these early secretary-managers were relatively poor and few if any secretary-managers had any previous playing experience (Carter, 2006). In this regard, the ideology of the time was one that drew on Britain's practical tradition of 'learning by doing', in which knowledge was passed down through the generations. Thus, secretary-managers were not viewed as specialists but more a product of British management's practical tradition, which eschewed the concept of professional management training and vocational education (Carter, 2006; Walvin, 1986). The job was not seen as a 'profession' and did not require any formal training or qualifications. During this period, there was no set job description for a football manager and despite the delegation of a number of responsibilities to secretary-managers, directors still maintained considerable control over player recruitment and team selection at their clubs (Young, 1968; Carter, 2006).

### The recruitment of players

Throughout this period, football club secretaries, committee members and directors began to recognise the importance of recruiting star players in the process of building successful teams and were all involved in the process of player recruitment. In terms of player recruitment, some football clubs placed advertisements in local newspapers, while other clubs developed networks of personal contacts that informed them of promising players. In addition, a number of football clubs, such as Aston Villa and Middlesbrough, employed agents to recruit players (Carter, 2006), while the practice of poaching players from rival clubs was common (Garnham, 2002; Mason, 1989).

Following the introduction of transfer fees in 1891, the first £1,000 transfer fee for a player was recorded in 1905 (Dabscheck, 2000) and by 1928, the transfer record had reached £10,000 as clubs bid against each other to secure the services of star players. In trying to compete with other football clubs, most clubs developed financial incentives and bonus schemes in addition to the basic wage to attract star players (Taylor, 2001). In addition, it was not uncommon for football clubs to offer players jobs and tenancies in local pubs (Collins & Vamplew, 2000; Dixon & Garnham, 2005). However, paying players raised a number of contentious issues. Taylor (2001) argued that the maximum wage shaped the occupational culture of English football in the twentieth century. Specifically, one aspect of the culture of professional football – arguably one that is still prevalent today – concerned illegal and under-the-counter payments, which were widely practised by the majority of football clubs (Tischler, 1981; Taylor & Ward, 1995). Nearly all Football League clubs in some way broke the maximum wage agreement. In 1905, Manchester City were punished for illegal payments and bribery and in 1912 Leeds United were closed down by the English FA for making illegal payments to their players (Mason, 1989).

## *The discipline and control of players*

During this period, maintaining control and discipline of players was a contentious issue. Few, if any, directors had any experience of how to manage players and usually drew on their own professional background. However, some players were now viewed as football clubs' main assets and directors and secretary-managers attempted to maintain a balance in terms of how they disciplined and treated them. It was widely felt that players needed discipline in relation to both their on- and off-field behaviour. For example, in 1893, Fred Rinder of Aston Villa commented that 'drink was the curse of the team' (Carter, 2006: 40). Alcohol consumption was seen as a major problem during this period and most football clubs had strict guidelines pertaining to players' (excessive) consumption of alcohol (Dixon & Garnham, 2005). Some football clubs adopted more covert means to monitor their players' drinking activities, such as Aston Villa, who resorted to spying on players (Carter, 2006), while West Ham United fined players whom they thought might have a drinking problem (Vamplew, 1988). The most obvious way to control and discipline players was through their pockets. Most football clubs fined players a day's wages if they did not train and players were also liable to a suspension and/or a forfeit of their daily meals. However, the rules and regulations reflected the attitudes within the particular football club's management and so varied from club to club.

### Training and match preparation

The growing competitiveness of football and football clubs' desire to improve team performance in particular influenced the emergence of the football manager. Towards the end of this period, the training and preparation of players had little to do with the secretary-manager as more and more football clubs began to employ specialist trainers. However, it was uncommon for trainers to possess any football knowledge and their man-management skills were poor (Carter, 2006). The club trainer was employed to train and supervise the players and was viewed by many as 'a quasi-NCO figure' (Carter, 2006: 39). This recognition of the importance of preparation and training of players was not new; a number of football clubs had employed specialist trainers, quite often from athletics, as early as the 1890s. However, in 1899, John Cameron published a book that focused on the preparation, conditioning and training of players, which reflected a growing awareness of the need for a more scientific approach to the training and coaching of players. One consequence of this development was that more consideration was given to the players' physical well being, diets and the treatment of injuries. However, despite these new ideas, many improvements took place on an ad-hoc basis. During this period, club trainers and secretary-managers were requested to report the condition of the players to the clubs' boards. There is evidence to suggest that around the 1900s, some club directors were beginning to leave the assessment and recruitment of players to their trainers and/or secretary-managers, whose authority was nevertheless still limited.

### The role of the media

The popularity of football during this period was enhanced by the expansion of the newspaper industry. In particular, from 1887 the *Athletic News* – whose editor, J. J. Bentley, was president of the Football League – became the voice of the professional game (Mason, 1989). Newspaper coverage of professional football had major implications for the role of the secretary-manager. At this time, football clubs used the press as a means to promote themselves and communicate important signings and ticket arrangements. More specifically, the secretary-manager became the main link between the press and the football club. This was important as reports on football clubs previously focused on directors, the majority of whom were still responsible for picking the team. However, due to the game's increased levels of competitiveness and the growth in newspaper readership, scapegoating developed. Quite often, supporters wanted someone to blame for poor performances on the pitch and these frequently angry displays were viewed with some disquiet by club directors, who ultimately bore the responsibility for the team's performance. Thus, in an attempt to escape from the position of responsibility, directors were now anxious that some public figure other than them should become the focus of the passionate interest that people took in their football club. As a result, secretary-managers now experienced considerable attention and scrutiny from the press and some used this media attention as a means to cultivate their own reputation. As a result, by 1920 secretary-managers had gradually gained greater importance and a number of them attempted to forge a professional identity using the expanding press coverage to help achieve this aim. The gradual growth in the importance of the secretary-manager was not only recognised by the press but, more importantly, by football clubs. It has been argued that George Ramsey, the secretary of Aston Villa, was football's first paid manager (Carter, 2006); however, Tom Watson – who, during his time at Sunderland and Liverpool, was always referred to 'as a manager pure and simple' (Carter 2006: 31) – was probably the game's first prototype football manager. Although early football managers did not enjoy the high profile of their modern counterparts, they began to form a distinct group within the game and in 1907 the Secretaries' and Managers' Association was formed.

## 1920–1940

By the 1920s, a number of ex-players were appointed as secretary-managers and there were signs by the early 1930s, due largely to the increased press coverage, that the secretary-manager was becoming more closely associated with team performances (Wagg, 1984). During this period, both the practice of managerial scapegoating and the prevalence of illegal payments as a means of circumventing the maximum wage continued (Mason, 1989).

### *Managerial roles and duties*

The majority of secretary-managers saw little of their players during the week and quite often it was the trainer who took charge of the team. Instead, much of the secretary-managers' time involved administrative tasks, watching games and liaising with club directors and owners regarding the recruitment of players. However, Major Frank Buckley and Herbert Chapman began to adopt a more professional approach in the management of team affairs. Contemporary football management is 'based largely on the pioneering work of Buckley and Chapman, two of the most influential managers of the first half of the twentieth century' (Young, 1968: 182), who realised the direction that football was taking and instigated a changing ideology towards football management.

Buckley possessed considerable managerial experience with Norwich City, Blackpool and Wolverhampton Wanderers and viewed football as a serious business in which the local football club was viewed as an asset (Wagg, 1984). Buckley trained and coached the players personally, and is often referred to as the first 'tracksuit manager'. In addition, his youth policies and football nurseries became the envy of many managers and he possessed the knack of buying young players, developing them and then selling them on for a profit (Young, 1968). Furthermore, Buckley introduced new training routines and watered pitches, and investigated the possibilities of psychologically analysing his players (Young, 1968).

Chapman viewed football as being 'too big a job to be a director's hobby' (Wagg, 1984: 49) and his most important legacy was to establish the manager as the most important person at a football club (Pawson, 1973). Chapman's ideology incorporated professionalism and he was responsible for introducing numbers on players' jerseys, the use of floodlights and tactic boards in pre-match talks. He also pioneered the use of team talks and denounced uninformed criticism of his players, and his 'intimate knowledge of the opposition enabled him to plan measures and counter-measures' (Young, 1968: 178). Chapman's previously unheard-of style of man-management was unique. For Chapman, if a football manager was to get the best out of his players, 'he must share their troubles, help them with any difficulties they had and, within the limits of discipline, be their pal' (Wagg, 1984: 51). However, most styles of football management were authoritarian and characterised by a tough, harsh, unsentimental masculinity. While Chapman's style of management was authoritarian (Young, 1968: 170), he did develop an intimate understanding of each individual player and his relationship with other players on the football pitch. Chapman viewed the football manager as being responsible for picking the team, and organising victory (Carter, 2006). For Chapman, a player's attitude and off-field behaviour were considered as important as his playing ability. In this regard, when recruiting players, Chapman would always enquire about a player's behaviour, and preferred 'decent fellows' in the dressing room (Wagg, 1984: 49). Significantly, Chapman recognised the importance of delegating duties to specialist staff and appointed a physical fitness specialist, Tom Whittaker, 'who brought all the resources of modern science' when treating the players' injuries (Young, 1968: 175).

Chapman, Buckley and others like Bob Hewison (Bristol City), Harry Curtis (Brentford) and Jimmy Seed (Charlton Athletic) modernised football management and gave players a greater sense of involvement and of their own professionalism. As a result, a number of secretary-managers began to work more closely with their players, and players began to expect as much. However, it took considerable time for Chapman's ideas to be accepted and it was not until the 1960s and 1970s that his approach to management manifested itself in the game. While the above-mentioned changes did signal some recognition of the growing importance of the manager's role, other contributing factors were also significant.

## The role of directors and owners

Since the game's professionalisation, considerable hostility had existed between players and club directors (Mason, 1989; Carter, 2006). Much of the players' hostility concerned directors' curt and condescending treatment of them, their total ignorance in relation to football matters, their total control over player recruitment and team selection and their limited understanding of the media's and public's growing expectations on players (Carter, 2006; Wagg, 1984, 1998). As a result, players sought an independent managerial figure who was well versed in football matters and began complaining if their manager did not fit the bill; in 1931, Blackburn Rovers' players signed an expression of dissatisfaction with their manager Bob Crompton. Similar developments occurred at Tottenham Hotspur and Everton following the appointment of Chapman's successor at Arsenal in particular. Secretary-managers were also quite hostile towards club directors and owners and began looking for greater autonomy in decisions concerning team selection and player recruitment (Russell, 1997). The success of Chapman, at both Huddersfield Town and Arsenal, gradually persuaded some club directors to appoint a football expert to run the team (Mason, 1989). However, it wasn't until the mid-1950s that the football manager became a prominent figure as most club directors and owners were still responsible for team selection.

## The role of the media

The advent of radio coverage of professional football in the 1930s resulted in a significant increase in media attention and the public's growing interest in match reports, players' off-field affairs, proposed transfer dealings, player injuries and team selection (Crolley & Hand, 2006). Moreover, secretary-managers became the media's central focus due in part to players being forbidden in their contracts to speak to the press and the media viewed club directors and owners as inappropriate and in some cases too high-handed and resentful of their intrusion (Carter, 2006). This suited the increasingly publicity-conscious secretary-managers, who drew great satisfaction in communicating their own personal views, while for those secretary-managers who were viewed as powerless clerks at their clubs, it provided a means of chastising their respective directors. More importantly, by the 1930s, the secretary-manager, through the press, was becoming more closely associated with the team's performance (Russell, 1997; Wagg, 1984). During this period, 'public relations became part of a manager's job' (Carter, 2007: 222) and a mutually beneficial relationship between secretary-managers and the media steadily developed (Wagg, 1984).

### Coaching

There was limited acceptance of the importance of coaching in professional football from players, owners, administrators and the media. In response, following his appointment as English FA secretary in 1934, Stanley Rous set about changing these attitudes towards coaching in England. Despite the English FA's refusal to acknowledge the importance of coaching qualifications, Rous began initiating coaching courses, reasoning that formal qualifications would help raise the status of football as a profession. Despite hostile attitudes, there seemed some, albeit slow, acknowledgement of the importance of coaching and management in professional football following the English FA's invitation to Herbert Chapman in 1933 to accompany the national team as their unofficial manager. While the introduction of coaching schemes by the English FA during the 1930s and 1940s reflected an attempt to professionalise and modernise management in professional football, Rous was acutely aware of the rapid progress being made in football coaching in other parts of the world. However, it took a considerable time before the English FA, media and players would accept the idea of coaching in general and with the England team in particular.

## 1940–1970

During this period, three factors had a significant impact in shaping the role of the football manager: the promotion of coaching by the English FA, the abolition of the maximum wage and the growth in media coverage of professional football.

### Coaching qualifications

In 1946, Walter Winterbottom was appointed as the English FA's first-ever Director of Coaching. Winterbottom's previous playing experience with Manchester United and his results as England manager disarmed much of the criticism and hostility towards coaching. The campaign to introduce coaching qualifications began with the English international team. However, the views of the English media and international players towards coaching were mixed, with some established international players relishing Winterbottom's coaching and training methods while others, such as Stanley Matthews, were rebuked by the English FA for publicly attacking them (Wagg, 1984). Much of the hostility of the general public, media and players towards coaching was a reflection of their distrust towards anything theoretical. Furthermore, coaching challenged the widely held belief among players that English football was based on individual skill and masculine toughness; English football was perceived to be the best in the world, where players learned all they needed to know about the game on the cobbled streets.

During this period, there existed a certain reluctance to embrace reform and change, not just in professional football, but in English society in general (Carter, 2006), resulting in English football being considered old-fashioned in style and outdated in comparison to other more developed and technically superior teams abroad (Carter, 2006; Crolley & Hand, 2006). During the early 1960s, the majority of the more successful international teams and European clubs were only interested in appointing managers who possessed coaching qualifications. Moreover, in 1946 the Italian FA introduced its first-ever football management course, a clear recognition of the importance of formal coaching and management qualifications. However, it was not until the 1960s that the English FA attempted to establish similar coaching and management courses. This was partly in response to the growing pace of managerial turnover during this period (Allera & Nobay, 1966). The English FA felt that such courses would better prepare the vast number of ex-players who had secured management positions. However, the English FA was frustrated in its efforts, due mainly in part to managers' reluctance to participate in these courses. As a result, like their counterparts in industry, football managers continued to learn their job 'on the job' (Carter, 2006: 48). In addition to coaching qualifications and in line with other professions, the English FA attempted to establish a formal appointments procedure for football managers. However, such proposals were rejected by club directors and owners, who did not want to be restricted in terms of whom they could appoint as managers, while managers were not in favour of a system that may have decreased their chances of securing management positions.

Despite little media interest in England's defeat by the USA in 1950, England's home defeat to Hungary in 1953 and subsequent defeat in the return game, styled the 'disaster on the Danube', was attributed by the press to the England team's lack of coaching and tactical preparation. The media angrily attributed England's failure to win the World Cup in 1958 and 1962 to poor selection and insufficient preparation. The manager and those responsible for the administration of the team were blamed and subjected to increased media scrutiny. This, it is argued, was the symbolic moment when it became clear that English football would have to 'go back to school' and adopt a more scientific approach. It was inevitable in such a climate that Winterbottom's successor, when he resigned in 1963, would be chosen from among England's Football League club managers. As a result, Alf Ramsey, an ex-international full back, was appointed. Ramsey had the qualities now widely prescribed by directors, players and the press: 'a distinguished playing career, tactical competence and success' (Wagg, 1984: 93).

While the general public's hostility towards coaching diminished and many English international players began to develop a more positive attitude to the idea of coaching qualifications, hostility towards the English FA's coaching initiatives among Football League club managers was still prevalent for a number of reasons. While such hostility was partly a reflection of the perceived threat to managers' authority from players (Carter, 2006), it was also due to the fear that people with no professional playing experience, but who possessed coaching qualifications, might now secure management and coaching positions at Football League clubs. As a result, from the 1940s a strong occupational ideology developed among professional football managers. This ideology involved an often fierce contempt for outsiders or, more specifically, those with limited previous playing experience. During this period, the ideology of 'We are the professionals – what do *they* know?' was frequently invoked and the notion of 'insiders' and 'outsiders' was particularly evident among both players and managers (Wagg, 1984: 184). For example, Peter Taylor stated that, as Middlesbrough players in the 1950s, both he and Brian Clough 'resented schoolmasters who posed as authorities on a game of which they had no professional experience' (Wagg, 1984: 93). In this regard, the widely held view among players and managers was to 'leave professionalism to the professionals'. However, during the 1970s and 1980s there were some managers with limited professional playing experience, such as Bertie Mee (Arsenal), Richard Dennis (Newcastle United) and Lawrie McMenemy (Southampton). In particular, McMenemy struggled to gain the respect of players, and a close associate of McMenemy stated:

> to be accepted as a manager of a League football team, you have got to have been a professional player. Lawrie's broken through this and I would say it's a hell of a breakthrough you've got to make because players don't basically admire someone coaching them football that hasn't been a player of some standing.
>
> (Wagg, 1984: 96–7)

By the end of the 1960s, a growing number of managers began acquiring coaching qualifications, which represented an ideological change in the perception and importance of coaching in football, and professional football now began to acquire greater respectability by adopting the rhetoric of efficiency, professionalism and science (Wagg, 1984). Moreover, the growing emergence of the 'tracksuit manager' was a reflection of the growing demand by players and club owners of a more professional and scientific approach to training and, although not a prerequisite for the job, some club directors began requesting coaching qualifications and questioned prospective managerial applicants about how much time they intended to spend working with the players. Similarly, players began demanding more specialist knowledge on the training field and resentment of desk-bound managers grew. As the number of managers with coaching qualifications grew, expectations that they could produce results were obviously legitimised. The general consensus was that if a team won a game, then it was because of some managerial master plan; if they lost, then it was associated with inadequate coaching.

## The role of the media

In 1955, the establishment of 'commercial television (ITV)' raised the profile and changed the perception of the football manager in a number of ways (Carter, 2007: 224). First, while television coverage of professional football attracted considerable public interest, programmes devoted to football, such as *Grandstand*, began incorporating managers in their commentary panel. Second, television's increased involvement in football partly usurped the role of the radio and press. The advent of competition in football's media coverage stimulated an increase in the extent and quality of football coverage in the print media with the football manager becoming the obvious focus (Crolley & Hand, 2006). The growing importance of the football manager was particularly evident following England's success in the 1966 World Cup; England were referred to by the press as 'Ramsey's winning team' (Crolley & Hand, 2006: 24). Elsewhere, other managers such as Sir Matt Busby, Bill Shankly and Don Revie received similar media attention. Both the increased media attention and the assumption of greater importance (Crolley & Hand, 2006) resulted in the manager becoming one of the most prominent figures in professional football (Mason, 1989) and, with the possible exception of Herbert Chapman, the notion of managers as celebrities was inaugurated in the 1960s (Wagg, 2007).

However, the involvement of television in professional football created managerial problems, particularly at the highest level. For example, with increased revenue from television and advertising, participation in European club competitions – previously discouraged by the English FA – became a universal aspiration among managers in the top league. Moreover, due to the escalation of players' wages, 'getting into Europe' now became a priority for leading English clubs (M. Taylor, 2008) and top-level managers faced greater expectations to qualify for European competitions. In addition, the media had highlighted that other national football associations had given full control of team matters to their managers. Tom Finney's description was typical: 'Appoint the right man. Give him full control. If his team fails, then let him take the consequences. If his team succeeds, give him the credit' (Wagg, 1984: 89). Crucially, the media now linked managerial responsibility and team performance. This idea gained acceptance not only on the terraces but also among club directors and owners, who were now more demanding and had greater expectations of their managers, making the practice of scapegoating and the apportioning of blame to unsuccessful managers common practice in the 1960s.

## The abolition of the maximum wage

Since its formation in 1907, the Players' Union had fought for the abolition of both the maximum wage and the retain-and-transfer system. However, no real progress was made in relation to either of these issues until the late 1950s, when tension and hostility escalated between players and clubs in general and between the Football League and the Professional Footballers' Association (PFA) in particular (Stewart, 1986). Factors that contributed to the reform of both the maximum wage and the retain-and-transfer system are well documented. First, the appointment in 1958 of the PFA's new chairman Jimmy Hill was seen as the catalyst for those who wished to end the maximum wage. Second, since the introduction of the maximum wage, the exodus of players from the English game began around 1910 and a number of leading British players such as Jimmy Greaves, Denis Law and John Charles took up offers to play professional football abroad, attracting considerable media attention. Third, prior to the Eastham case, the maximum wage had become increasingly discredited. In particular, there were numerous allegations concerning financial irregularities and illegal payments at a number of football clubs (Harding, 1991). The prevalence of illegal payments or 'boot money' considerably strengthened the hand of the PFA (McArdle, 2002).

In 1961, following a threatened strike by players, negotiations between the PFA and the Football League resulted in the abolition of the maximum wage (Mason, 1989; Dabscheck, 1986, 2000). In 1963, following the landmark George Eastham case,[2] the retain-and-transfer system was found to be an unreasonable restraint of trade, though not illegal (Dabscheck, 1986). The Eastham case resulted in only limited reforms to the domestic transfer system and 'didn't result in the game being shaken out of its myopia and complacency' (McArdle, 2002: 265), as football clubs still had the power to decide whether or not they would retain or transfer a player (Dabscheck, 1986; Mason, 1989). The 'transfer' aspect of the retain-and-transfer system remained largely untouched until the Bosman ruling in 1995. The freedom of players was still very limited and it was not until 1973 that the 'retain' aspect was finally abolished and 'freedom of contract established for the 1978–79 League season' (Speight & Thomas, 1997: 223). Players now had a greater degree of freedom than ever before and disputes between football clubs and players could be referred to the newly formed 'Independent Transfer Tribunal' (McArdle, 2002: 265), as it was not uncommon for a 'vindictive' football club to bring a player's career to a premature end by adhering to the registration scheme (McArdle, 2002).

As a result, the number of professional players employed by the 92 Football League clubs fell by approximately 20 per cent (Mason, 1989), players' wages escalated throughout football and in the top division in particular (Walvin, 1986; Mason, 1989) and transfer fees increased dramatically (Sloane, 1969). The financial management of many clubs was deficient (Walvin, 1986) and over half of all Football League clubs were now operating at a loss (Sloane, 1969). In addition, the Chester Report identified that by 1966/67 the ratio of apprentices to players had dropped considerably. Therefore, costly though training young players was, it appeared to be less costly than employing senior players (Sloane, 1969). Finally, because football clubs could not hold on to top players against their will, clubs began offering longer contracts to those players considered more important (McArdle, 2002). As a result, many club directors and owners now felt that these well-paid professionals required closer attention by someone who had played and knew the game and demanded greater general care and tactical preparation accorded to what were now viewed as important club assets. This new culture of commercially liberated professionalism in the football world could no longer support a manager distanced from his players, in his traditional suit and tie. Thus, the manager's place was now seen to be on the training ground and managers were now expected to 'man-manage'.

## Player management

The balance of power had already begun shifting towards players even before the lifting of the maximum wage as players were driving a hard bargain in relation to boot money and bonuses. Club directors were now placing greater demands on managers to negotiate with and persuade players, especially those who were considered more valuable, to stay with the club. Most managers had limited preparation or training in the skills of negotiating and bargaining and drew primarily on their previous experiences as players.

In addition, club managers were now dealing with a smaller number of well-paid players (Walvin, 1986) and quite often had to deal with feelings of jealousy and resentment among players concerned about the considerable wage differences that the abolition of the maximum wage brought about. Club managers now became closer to their playing staff and their relationship with players changed somewhat. Many club managers during this period differed from the early authoritarian styles of management epitomised by Stan Cullis and Major Frank Buckley. Taylor (2006: 215) noted that many post-war managers 'combined an authoritarian hand with a personal touch, perhaps reflecting the less deferential nature of society after 1945'. For example, Sir Matt Busby was viewed as a manager who balanced the task of disciplining players with a greater concern for their welfare and was disturbed by the 'seemingly unbridgeable gulf between players and management' and also of the 'indignities that were heaped on players' (Wagg, 1984: 167). However, most club managers were anxious to maintain some social distance between themselves and their players, and despite closer relationships between managers and players, the style of management during this period was still authoritarian (Carter, 2006; Pawson, 1973). For example, Brian Clough at Derby County and Don Revie at Leeds United developed publicly protective relationships with their players; however, behind the scenes they were viewed by players as ruthless, authoritarian and strict yet ferociously loyal, combining elements of a regimental sergeant-major and an elder brother in the relationships they formed with players.

## Player recruitment

During the 1960s and 1970s, the more successful players were exposed to increased media attention and greater financial rewards. Because players' association with gambling, womanising and boozing attracted considerable media attention, managers were careful to avoid signing any potential troublemakers who would negatively affect their clubs' image. For example, George Best's off-field behaviour, rather than his excellence on the pitch, became the focus of considerable press and television attention (Mason, 1989). In addition, the tougher and more competitive professional game of the 1960s and 1970s could not accommodate as many heavy drinkers. As a result, many club managers began investigating players' backgrounds in the assessment and recruitment process. For example, one First Division manager said, 'I've never yet signed a player . . . that I haven't done a great deal of homework on regarding his character and his home life and what he is like off the field as well as on' (Wagg, 1984: 173). With rising transfer fees, managers began developing networks of contacts with other managerial colleagues and former/current players and trainers to safeguard against making poor player recruitment decisions (Wagg, 1984; Mason, 1989) and for advice concerning possible football management opportunities. Many managers in the 1960s and 1970s owed their jobs to the likes of Sir Matt Busby, Don Revie and Joe Mercer. In 1968, the English FA and the Football League banned players from using agents; however, by 1978 most players were employing agents to represent them, flagrantly disregarding the ban despite the potential formal sanctions they may have faced (Mason, 1989).

## Managerial appointment and turnover

Throughout this period, managerial scapegoating continued and between 1945 and 1975 802 managers lost their jobs. In the search for managerial replacements, club directors and owners also utilised their own contact networks while a number of coaches/trainers were promoted internally. Another trend that emerged was that of the position of 'general manager', or 'director of football', as it is commonly referred to today. Quite often, if managers were the subject of media pressure and public dissatisfaction but club directors were reticent to fire them, an ill-defined post of general manager was created to facilitate them staying on the payroll.

By the 1960s, the manager had become a dominating figure in professional football (Mason, 1989) and in 1961 the English FA defined the manager's responsibilities to include the signing of players, the negotiation of players' salaries, the organisation of the club's scouting system, the planning of tactics and coaching and the overall management of all staff (M. Taylor, 2008). In 1965, a survey of 76 clubs found that at 73, one manager was responsible for all spheres of the club's activities – playing, administrative and financial – with only three employing a general manager (Allera & Nobay, 1966). However, at many clubs, directors still controlled the selection and recruitment of players (Carter, 2006; M. Taylor, 2008). Prior to his appointment at Liverpool, Bill Shankly was bluntly told by directors that they reserved the right to change the team, while at Manchester United Sir Matt Busby fought repeated attempts from the club chairman to interfere in player trading decisions.

## 1970–2000

Following events such as the Heysel Stadium disaster, the Bradford City fire and the Hillsborough tragedy, professional football experienced a 'revolution' (Taylor, 2006) in which it was transformed, restructured and commercialised due mainly to the influx of new owners and increased television revenue.

### Coaching and management qualifications

In 1969, the English FA, in partnership with the Football League and the PFA, initiated its first-ever course in professional club management at Loughborough University. However, by 1973, after only two intakes, the Football League withdrew its support for the programme. Similarly, in 1982, formal managerial training initiatives such as the Advanced Coaching Diploma were discontinued due to a lack of numbers. The English FA was acutely aware of how much it lagged behind its European counterparts in the provision of coaching qualifications. For example, 'by 2000, whereas in France there were 17,000 UEFA-qualified coaches and in Germany 53,000, there were only 1,000 qualified coaches in England' (Carter, 2006: 127–8). Elsewhere, coaching qualifications were a mandatory requirement to manage professional football clubs in France and Germany (McCutcheon, 2002). In Germany, any aspiring manager (head coach) required both coaching qualifications and two years of managerial experience in order to manage a club in the Bundesliga. While formal coaching qualifications were introduced in Germany in 1947, in 2000 the German FA instigated a number of changes to coach and manager training and development designed to assist in reforming German football (Price, 2015). Possible reasons for the continued resistance towards the idea of coaching qualifications in England included managers' and players' distrust of anything theoretical. While qualified coaches were regularly stigmatised as 'schoolteachers' by many in the game, previous experience of playing professional football still remained a key managerial attribute.

Attempts by the English FA to modernise and formalise the process of appointing football managers continued throughout the 1970s and 1980s. Proposals to implement a European-style licensing system were rejected by club directors, who did not want to be forced to choose managers from a list of qualified candidates but also, more importantly, did not regard professional qualifications as necessary for management. In 1992, the League Managers Association (LMA) was formed. One of its main aims was to campaign for the introduction of mandatory qualifications for managers. However, it was not until 2003 that the English FA was successful in introducing a licensing system.

## The role of the media

During this period, television played a key role in transforming professional football. The formation of the FA Premier League and subsequent separation from the Football League in 1992 were prompted by the desire of the top clubs to retain control of TV income (Buraimo et al., 2006; Taylor, 2006). The BBC and ITV had the rights to televise live matches before the Premier League, but neither had the rights to televise live Premier League games, only highlights. Instead, television coverage rights were sold to a pay-TV broadcaster, BSkyB, leading to an explosion of income for Premier League clubs, with the price generated by successive auctions of broadcasting rights rising tenfold since the 1980s. In 1992, Sky TV secured the broadcasting rights for the English Premier League for £302 million (Antonioni & Cubbin, 2000) and by 1996 this figure had risen to £670 million (Magee, 2002).

## Commercialisation

With an economic platform founded on the influx of television money, professional football in England during the 1990s was transformed and experienced enormous upheaval, during which many aspects of the game changed beyond recognition (Garland et al., 2000). The hooligan-ridden game of the 1980s (Harris, 2006) gave way to a classier, more spectator-friendly sport (Magee, 2002), aided by the rapid commercialisation and transformation of the game into a multi-million pound industry (Crolley et al., 2002; Conn, 1997; Banks, 2002). While professional football in the UK changed dramatically during the 1980s, the pace of change accelerated throughout the 1990s (Grundy, 1998; Nash, 2000a). By the mid-1990s, football in England 'embodied the central features of a modern high- profile sport' (Horne et al., 1999: 52). During this period, many clubs converted to public limited companies, constructed new stadiums incorporating hospitality suites and developed new revenue streams from sponsorship and merchandising. Numerous academic studies have analysed the intensifying rationalisation, globalisation (Duke, 2002), transformation (Giulianotti, 1999, 2005; King, 1997; Conn, 1997; Russell, 1997; Grundy, 2004; Boyle & Haynes, 1998; Hamil et al., 1999) and commercialisation (Morrow, 2003; Szymanski & Kuypers, 1999; Conn, 1999; Nash, 2000b) of professional football in the late twentieth century. However, there were other changes that dramatically altered professional football not just in England but throughout Europe.

## The Bosman ruling

Since the Eastham decision, there had been few legislative changes in relation to the employment status of players in England. However, throughout this period, there were considerable modifications to the employment status and mobility of professional football players. In 1978, the PFA and the Football League negotiated a new transfer compensation scheme, which recognised the right of a player to change football clubs at the end of his contract (Dabscheck, 1986). More significantly, professional football was beginning to attract considerable criticism from the European Parliament (Parrish, 2002; Crolley *et al.*, 2002), which in 1989 stated that UEFA's transfer system was a 'latter-day version of the slave trade, a violation of the freedom of contract and the freedom of movement guaranteed by the Treaties' (Morris *et al.*, 1996: 894).

In 1995, the European Court of Justice (ECJ) ruled in favour of Jean-Marc Bosman, deciding that the existing football transfer system was in breach of EU law. Specifically, the ECJ demanded that regulations concerning player transfers and foreign player quotas be amended immediately. The ECJ held that 'the imposition of national quotas on teams participating in European competitions violated the right of free movement' (McCutcheon, 2002: 312). In addition, an important consequence of this ruling was the elimination of national quotas in domestic competitions (McCutcheon, 2002). A number of academic studies have examined the Bosman ruling (Antonioni & Cubbin, 2000; Simmons, 1997; McArdle, 2000, 2002; McCutcheon, 2002; Crolley *et al.*, 2002), its financial impact on football clubs (Morris *et al.*, 1996; Szymanski & Kuypers, 1999) and its major consequences for the freedom of movement and freedom of contract (Morris *et al.*, 1996; Antonioni & Cubbin, 2000). In terms of freedom of movement, one important consequence of this ruling was the elimination of national quotas in domestic and European competitions (Lanfranchi & Taylor, 2001; McCutcheon, 2002). Freedom of contract established the free movement of players between football clubs within EU member states. Thus, once a player's contract had expired, he was free to discuss and negotiate a deal with a new club and move without a fee being paid. The Bosman ruling did not affect the transfer of in-contract players (Antonioni & Cubbin, 2000) and therefore only affected a minority of potential transfers.

The ECJ ruling had a number of important implications. First, the removal of foreign player quotas resulted in increased migration of foreign footballers throughout the major leagues in Europe (Frick, 2009; Magee, 2002) and in particular to England (Magee, 2002; Maguire & Stead, 1998; Stead & Maguire, 2000). By the end of the 1999/00 season, almost 40 per cent of the registered professional players playing in the English leagues were foreign nationals (Lanfranchi & Taylor, 2001). On Boxing Day in 1999, Chelsea became the first English team to field an all-foreign starting XI (Harris, 2006). In addition, by 2001 there had been a dramatic increase in the number of senior international players registered with professional clubs in

England, particularly in the top two leagues (Dabscheck, 2006). Second, there was a steep rise in players' wages in both the English Premier League and Championship (Magee, 2002; Cashmore, 2000; Kesenne, 2003). In the 2000/01 season, the total wage bill for English Premier League clubs was £706 million, with at least 100 players earning in excess of £1 million a year (Sugden & Tomlinson, 2002). Third, in the post-Bosman era of professional football, with greater-value contracts on offer, as well as more out-of-contract footballers seeking to maximise their career potential, there was a considerable increase in the number of players using agents (Horne et al., 1999). In 2001, there were 179 FIFA-registered agents in England, compared to 88 in France and 80 in Germany (Banks, 2002).

Finally, it was argued that the ECJ ruling resulted in clubs recruiting cheaper, more experienced foreign players rather than relying on indigenous youth development schemes. While the widely held view at this time was that home-grown players were more costly than foreign players, Madichie (2009) argued that the influx of foreign players extinguished the potential development of home-grown players. Specifically, English Premier League clubs had the lowest number of scholars/apprentices of all four divisions. Related to this was the argument that English Premier League clubs were hoarding players (Dabscheck, 2006). For example, the average number of professional players at English Premier League clubs in the 2000/01 season was 48 and the average number of players who played league games was 28. In particular, Manchester United had a squad of 70 registered professional players, 38 of whom had never played a first-team game. Dabscheck (2006) concluded that English Premier League and Championship clubs were stockpiling players. It was argued that the increased numbers of players in their squads posed considerable problems for managers in terms of selection and also in terms of maintaining harmony within the squads.

However, English clubs were not able to recruit from abroad until 1978, when the PFA lifted its ban on overseas players. This move has given rise to well-founded concerns about the influx of cheap foreign players – particularly Eastern Europeans – into the senior leagues of Europe. It has also been suggested that such moves enable rich clubs to monopolise the best talent and recruit foreign players as they wish. One particularly obvious consequence is that managers can sign proven players who can immediately make an impact on teams' performances. Considering the chronic insecurity of the manager's position, it is not surprising that some managers were unwilling to spend time recruiting young players.

It is not clear whether, or to what extent, the influx of foreign players can be attributed solely to the Bosman ruling (Frick, 2009). Lanfranchi and Taylor (2001: 222) argued that, in terms of player migration, the Bosman ruling 'did not revolutionize the migratory practices of professional footballers but merely gave added impetus to a trend already set in motion'. In this regard, they argued that other factors – the proliferation of agents, the emergence of cheap labour markets and the attractiveness of certain leagues – also contributed to the increased migration of players in the 1990s. Deloitte & Touche (2001) argued that the influx of foreign players could be attributed to the attractiveness of the wages in English football and to foreign managers' continental contacts. This improved position of power would extend most significantly to those players considered more valuable in terms of their playing talent, i.e. those players in demand.

### The foreign 'invasion'

During this period, labour migration in professional football was not restricted to players, and a number of clubs began to widen their managerial search abroad. Due to the increased number of foreign players in English football, the appointment of foreign managers seemed logical for a number of reasons. First, it was felt at the time that foreign managers possessed the necessary experience of dealing with foreign players and the necessary contacts for recruiting foreign players. Second, foreign managers were viewed as being more qualified and, in this regard, some club owners believed that these managers were more suitable candidates than their British counterparts. Initially, with the arrival of Jozef Venglos, who was appointed as manager of Aston Villa in 1990, there existed a deep-rooted British distrust of anything foreign.[3] In particular, Arsenal's appointment of Arsène Wenger in 1996 shook the football world. With limited previous professional playing experience, his appointment was greeted with scepticism by the media. However, Wenger has arguably become one of the most influential managers since Herbert Chapman. Foreign managers such as Gerard Houllier (Liverpool), Gianluca Vialli (Chelsea), Claudio Ranieri (Chelsea), Ruud Gullit (Chelsea and Newcastle United) and Jean Tigana (Fulham) soon followed (Harris, 2006; M. Taylor, 2008). It is interesting to note that since 1996, Chelsea have only appointed foreign managers. Similar developments took place elsewhere, particularly at international level with the appointment of Jack Charlton in Ireland, Sven-Goran Eriksson in England and Berti Vogts in Scotland (Wagg, 2007). The influx of foreign managers highlighted a number of differences with British managers. It was argued that their approach to management was more professional and specialised. In this regard, foreign managers – like foreign players – brought new styles and ideas to the British game. Significantly, the influx of foreign managers highlighted how the British approach to football management, with its practical and traditional orientation, was outdated in comparison to football management in other European countries.

### Club ownership and governance

In 1981, payments to full-time club directors were permitted, and rules restricting dividend payments were abolished in 1998. In 1983, Tottenham

Hotspur became the first English club to go public on the London Stock Exchange. During the 1990s, this trend continued and, by October 2002, 20 UK clubs had listed on the London Stock Exchange (Morrow, 2003). Clubs viewed flotation as an opportunity to generate increased revenue for stadium development and player acquisition, and between 1991 and 1997 clubs spent over £500 million on ground improvements or new stadiums (M. Taylor, 2008). Following this flotation culture, a new breed of entrepreneurial director and owner emerged (King, 1997; Russell, 1997). Club owners such as Elton John (Watford), Robert Maxwell (Oxford United), Alan Sugar (Tottenham Hotspur) and Sir John Hall (Newcastle United) emerged from the worlds of finance, property development, entertainment and the newspaper industry (Mason, 1989; Walvin, 1986). As a result, the local commerce-orientated owners of the 1960s and 1970s were replaced by successful national and multinational executives in the late 1980s and 1990s. These new club owners attracted considerable media attention and their motives aroused suspicion concerning share and property deals (Mason, 1989), while some seemed more concerned with the associated media attention than with the game itself (Wagg, 1998). New organisational structures emerged as clubs such as Manchester United employed financial controllers and chief executives whose main goal was making profits through the commodification and modernisation of the game. In particular, established directors such as Irving Scholar at Tottenham Hotspur, Martin Edwards at Manchester United and David Dein at Arsenal viewed football primarily as a business (M. Taylor, 2008). In addition, Horne *et al.* (1999) argued that the conversion of clubs to public limited companies shifted the emphasis towards meeting shareholders' rather than supporters' needs. During this period, there was also evidence of the bankrolling of clubs by wealthy individuals (Harris, 2006), such as Jack Walker's considerable wealth guiding Blackburn Rovers to the English Premier League title in 1994/95.

There were a number of implications of this new flotation culture for the football manager. First, there was a greater involvement by these new owners and directors in the decision-making process at clubs. For example, in 1996 Kevin Keegan was asked to resign prior to Newcastle United's flotation. It was argued at the time that the board wanted to hire a more 'credible' manager (Wagg, 1998). Second, a more worrying development concerned owners' and directors' growing involvement in player recruitment decisions, a trend that was to escalate further in later years.

### *Managerial responsibilities*

The game's rapid commercialisation during this period clearly affected the manager's role. During this time, club managers experienced a gradual decline in their overall powers and a refinement of their role particularly at the higher levels, whereby they had less involvement with financials side and became more concerned with the playing side. While each club had a different approach and the nature of the manager's role differed at each club, one of the problems was that football managers still had no job description. Football management underwent a new division of labour during the 1990s, and many clubs followed Liverpool's model of the 1970s and 1980s whereby the manager managed the players while a skilled administrator – like Peter Robinson – ran the club. In addition, a number of clubs employed chief executives to handle the financial responsibilities and to manage the day-to-day affairs. Even high-profile managers like Sir Alex Ferguson and Arsène Wenger were excluded from high-level boardroom decisions, with their responsibilities limited to team matters. In addition, chief executives such as Peter Kenyon at Chelsea were responsible for transfer and contract negotiations with players and/or their agents. Towards the end of this period, other responsibilities such as youth development and player recruitment were quite often delegated to a 'director of football'.

However, the steady dilution of the manager's powers was not a linear process. A number of club managers resisted the reduction in their powers, highlighting the ongoing tensions between commercialisation and traditional attitudes towards football management. For example, Martin O'Neill – at both Leicester City and Glasgow Celtic – insisted on being given full control of the playing side without any interference from directors. O'Neill also insisted on bringing in his own backroom staff. In this regard, although not a new development, managers began delegating greater responsibilities to their backroom staff, who now included sports scientists and psychologists. Due to the game's increased competitiveness, football became more scientific in its preparation of players, precipitating a further process of specialisation within its management. While there was an initial reluctance to embrace new and innovative ideas, Arsène Wenger was at the forefront of this new scientific approach when he hired a number of French health and fitness experts to assist his players.

## 2000–2010

The influx of foreign owners and the steady flow of foreign managers into the UK continued throughout this period and had a number of important implications for the role of the manager. Other important developments related to coaching qualifications in general and sports legislation in particular. More recent developments impacting on specific aspects of the manager's role will be discussed later.

### *'Bosman II'*

After the Bosman ruling, the European Commission (EC) began to take a greater interest in professional football and in 1998 challenged the payment of fees for players who wished to change clubs while still under contract (Dabscheck, 2006; Foster, 2001). In 2001, the EU ruled that the European football transfer market was in breach of EU employment regulations and ordered UEFA to modify its employment regulations. In effect, this reversed the Bosman ruling and threw the football world into chaos (Magee, 2002). However, labelled 'Bosman II', these new regulations were viewed as vague (Simmons, 2001), potentially illegal (Foster, 2001), contradictory and akin to slavery (Dabscheck, 2006). In response, both FIFA and UEFA lobbied the EC to reverse its position and agreed on new regulations and their application. This involved two new standardised transfer windows (Simmons, 2001; McCutcheon, 2002; Foster, 2001), the transfer and payment of fees (both international and domestic) for players under contract and the resurrection of compensation fees for players under the age of 23 (Simmons, 2001; Foster, 2001; Dabscheck, 2006; Crolley *et al.*, 2002).

It was envisaged that such proposals would protect and maintain contract stability and prevent opportunistic behaviour by players and/or clubs (Dabscheck, 2006) while the compensation scheme for players under the age of 23 was an attempt to stop clubs and/or agents luring players from South America and Africa (Dabscheck, 2006). In addition, the international transfer of players under the age of 18 was only allowed in certain circumstances (Dabscheck, 2006). This related to the allocation of a reward or training compensation for those clubs who developed young players (Simmons, 2001; Foster, 2001). In short, these new changes, disguised as compensation for training costs (Foster, 2001), were intended to preserve suitable incentives for clubs in the training and development of young players, while compensation was an attempt to address the practice whereby players break or 'jump contracts' without 'just cause' (Foster, 2001: 6) and to prevent the poaching of young players.

## Managerial turnover

Since the formation of the English Premier League in 1992/93, there has been, across all four divisions, an average of 43 managerial terminations every season. In this regard, a number of academic studies have examined the determinants of managerial survivability (Audas *et al.*, 1999; Scully, 1994), team performance following a change in manager (Peiser & O'Franklin, 2000; Audas *et al.*, 1997, 2002; Bruinshoofd & ter Weel, 2003; Koning, 2003) and the contribution of the manager to the performance (Audas *et al.*, 1997; Dawson *et al.*, 2000; Dawson & Dobson, 2002). 'Almost half of first-time managers (49.07%) get only one chance to prove themselves and are never appointed again to management posts' (Bridgewater, 2006b: 8). Thus, the high exit rate suggests that football management is more like an aggressive form of musical chairs rather than resembling a merry-go-round (Bridgewater, 2006b). Across all four divisions in England, the average tenure for managers is 1.52 years. It is worth noting that the average tenure of a coach (manager) in Holland is between two and three years (Murphy, 2002). In short, the average length of tenure for English managers is declining and the overall rate of managerial dismissals is increasing.

## *Coaching qualifications*

In 2000, UEFA introduced regulations to standardise coaching qualifications across Europe for the 2003/04 season. As a result, the UEFA Pro Licence, which is the apex of a pyramid of awards, became a mandatory requirement to manage in the top league in each nation and in European competition (Spencer, 2001). In 2000, following negotiations between the English Premier League, the PFA and the LMA, it was agreed to make coaching qualifications mandatory for English Premier League managers for the 2003/04 season. Three years later, English Premier League chairmen agreed to make the UEFA Pro Licence a mandatory requirement in the appointment of managers. However, during this period a number of managers, such as Glenn Roeder (Newcastle United), Gareth Southgate (Middlesbrough) and Paul Ince (Blackburn Rovers) were given special dispensations to manage in the English Premier League without the mandatory licence, whereas in Italy David Platt was prevented from managing Italian Seria A side Sampdoria for not having the appropriate qualifications.

The introduction of mandatory coaching qualifications in the English Premier League represented, in part, an attempt to professionalise football management. In 2001, the first 11 English managers enrolled for the UEFA Pro Licence. Interestingly, by 2003, 42 coaches had acquired the UEFA Pro Licence in Scotland, but only 11 in England. Coaches from other countries – including José Mourinho – had also taken the Scottish route. Nevertheless, a professional class of English football managers and coaches slowly emerged. By 2002, 60 of the 72 managers in the Football League had gained an advanced coaching licence. In the same year, the LMA launched its own business management course for football managers, the Certificate of Applied Management, run in conjunction with the University of Warwick's Business School.

## *Owners*

Since 2000, the influx of overseas owners has been particularly evident at English Premier League clubs, a trend that has spread throughout the lower leagues (Hope, 2003). Numerous studies have raised concerns about the increased numbers of foreign-owned clubs, threats of hostile takeover bids and the lack of transparency in clubs' ownership structure (FGRC, 2006; Hamil *et al.*, 2000; Jaquiss, 2000). More specifically, there have been accusations of fraud by senior club officials (Emery & Weed, 2006), dishonesty and corruption at boardroom level (Green, 2002; Holt, 2003) and illegal payments by club directors (Mason, 1980; Russell, 1997). In addition, numerous concerns surround wealth extraction and asset stripping (Emery & Weed, 2006) and poor management practices at boardroom level (Ozawa et al., 2004; Hamil et al., 1999, 2000; Carter, 2006). Conn (1997) concluded that the practices of many football club directors are deeply disturbing, while others have argued that greater accountability needs to be adopted in the recruitment and appointment of club directors (Cannon & Hamil, 2000; Green, 2002). However, it is also worth noting managers' alleged involvement in illegal (Taylor & Ward, 1995) and 'under-the-counter' payments (Taylor, 2001). In addition, numerous accusations concerning 'bungs', bribes and misappropriation of funds have been aimed at managers (Bower, 2003; Freeman, 2000). In particular, following a series of high-profile and damaging scandals surrounding transfer dealings between 1990 and 2005, managers' involvement in transfer dealings witnessed increased scrutiny.

### The role of the media

During this period, many football managers became national celebrities (Carter, 2006) and some, such as José Mourinho, Sir Alex Ferguson and Arsène Wenger, achieved celebrity on a global scale (Wagg, 2007). In particular, Mourinho, despite limited previous playing experience and only four years of coaching experience, won five major trophies with FC Porto. Following his appointment at Chelsea in 2004, he became one of the highest-paid coaches in the history of football. During his first term at Chelsea, he won the FA Cup and twice won both the Premier League and the League Cup. In 2006, Mourinho – backed by the Russian billionaire Roman Abramovich – spent in excess of £200 million in wages and transfers to generate a Premier League-winning side for Chelsea. Contemporary football management, epitomised by managers such as Mourinho, Ferguson and Pep Guardiola, incorporates the application of science and technology in exploring avenues to pursue success. However, the considerable influx of foreign owners has had important implications for both the role and the security of the football manager.

## Conclusion

Taylor (2008a: 1) has recently noted that 'British football has a powerful sense of its own history. The culture of the game is replete with reminders of the past.' As we have seen, a recurring theme has concerned the relationship between continuity and change. More specifically, professional football clubs have become increasingly modernised, incorporating increased levels of financial, marketing, legal and administrative expertise. However, despite the professionalisation and bureaucratisation of many aspects of the management of professional football clubs, one key aspect of clubs – the role of the manager – has, as we shall see, remained remarkably resistant to such changes. The question at the heart of this research concerns the role of the manager in professional football. In particular, the book focuses on aspects of the role of the contemporary football manager including the recruitment and appointment of managers, the assessment and recruitment of players, the process of establishing discipline, the role of agents and the relationship between managers and directors/ owners.

## Notes

1  The retain-and-transfer system allowed clubs to keep a player's registration, which prevented him from moving to another club. Clubs could also refuse to pay players if they had requested a transfer to another club.
2  George Eastham won a court case against his employers Newcastle United. The case concerned Newcastle's failure to provide him with an alternative source of income and appropriate lodgings and their refusal to allow him to move to another club when his contract has expired. Because he was unable to move from the club, Eastham went on strike and took the club to the High Court in 1963 and won. Backed by the PFA, his central argument was that the retain-and-transfer system was an unfair restraint of trade. The 'retain' aspect was revised and a tribunal for resolving disputes between players and clubs was established.
3  South African Peter Hauser was actually the first foreign manager in English football, managing Chester City from 1963 to 1968. However, the appointment of Venglos was particularly significant because he was the first foreign manager in the top flight.

# Chapter 2

# Managerial recruitment and appointment

## Introduction

For some, securing a managerial position in professional football may be unplanned, arising as a result of a fortuitous opportunity, while for others it may provide an opportunity to recapture or prolong the success experienced as a player. While a love of the game and ego fulfilment appear to be obvious but incomplete explanations for entry into management (Perry, 2000b), some individuals may be drawn by the perceived prestige, image and celebrity-like status associated with football management. The process of securing a management position in professional football is dependent on a complex mixture of factors such as formal qualifications, personal contacts and previous playing experience. While Chapter 3 examines specific competencies that distinguish the more successful professional football managers from their less successful counterparts, this chapter looks at the managerial recruitment and appointment process in professional football. In particular, the chapter explores traditional forms of authoritarianism in football management, such as the establishment of managerial roles and responsibilities and the process of appointing backroom staff.

## Personal contact networks

As noted in Chapter 1, uncertainty and insecurity are pervasive features of management in professional football. Therefore, an obvious question concerns how football managers cope with these insecurities, which are a permanent feature of their working lives. One way in which all employees, including football managers, alleviate the problem of uncertainty in workplaces is by drawing on a network of personal contacts as a form of support and to take advantage of employment opportunities (Blair, 2001). Within the sociological literature on job searches, social resources such as informal networks, referrals and personal contacts facilitate access to information about possible job opportunities (Lin, 1999; Marsden & Campbell, 1990; Marsden, 1994; Granovetter, 1973, 1974). For example, in professions such as engineering, film-making and academia, individuals establish personal contact networks that are useful in providing information about possible job opportunities (Katz, 1958; Blair, 2001). Personal contact networks may also be used by employees 'to feed into the fact that they are not too happy' in their current employment (Katz, 1958: 52). In professional football, 'friendship networks generally fulfil the functions of directly offering a job opportunity, informing a person of a potential job opportunity, or recommending a potential employee via a third party' (Roderick, 2006: 256). It is important to note that while relational ties may be comparatively weak (Granovetter, 1985), they may still prove crucial in providing employment opportunities within professional football. As we shall see in Chapter 4, personal contact networks also play a crucial role in the assessment and recruitment of players. Because relatively little is known about how personal contact networks influence managerial mobility in professional football (Taylor, 2010), their type, function, development and maintenance need to be explored. This provides a useful starting point in understanding the process involved in the recruitment and appointment of managers in professional football.

### Developing personal contact networks

When a decision is taken to dismiss a manager, most football club owners and boards of directors tend to draw up a shortlist of prospective candidates whom they wish to appoint. For clubs, it is important 'not to get in touch with the largest number of potential applicants; rather it is to find a few applicants promising enough to be worth the investment of thorough investigation' (Rees, 1966: 561). Because the appointment of a particular manager may be complicated by the fact that the club's 'ideal candidate' is currently employed elsewhere, it is not uncommon for the managerial recruitment process to have already commenced prior to the manager's dismissal and, more worryingly, without his knowledge. In this regard, as we shall see later, the practice of 'tapping up' prospective managers is not uncommon (Perry, 2000a, 2000b). Employee mobility in professional football is all about 'who you know' and while some clubs may formally advertise a vacant managerial position, managerial appointments are usually facilitated by personal relationships and contacts in the game (Taylor, 2010; Wagg, 1984; Lear & Palmer, 2007). Because club directors and owners are viewed as the gatekeepers to managerial positions in professional football (Morrow & Howieson, 2014; Bridgewater, 2010), gaining access to these gatekeepers would seem an obvious strategy for managers in general and novice managers in particular. This is because, as we shall see, the accumulation of social capital (Bourdieu, 1986) facilitates access to information concerning potential management opportunities.

For professional football managers, developing personal contacts and gaining membership of particular networks 'can be seen as a deliberate pursuit of goals in which such membership may provide expectations of an immediate or some future benefit' (Weber, 1968: 102). For example, membership of formal groups, such as the League Managers Association (LMA), provides a set of privileges and associated obligations that assist current and former professional football managers in a number of ways. The LMA, as a collective representative voice for all professional managers, provides a range of support services such as legal, financial, contractual and personal advice. However, all of the managers interviewed mentioned the importance of developing informal networks of personal contacts. More specifically, a recurring theme in all of the interviews with managers was how personal contacts are developed by attending coaching courses and particularly football matches. Moreover, personal contacts were viewed by managers as a means of sharing information between themselves on topics such as dealing with the press, potential signings and job opportunities. For example, one former English Premier League manager stated:

> Well, there's a group of us [managers] who meet up quite a bit. Like, some of them I would have known from playing against them or maybe they were a coach somewhere else, and we talk about stuff. Like "How did you deal with the player getting sent off last week?" or "How did you find that referee?" – stuff like that. We also talk about new managers and players in the league and how they are doing. We would always go for a drink in the office after a game, where nobody can see us and have a good chat. But there's only a few of them [managers] that I would openly chat to about confidential stuff. I would also text these guys a lot with information and stuff like that.

Implicit in the above comments is how personal contact networks and membership of managerial cliques in particular provide support and evolve in a slow process, commencing with low-risk minor transactions that facilitate access to information (Portes, 1995; Shapiro, 1987). Regarding support, back in 2008, following his appointment at Sunderland, Roy Keane stated that 'Rafael Benitez couldn't be more helpful' while 'Arsène Wenger has been brilliant' (Buckley, 2008). Moreover, a recurring theme in the manager interviews concerned how the level of information shared, within these managerial cliques, was dependent on interpersonal trust. What this means is that repeated interactions between people enhances the probability that trust will emerge between them. This forms a sort of 'knowledge-based' trust that is grounded in other people's predictability and, as a result, we can anticipate and predict, to a certain extent, other people's behaviour (Lewicki et al., 1998). Brewer (1981) identified a number of reasons why membership of a salient category may provide a basis for presumptive trust. First, shared membership of a given category can serve as a 'rule for defining the boundaries of low-risk interpersonal trust that bypasses the need for personal knowledge when interacting with members of that category' (Brewer, 1981: 356).

Second, because of the cognitive consequences of categorisation and in-group bias, individuals tend to attribute positive characteristics such as honesty, cooperativeness, and trustworthiness to other in-group members (Brewer, 1996). What this means is that football managers may confer a sort of depersonalised trust on other managers that is predicated simply on awareness of their shared category membership. It would be useful to know how inexperienced managers in particular, with less extensive personal contact networks and limited access to privileged information, develop personal contacts with key stakeholders in the game.

The importance of developing personal contacts was identified during an interview with a relatively inexperienced manager. Following his retirement from professional football as a player, he was appointed as the manager of an English League Two club. In addition to describing his approach to recruiting players, this manager stated how he needed 'to get out there more often' and provided an understanding of how personal contacts are developed in professional football:

MANAGER: Well I need to get up and see xxxx [English Premiership player] next week. Then there's a boy in Ireland that I'm going to watch.
SK: Are you going to sign that player in Ireland?
MANAGER: Probably not, but I need to speak to the guys over there and see what's happening. I haven't been over there for a while. It's amazing what happens in a few months.
SK: So there seems to be a lot of travelling involved?
MANAGER: F****** hell, I've been up and down the motorway all week. I wouldn't mind but it's only because I'm a nosy c***. Like, half the time I've no interest in the games, but it's just to be seen to be at the games, particularly as I'm new to this. But as well as that, you hear all the shit at games when you're up in the director's box. You hear all the latest gossip of who's looking at who and who's getting the chop and when.

While one recurring theme mentioned by all of the managers interviewed was the advantageous nature of personal contact networks in terms of offering support and advice, implicit in the latter manager's comments is the importance of developing personal contacts with more 'strategically' placed individuals such as club directors, owners and directors of football. In this regard, social capital can be both 'relational' and 'structural', with the former referring to one's personal relations with others and the latter referring to one's position within the network of social relations in which one belongs (Granovetter, 1985). Therefore, the structural nature of one's position within the network of personal contacts and with strategically placed contacts 'in the know' in particular is crucial for gaining access to information about potential management opportunities. The importance of developing contacts with those 'in the know' and with more experienced managers in particular was a recurring theme throughout the manager interviews. This seems an obvious strategy considering experienced managers' knowledge relating to aspects of management but also in terms of gaining access to their dense networks of personal contacts. For example, experienced managers such as Arsène Wenger and Sir Alex Ferguson possess dense networks of personal contacts that they have built up over numerous years. It is worth noting that a number of the managers interviewed identified the significant role Sir Alex Ferguson played in terms of offering them general advice and information on aspects of management, and on player recruitment and assessment in particular. Membership of personal contact networks comprising experts of refinement, such as Sir Alex Ferguson, is viewed as a form of embodied cultural capital (Bourdieu, 1986) characterised by 'knowledge channelling', whereby information is circulated concerning potential management opportunities (Elliott & Maguire, 2008). As we shall see in Chapter 6, the ability of a football manager to develop personal contacts with strategically placed individuals, such as agents, is deemed crucial in terms of accessing information concerning the assessment and recruitment of potential players.

### *Personal contact networks and managerial appointments*

In some organisations, promoting from within has become an institutionalised practice or 'custom' (Doeringer & Piore, 1971). Traditionally, professional football clubs have adopted a promotion-from-within policy whereby appointments to positions such as club doctors, coaches, physiotherapists and public relations officers are often made informally, without an interview and on the basis of recommendations from personal contacts (Lear & Palmer, 2007; Taylor, 2010; Waddington, 2001, 2002; Taylor et al., 1997; Bridgewater, 2006b). In professional football, Perry (2000b: 7–8) provides 'evidence of huge on-the-job research, sophisticated networking and intelligence gathering'. Professional football is often described as a 'who-you-know sport' (Lear & Palmer, 2007: 20), in which the 'grapevine' is highlighted as a central point of recruitment (Magee, 1998: 107). All of the managers interviewed identified the importance of personal contact networks in terms of securing information about potential job opportunities. One former English Championship manager described the importance of keeping in contact with those with whom he had worked previously. In addition, he identified how a former player whom he had managed previously had recommended him to the club chairman. The following is a description of how this manager was appointed at the club:

> A former player of mine rang me up and told me that their manager was just [leaving] after resigning. He said to me, "You would do a job, you

would definitely do a job here – it was made for you". So I put my name forward to the chairman. He [chairman] says to me, "Come over for an interview". So that was on a Wednesday, and I went over for an interview and we had a chat. So I went in and they [boardroom members] seemed impressed – there were three of them there. They said they would meet me again on Sunday morning, so I met them again. They said that they had gone through my stuff and said, "The job is yours – can you start in the morning?" So I said, "Would you mind if I start on the Tuesday?", and they said, "Fine".

While privileged access to valuable information 'obtained through social capital [has], from the point of view of the recipient, the character of a gift' (Portes, 1998: 5), it would be a mistake to assume that all managerial appointments are as fortuitous as the above manager suggests. As we know, only a few of the more experienced and successful managers are in such a privileged and powerful position and can, when their contract is terminated, find a comparable position at another club in a relatively short space of time (Dawson & Dobson, 2006; Bridgewater, 2010; Audas et al., 1997). What tends to happen is that when a club draws up a list of prospective managerial candidates, club officials speak to and confide in personal contacts such as current and/or former players and managers in attempting to ascertain the suitability of the prospective manager. For example, in 1996, having identified Arsène Wenger as a suitable candidate, Arsenal decided to wait until his contract at Grampus Eight had expired. Depending on the availability of their 'ideal candidate', football clubs may decide to appoint managers on a short-term or trial basis. While older, more experienced football managers tend to perform better than younger managers (Bridgewater, 2010), one trend in professional football is the tendency to appoint high-profile players as managers. I will return to this point in the next chapter.

Personal contacts not only provide managers with information about potential employment opportunities but also assist managers in making more informed decisions about whether or not to apply for, and if offered, accept particular managerial positions. For professional football managers, being able to secure as much information as possible about potential opportunities from personal contacts in general and from trusted colleagues in particular assists them in establishing their suitability for a particular job. This point was borne out during an interview with a manager who possessed considerable managerial experience in both the UK and Ireland:

> I'd always get a second opinion about a job. Like when I got offered a gig back in Ireland. Oh god yeah, I'd always speak to managers that I trust before I take any job. Like the job at xxxx [Irish Premier League club] – I spoke to five different managers, who all have managed there. The biggest thing about asking them, in terms of how should I approach

the job, every one of them said, "Just be yourself, don't try and do anything different. Put your own stamp on it and be the way you are."

In his autobiography, Bryan Robson described the importance of maintaining friendship networks in professional football. Robson described how, prior to being interviewed by the Football Association of Ireland, he gathered information about the vacant Irish manager's position from his ex-playing colleagues:

> I did my homework and got in touch with people who knew about the set-up of the Irish camp. I spoke to Roy Keane, Andy Townsend and Denis Irwin, all experienced former Ireland internationals, knowing I'd get three honest and different opinions.
>
> (Robson, 2006: 263)

Throughout their experience in professional football, managers develop interdependent networks of personal relations with current and/or former players, directors, owners, managers and agents. However, once developed, these personal contact networks are not self-sustaining but are developed through various forms of engagement activities that are the 'result of a process of construction and recomposition that takes place over time' (Bidart & Degenne, 2005: 283) and quite often involve some level of personal interaction (Mohon & Mohon, 2002). Personal contact networks consist of superimposed 'layers of relationships, with varied origins and ages, which are the result of the subject's personal history and the various socialization processes the subject engages in the course of his or her life' (Bidart & Degenne, 2005: 283). These comments illustrate how a 'combination of the amount of time, the emotional intensity, the intimacy (mutual confiding), and the reciprocal services which characterize the tie' influences the strength of a personal contact (Granovetter, 1973: 1361). In addition, the comments support the view that the sharing of information about potential job opportunities between managers and players often produces a greater disposition to trust each other (McGovern, 2002; Mohon & Mohon, 2002). Moreover, implicit in this sharing of information is the expectation of reciprocity at some point in the future (Portes, 1995). What this means is that reciprocity – the giving of benefits to another in return for benefits received – facilitates the development of bonds of trust (Molm, 2010). Thus, reciprocity is viewed as a considerably important aspect 'of creating social capital through networks of relationships and through embeddedness' (Molm, 2010: 126).

It is worth noting that personal recommendations and referrals 'may also result in a higher-quality stream of applicants, if the person making a referral is selective about those to whom she or he passes information, thus serving to screen or vouch for the people referred' (Marsden, 1994: 981). Moreover, personal contact networks may be viewed as an aid to securing a managerial position but may also act as a form of 'sanctioning device' by alerting prospective employers to the availability of a potential recruit (Katz, 1958: 54). In this regard, personal contacts can provide credible, realistic job previews as they are 'sources of accurate, subtle information for both potential employees and employing firms' (Granovetter, 1974). However, recruitment through informal channels may not yield heterogeneous applicant pools, as quite often employees are likely to convey information to socially similar persons (Granovetter, 1974). In addition, it is questionable what impact, if any, personal recommendations and referrals play in reducing the uncertainty that characterises labour as a commodity – a point that was particularly evident in the appointment and subsequent sacking of David Moyes at Manchester United. Despite these limitations, what is evident from the interviews with managers is the central role that personal contact networks play in obtaining information about potential employment opportunities. This is perhaps one reason why football managers are continually trying to establish and develop personal contacts in general, and contacts with key stakeholders in the game in particular.

## 'Reluctant maidens'

Dawson and Dobson (2006) argued that the greater the probability of a manager being dismissed, the greater the intensity with which he would search for alternative employment opportunities. Following a dismissal, while the more successful managers tend to find a comparable position at another club in a relatively short space of time (Dawson & Dobson, 2006), most are faced with considerable difficulties in securing further managerial opportunities (Bridgewater, 2010). Considering the insecure and cut-throat nature of football management, quite often football managers assume the role of 'reluctant maidens' (Granovetter, 1974), whereby they continue searching for potential job opportunities while still employed at a particular football club. This was certainly the case for a number of the managers interviewed. For example, one current English Championship manager noted how he was 'always on the look-out' for potential job opportunities. Similarly, another former English Premier League manager stated that he 'would always keep his ear to the ground' for potential job opportunities. Within the professional football industry, there is a constant flow of gossip and rumours between players, managers and agents in general, and in the context of players and managers who are under pressure and facing the prospect of being dropped or dismissed in particular.

While Chapter 4 examines how managers use personal contacts, such as agents, to informally tap up players, the practice of tapping up managers, doctors and physiotherapists is also widespread in professional football (Waddington, 2002; Roderick, 2006; Magee, 1998). The practice of tapping up potential employees quite often incorporates the classic 'off-the-record phone call' and may involve conversations that 'never take place' (Waddington, 2002: 58). Moreover, the practice of tapping up is designed to 'test the water' and identify prospective employees' level of interest and availability for a particular opportunity. In this regard, there is some evidence to suggest that managers adopt a more brazen or devious approach in sourcing information about potential job opportunities. For example, an interesting situation developed during the course of an interview with a former English Championship manager. During the interview, the manager received a telephone call from another manager, the purpose of which was to enquire about the performances of a player who was on loan at the Championship club. During the telephone conversation, this manager also enquired about possible coaching opportunities at the Championship club. The interviewee seemed quite irate and agitated, and was cursing profusely under his breath as he slammed the phone down following the conversation. When I asked him 'What was that all about?', he said:

MANAGER: Like, he knows how the f****** player is doing, he doesn't need me to tell him that. He's only ringing me to see what's happening down here. F****** twat.

SK: What do you mean?

MANAGER: Well, I'm under serious pressure, like – everyone knows that and it's a big bloody club, so he knows the story. He's only ringing me up to suss out the situation and see if there are any jobs or anything going down here.

When questioned if this was common practice in professional football, the manager replied, as he raised his eyebrows to the ceiling, 'It goes on *ALL THE F****** TIME*'. A similar situation developed during the course of an interview with a current English League Two player. The League Two club were experiencing a poor run of form and the manager was under considerable pressure. During the course of the interview, the player answered a telephone call from a former manager. Following the telephone conversation, the player raised his eyes up to the sky and said, 'F***** hell'. When I asked the player if everything was OK, he replied:

PLAYER: No, it's grand. That was xxxx [former manager] ringing me to see how I was.

SK: To see how you are getting on?

PLAYER: Yeah right. Cute f*****, he knows the story. Like, it is obvious xxxx [current manager] is under a bit of pressure and the chairman has pumped a wad of money in. Like, potentially it's a huge club, new owners, loadsa money and a new ground. *YOU* know the story.

SK: So was he trying to see how things were down here?

PLAYER: Yeah, course he was. No harm in keeping him sweet, though.

While not a recurring theme, implicit in the latter two interviewees' comments are the somewhat questionable methods some managers may adopt in attempting to obtain information from personal contacts concerning potential job opportunities. It could be argued that the probability of such telephone conversations occurring during the course of a research interview reinforces the former interviewee's comments about how tapping up in professional football 'goes on ALL THE F****** TIME', which is an obvious reflection of the considerably insecure and uncertain nature of professional football management. Moreover, the fact that the average length of tenure for English managers is declining and the overall rate of managerial dismissals is increasing may lead some managers to adopt such devious approaches. Thus, an interesting dichotomy exists. On the one hand, we have seen how personal contact networks are crucial in providing information concerning potential employment opportunities within professional football. On the other hand, personal relationships or networks of such relations can facilitate the generation of trust and the discouragement of malfeasance (Granovetter, 1985: 490). Moreover, implicit in the latter two interviewees' comments is that

> while social relations may indeed often be a necessary condition for trust and trustworthy behavior, they are not a sufficient condition to guarantee these and may even provide occasion and means for malfeasance and conflict on a scale larger than in their absence.
>
> (Granovetter, 1985: 490)

This is important because 'the trust engendered by personal relations presents, by its very existence, enhanced opportunity for malfeasance' (Granovetter, 1985: 491). It is well known that distrust is viewed as a lack of confidence in other people whereby a concern exists that they may act in a hostile or harmful manner towards oneself (Lewicki et al., 1998; Sztompka, 1999). This is not normally the case but considering the limited number of managerial opportunities and the insecure nature of football management, some football managers may engage in 'potentially injurious behavior towards other' managers (Lewicki et al., 1998: 677). As we shall see later in this chapter, the pervasive generalised climate of suspicion, characteristic for the 'syndrome of distrust' (Sztompka, 1999) or 'culture of cynicism' (Stivers, 1994) is particularly evident in the appointment of a professional football manager's backroom team.

An examination of the recruitment of managers in professional football does not appear, based on the data gathered, to involve the use of formal contacts. Instead, the recruitment of football managers is facilitated by communications with informal personal networks. Thus, these personal contacts are viewed as a resource, as a form of social capital (Bourdieu, 1986) through which links to potential employment opportunities can be developed and information valuable both to the potential manager and to the potential employer can be circulated. It is argued that managerial mobility, like player mobility generally, is 'a network-creating and network-dependent process' whereby 'recruitment patterns are embedded in a range of social ties and networks' (McGovern, 2002: 26). For football managers, personal contact networks are viewed as highly valuable in terms of sourcing knowledge about potential employment opportunities and can be seen to constitute the most effective means of securing management positions.

## Roles and responsibilities

One of the problems facing football managers in general and newly appointed managers in particular is the lack of clearly defined job descriptions and roles (Perry, 2000a; Penn, 2002). Misunderstandings often arise because it is not obvious where the manager's responsibilities end and where those of others, such as coaches, directors of football and directors/owners, start. Perry and Davies (1997) highlighted the value of developing both person and job specifications that articulate both the requirements of the individual and of the role. A number of academic studies (Perry, 2000a, 2000b; Perry & Davies, 1997) have identified the many roles that a football manager may assume but, perhaps unsurprisingly, few managers – if any – do all of these things, confirming Cook's view (cited in Perry & Davies, 1997) that the job will be shaped by the club, the available resources and the owner/chairman of the club. This point was a recurring theme throughout all of the manager interviews. More specifically, all of the managers identified a lack of any clearly articulated criteria and objectives, and job descriptions varied considerably from club to club. In professional football, an 'appointment is hardly ever accompanied by any terms of reference' (Allera & Nobay, 1966: 123). This is not generally the case in other industries, where employees' duties and rights are clearly defined and the allocation of both rights and obligations is clearly prescribed in advance. One manager, with considerable experience in both the UK and Ireland, described the only job interview he had had in professional football. During the course of the interview, his duties and responsibilities were identified. Interestingly, the interview took place after he had been appointed caretaker manager. He said:

> When I got the job, they [club owners] said, "Take it for four games, as caretaker, while they [club owners] put the word out". So we won three and drew one. So I still had to go through the official interviewing process, and faced the questions. I just put my case forward, and so they gave me the job on a two-year contract, and they just said, "Try and keep us in the Premier League".

In the UK, the LMA provides a standard contract of employment for football managers in which their tasks are clearly identified. One former English

Premier League manager described employment contracts as 'pretty standard, with all the basic stuff, nothing too specific'. One thing is clear though: the prospective manager will certainly realise that he will be judged in terms of the club's success. However, 'success' is an ambiguous term and might mean winning trophies, avoiding relegation or even maintaining financial solvency. Moreover, professional football is a results-based industry (LMA, 2009; Gilmore & Gilson, 2007) in which a manager's tenure is highly dependent on team performance and success (Wilders, 1976; Audas et al., 1999). During his time as Everton manager, David Moyes identified the importance of getting off to a good start in football management and stated: 'When your first chance at management comes along, you are judged very quickly. Lose the first six games and you could be out of a job' (LMA, 2009: 9). For managers in general, and as Moyes was to later experience at Manchester United, professional football is a results-based industry in which previous reputations are meaningless. One consistent theme that emerged from the manager interviews concerned the importance of success, in terms of results on the field. For example, one experienced manager stated that, despite there being no specific criteria or objectives stipulated in his contract, the message was unambiguous:

> The objective here is obviously to win the league every year, which is not possible, but people expect it because there's so much goes into it. But no one said to me, "You've got to win the league or else you'll lose your job" . . . [I've been] around long enough to know what's expected of a manager. If you don't win things . . . you won't be around too long.

In contrast to other industries, implicit contracts (Doeringer & Piore, 1971) consisting of unwritten understandings are a common aspect of management in professional football. Moreover, while success-related expectations are not always explicit, they are clearly implied. While this can partly explain the lack of formal job descriptions, which may include specific criteria in terms of success, it also raises an interesting dichotomy. On the one hand, if there are clearly articulated criteria and responsibilities in a manager's contract, and if he meets such criteria and fulfils such responsibilities, then the club has severely restricted grounds on which to terminate the contract. On the other hand, the presence of a job description could severely constrain a football manager's authority. This may be one possible reason why both football managers and clubs have continually resisted attempts by the English FA to introduce detailed job descriptions and establish a formal appointments procedure in professional football.

Several commentators have argued that, particularly in the last few years, the overall powers and roles of English Premier League managers – in contrast to managers at lower-league clubs – have become more narrowly defined. For example, Carter (2006: 122) noted how at the top level some English clubs have moved 'not without some cultural resistance towards a more European style of management'. This, in general, has resulted in managers' responsibilities being limited to controlling team matters while responsibilities for youth development and scouting have, in some cases, been allocated to other people, such as general managers or directors of football. Moreover, Carter (2006) noted how a number of managers have resisted this dilution of their powers. For example, prior to the appointment of Brendan Rodgers at Liverpool and Harry Redknapp at Tottenham Hotspur, both managers insisted on total control of player recruitment, with the latter insisting that this was explicitly stipulated in his employment contract. In 2008, Kevin Keegan resigned as manager of Newcastle United. Despite assurances from the club's owner, Mike Ashley, that he would have the 'final say' over player recruitment decisions, Keegan felt his position at the club had become untenable following the recruitment of an unknown player, Ignacio Gonzalez, against his express wishes by the club's director of football, Dennis Wise – a move calculated to further the club's 'commercial interests' and curry favour with two South American agents rather than to improve the playing squad. Following a subsequent tribunal, it was found that Keegan was constructively dismissed by Newcastle United concerning breach of contract. The terms of Keegan's contract were revealed to be very vague, stipulating that he should 'perform such duties as may be usually associated with the position of a Manager of a Premier League football team'; the tribunal ruled that this included the duty, or right, to have the 'final say' on transfers.

Total control by football managers over team selection and player recruitment is an important and considerably prominent aspect of the professional football manager's role, particularly in the higher echelons of English football. First, it 'highlights the ongoing tensions between commercialization and traditional attitudes towards football management' (Carter, 2006: 130). Second, insistence on total control over team matters is a reflection of a desire by managers to maintain their authority in defining and resisting any possible interference in their role. This was a common theme in the comments of all of the managers interviewed. In particular, all of the football managers described their insistence that they have total control over the 'playing side of things'. This concerned a desire by managers for total control of team affairs, including issues such as evaluating the squad, signing or releasing players and team selection. In addition, several managers described how they would insist that this is explicitly documented in their contract. The following manager provided a description that was typical of all of the managers interviewed:

SK: When you got the job, did you have a contract?
MANAGER: Yeah, I should have brought you the contract, from England. It's a standard nine-page contract.
SK: Were your responsibilities and duties outlined in this contract?
MANAGER: Not really. Well, it's pretty straightforward – there's nothing to them [contracts]. Sure they mean f*** all anyway. But I also

insisted on [controlling] all footballing duties – I would *always* insist on that.

These comments challenge the assumption that the labour market for professional football managers is essentially an open and competitive arena in which information concerning job specifications and the necessary skills and competencies is widely diffused. In addition, the authority of the football manager continues to be based on traditional forms of authoritarianism and this allows managers an unusually high degree of autonomy in defining their own role. Based on the data collected, it seems that very few football managers have clearly defined job descriptions and their roles remain quite vague. The limits of the managers' authority, unlike those of most managers in other modern industries, are not clearly defined or limited by formal rules and regulations, but are largely left for each manager to define for himself. A central characteristic of traditional authority is that it is not rule-bound and regulated in a stable and systematic way, as is rational-legal bureaucratic authority. Within rational-legal bureaucracies, as defined by Weber (1968: 956–9), each managerial position has 'a defined sphere of competence in the legal sense, which is ordered by rules and/or administrative regulations'. What this means is that the regular activities carried out by the holder of a given position are assigned as official duties – as in a job description.

It is clear that although the professionalisation and bureaucratisation of football clubs in recent years have involved the increasing application of rational modes of coordination and control to areas such as sales of match tickets, marketing of club merchandise, sponsorship and public relations, the role of the football manager has remained remarkably resistant to these processes. Even a cursory glance at the role of the football manager is sufficient to indicate how little it has in common with managerial posts in most modern organisations. Penn (2002: 44) has noted that 'despite the centrality of the manager within the organizational structure of the modern club, his role remains organizationally vague'. The degree to which the manager's role stands outside of the formal organisational structure of the club is highlighted in Penn's study of the management of Blackburn Rovers. Penn notes that since the mid-1980s, 'Blackburn Rovers have developed an increasingly complex organizational structure. The organizational form is typical of the modern corporation: differentiated functions and clear lines of responsibility.' However, and very significantly, he adds that the management of the team does not even feature within the club's own organisational chart (Penn, 2002: 42)!

Perhaps a number of lessons can be learned from the Dutch approach to club management. In the Netherlands, when a manager is offered a job, he is informed of the conditions under which he will be required to work. These include criteria by which his performance will be judged. These pertain to issues such as the size and quality of the squad, the emphasis placed on youth development and the resources available for purchasing players.

Following this, if the manager does not think that he can achieve the success required by the club under the specific conditions, he should decline the job (Murphy, 2002).

The following section explores another traditional aspect of the role of the manager, the appointment of backroom staff.

## The appointment of backroom staff

Quite often, a newly appointed football manager will bring with him to his new club many backroom staff with whom he has worked at one or more previous clubs. This typically involves an assistant manager and other support staff such as a chief scout, goalkeeping coach and physiotherapist. Granovetter (1974) suggests that succession at the top sets off a chain reaction. The successor, particularly if he is new to the club, often finds it necessary to bring new people into the organisation to support his policies and buttress his position. The need to find an ideal management partner is firmly ingrained in football as an important strategy (Rogan, 1989). Moreover, the appointment of an assistant manager is viewed by managers and players as a crucial factor contributing to their success. For example, the partnership of Brian Clough and Peter Taylor is considered as one of the most famous and successful partnerships in English professional football (Wilson, 2011). Many have argued that it was Taylor's 'eye for a player' that contributed greatly to Clough's success (Wilson, 2011). Other notable partnerships include Arsène Wenger and Pat Rice at Arsenal and Sir Alex Ferguson and Carlos Queiroz at Manchester United. In the context of the latter, it is worth noting Ferguson's considerable disappointment following the departure of Queiroz from the club and subsequent appointment as manager of the Portuguese national team.

A manager's backroom staff provide assistance and guidance that complement his core competencies and areas of expertise. What this means is that some managers may possess expertise in areas such as player motivation, while their assistants may have considerable acumen in the organisation of coaching sessions or in the assessment of opposing teams' players, game tactics and set pieces. Assistant managers and coaches also serve another critically important function. Quite often, the assistant manager is viewed by players as a 'go-between' between them and the manager. What this means is that assistant managers and head coaches are viewed by players as a means of discussing aspects of their playing performances in general and their role in particular. This is important because some players may feel intimidated and uncomfortable in speaking directly to managers in relation to obtaining feedback on issues such as why they were dropped. I will return to this point in Chapter 5. All of the players interviewed were asked to describe specific attributes and qualities that they associated with the more successful managers with whom they had worked in the past. A recurring theme in the interviews with players concerned the importance of a manager possessing good backroom staff. When questioned what makes a successful manager, one former English Premier League player expressed his view on the ability to assess players, the importance of a manager possessing good backroom staff and their level of tactical knowledge in particular:

PLAYER: An eye for a player is a massive thing – he's got to have good staff around him and the type of staff that he wants.
SK: Good backroom staff?
PLAYER: The manager needs good backroom staff around him . . . It's crucial – and the structure of the staff he wants as well. The staff he has around him – be that the physio or the fitness people or their assistants – need to be on the ball. And at the end of it would be tactically. He [assistant manager] would need to be quite clued up tactically nowadays as well.

Following Roy Hodgson's appointment as England manager in 2012, among his first staff appointments were his previous work colleagues Ray Lewington and Mike Kelly. In addition, the appointment of Gary Neville was rationalised by Hodgson, in part, due to his considerable experience of international football and his relationship with the England players. Bryan Robson, in his autobiography, describes how, following his appointment as manager at West Bromwich Albion, he wasted 'no time in contacting the man I wanted as my number two – Nigel Pearson. He had played for me at Middlesbrough, where he showed his leadership qualities as captain' (Robson, 2006: 268). In addition, Robson describes how, following his appointment at Middlesbrough, he brought in two ex-playing colleagues, Viv Anderson and Gordon McQueen. A similar theme emerged from the manager interviews. One manager stated that following his appointment at a particular club, he 'got rid of probably four of the six [existing backroom staff] and brought in my own people'. This involved bringing in a new assistant manager, kit man, physiotherapist and chief scout, three of whom were former playing colleagues of his. One former senior international manager reflected on his extensive managerial experience in general and his experience at an English Premier League club in particular. In addition, he also provided an insight into why managers normally bring in their own backroom staff:

> I think that a lot of them [managers] probably perceive that the person who was there before is the man's man as such, that has been there previously. I knew the people who were doing their jobs right and the people who weren't. But I just thought from that point of view it was time to change, to freshen [things] up because I knew the players weren't that happy regarding the training. I wanted to freshen that up a bit but from outside. I knew I needed to change it [backroom staff], and bring in new staff.

Central to understanding the appointment of a manager's backroom staff is the importance of friendship networks. As mentioned previously, managers are members of friendship networks with current and former managers, coaches and players. One manager interviewed, with considerable experience at Championship and League One clubs, described how he always appoints backroom staff with whom he has worked previously. He stated that 'this was the done thing in football', and described why managers usually bring in their own staff: 'I think that without a doubt they do that because it's someone they can trust and someone they've possibly previously worked with before'. Similarly, in other professional sports, such as American football, head coaches quite often appoint backroom staff with whom they have worked in the past and whom they trust (Fee *et al.*, 2006; Roach & Dixon, 2006). The importance of trust in professional football in general and in the appointment of backroom staff in particular was a common theme emerging from the interviews with managers. This point was borne out during an interview with a considerably experienced English Premier League manager who stated that:

> I would have always brought three people with me: a chief scout, a physio and a doctor. Key people, the people who you would trust and ask for advice and always get sound advice. Not always what I want to hear, not yes men. You need to be able to trust them implicitly.

Implicit in the above comments is how trust refers to an implicit promise from one party to protect, support, encourage and not to bring harm to others (Butler, 1991; Hosmer, 1995; Butler & Cantrell, 1984). The importance of loyalty and trust was identified by one English League Two manager who stated that 'it is important to employ backroom staff that are both loyal and trustworthy'. This manager then went on to describe a situation in which he brought in an assistant manager. However, in the months following his appointment, he stated that 'my assistant was annoyed at his lack of responsibilities'. The manager described a heated conversation with his assistant following one training session:

> He said to me, "Why am I f****** here . . . to put down cones every day and pump up footballs? I didn't come here to do this shit." I said to my assistant, "Listen, I have known you a long time, I need you here . . . you're here to watch my f****** back. Cos if I go, you're f****** gone as well."

Implicit in the above manager's comments are both the insecure nature of professional football and an obvious lack of trust in many of those around him. The role of trust and distrust in professional football will be discussed in greater detail in Chapter 7. In the context of appointing backroom staff, these comments support the view that personal ties are maintained with favourites, who are bound to the leader by ties of personal friendship, loyalty (Weber, 1964) and trust (Lewicki et al., 1998). What is also evident in the above manager's comments is how high levels of distrust are characterised by feelings of paranoia whereby undesirable eventualities and harmful motives are expected (Lewicki et al., 1998), referred to by Luhmann (1979: 72) as the 'positive expectation of injurious action'. We know that suspicion has been viewed as one of the central cognitive components of distrust (Deutsch, 1958) and has been characterised as a psychological state in which individuals 'actively entertain multiple, possible rival, hypotheses about the motives or genuineness of a person's behaviour' (Fein & Hilton, 1994: 168). It is certainly the case that 'when faced with the choice, individuals and organizations invariably opt to transact with those of known reputation or, better yet, with those with whom they have had past dealings' (Granovetter, 1985: 440).

However, managers may be restricted, for whatever reason, from appointing backroom staff with whom they have worked in the past. This point was borne out during an interview with a former assistant manager at an English League Two club, who described the importance of maintaining contact with ex-players and managers. In addition, he described how he secured his current position:

ASSISTANT MANAGER: I was still a player at xxxx [English League Two club] and the manager came in towards the end of the season. My contract was up and he released me as a player. But then he said there may be an opportunity further down the road or there might be an opportunity to do the reserves because he wanted to restructure the club. I kept in contact with him anyway . . . then he offered me the reserve post and a couple of weeks into pre-season he offered me the number two job.

SK: So the manager had initially planned on bringing in an assistant that he knew from a London-based club but, due to financial constraints, this did not materialise.

ASSISTANT MANAGER: Yeah, that's basically what happened, so he had to get someone who knew the club and who he could trust.

SK: That was quite a fortuitous opportunity.

ASSISTANT MANAGER: It was good for me obviously, but they also got a player, a reserve team manager and an assistant manager all for the price of one really, so it was quite handy for them as well.

| | |
|---|---|
| SK: | Because normally they tend to bring in their own staff, don't they? It seems to be the trend. |
| ASSISTANT MANAGER: | Yeah, yeah, I think that without a doubt they do that because it's someone they can trust and someone they've possibly previously worked with before, but just in my case I think that maybe the ones he wanted to get down here, he'd obviously not got the staff budget and with the people who might want to have come down with xxxx [English League Two club] being quite a way away. He's a London man himself with a lot of London connections, so you'd have to be offering them decent money to come down here. |
| SK: | So how do you get on? You have to forge a partnership then, haven't you? |
| ASSISTANT MANAGER: | Yeah. We get on very well anyway but we don't go out together socialising or drinking together or anything like that – the relationship is business. I think, with hindsight, he says it himself, it was better to do it that way as well for himself. |
| SK: | So it seemed important for him as a newcomer to the club to have someone knowing the ropes there at the club? |
| ASSISTANT MANAGER: | Yeah, I think that probably helped as well but because he didn't know me that well previously, it can be kept at just a working relationship really rather than friendship and he's come down here and it's his first managerial post as well. |

Implicit in the above assistant manager's comments is how relationships develop over time and that 'the more frequently persons interact with one another, the stronger their sentiments of friendship for one another' are (Homans, 1950: 133). Implicit also in the above comments is how thin interpersonal trust can be viewed as a 'standing decision to give most people, even people you don't know, the benefit of the doubt' (Putnam, 2000: 136). Moreover, when trust is not predetermined, the relationship needs to be 'worked upon' by all parties, involving a 'mutual process of self-disclosure' (Giddens, 1990: 121). Thus, if some level of trust is evident, it provides the basis for a relationship and it may be deepened to provide the means for further extending the relationship. In addition, implicit in the above comments is how aspects of personal contact networks, as a form of social capital, may also be cognitive in which trust may not only emerge from personal contact networks themselves but also regarding aspects of the trustees such as personal affection and likeability (Gambetta, 1988).

A central characteristic of traditional authority is that it is not rule-bound and regulated in a stable and systematic way, as is rational-legal bureaucratic authority. In this regard, Weber (1964) pointed out that while traditional authority is based on traditions that partly define the content of commands and the objects and extent of authority, it is also the case that tradition leaves a certain sphere of action open for the leader's 'free personal decision'. This means that traditional authority is characterised by what Weber called a 'double sphere', on the one hand, of action that is bound to specific tradition, and, on the other hand, of action that is free of any specific rules (1964: 342). As Weber noted, this means that the person who exercises traditional authority 'is free to confer grace on the basis of his personal pleasure or displeasure, his personal likes and dislikes, quite arbitrarily' (1964: 342). Therefore, in the exercise of traditional authority, unlike the exercise of legal-rational authority, the extent of the leader's authority is not specified and delimited clearly. On the contrary, there is scope for the arbitrary exercise of power. As previously identified, it is common practice in professional football for a newly appointed manager to bring with him to his new club many backroom staff with whom he has worked at one or more previous clubs. Weber (1964: 341) noted that, in appointing their administrative staff, traditional leaders typically do not appoint people who have been selected as the result of the operation of a regular system of appointments based on technical qualifications but, rather, people who are personal 'favourites' and who are already bound to the leader by ties of personal friendship and loyalty. However, these ties of personal dependency between support staff and the manager may be problematic in a number of respects and may detract from what is regarded as good practice, for example in relation to the treatment of players' injuries (Waddington & Roderick, 2002). More specifically, 'when a manager brings in his own people, that is where there is concern because this person is relying on the manager for his job and he's not going to go against the manager' (Waddington, 2000: 84). There are a number of additional problems concerning these ties of personal dependency between support staff and the manager.

First, while trust may be an important determinant in the selection of a manager's backroom staff, of equal importance is their level of competence in their roles. While some managers may adopt arbitrary rules in the appointment of backroom staff, each of these rules must have some relevance to job performance (Rees, 1966). This is important because reliable and valid selection systems enhance initial person–job fit and person–organisation fit (Rees, 1966). While the latter refers to matching individuals' values and goals, the former relates to matching their knowledge, skills and abilities for the role. This is an important point because, while the lack of specific qualities or skills may be compensated for by the presence of other skills (Rees, 1966: 561–2), a number of studies have identified how backroom staff characteristics, such as previous playing and coaching experience, impacts positively on team performance (Cunningham & Sagas, 2004; Lear & Palmer, 2007). Moreover, an acceptance within, and understanding of, the culture of professional football in addition to an ability to develop a rapport with the players are obviously important justifications for employing personal contacts as assistants. However, the hiring of internal employees, such as former players, 'may lead to a backroom team that think alike and are resistant to change' (Roach & Dixon, 2006: 140). In response, managers could adopt critical reflective practices, involving discussion and debate, with their backroom staff. This is important because, when discussing aspects of player assessment or coaching practices, such critical thinking practices may assist in alleviating any potential confirmation bias and groupthink and facilitate a more critical and consensual decision-making process (Tversky & Kahneman, 1973).

Second, personal contacts can also be viewed as an exclusion mechanism that may limit employment options for those who are not connected to dominant flows of knowledge (Elliott & Maguire, 2008). In particular, utilising personal contacts may lead to diminished access to important, specialised knowledge and sources of new and innovative ideas (Roach & Dixon, 2006: 140). This may limit a manager's backroom staff competencies and knowledge regarding developments in sports science, coaching practices and performance analysis in particular. In this regard, the personal contact network may not only 'be an aid to getting a job, but also a sanctioning device' by virtue of alerting potential employers to the availability of specific individuals (Katz, 1958: 54) and new coaching talent and ideas in particular (Roach & Dixon, 2006).

Finally, what happens when clubs appoint assistant managers and backroom staff without the input of the manager? This is an important point in light of recent events in professional football and at a number of English Premier League clubs in particular. Weber's analysis of the routinisation of charisma and the problem of charismatic succession (1968: 246–54, 1121–57) provides a useful model for understanding the transition from embeddedness to impersonal trust and the dilemma of selecting trustworthy agents from among unfamiliar candidates. The designation of successors by the leader represents an important gatekeeping mechanism regulating trustee roles. What this means is that when a manager is required to work with backroom staff with whom he is unfamiliar, they must build and develop trust (Shapiro, 1987). Thus, trust is based on reputation and that 'reputation has ultimately to be acquired through behaviour over time and in well-understood circumstances' (Dasgupta, 1988: 53). However, due to the insecure nature of their position, quite often managers do not have sufficient time to build this trust and this is one possible reason why managers bring in their own staff. Moreover, the practice of clubs and their owners appointing coaches and assistants without the consent of the manager poses a number of problems. In particular, any possible interference in the manager's role can certainly strain the relations between the manager and his assistant – a point particularly evident in the appointment of Clive Woodward as performance director at Southampton in 2005 (Clifford, 2005). Interference in the role of the football manager will be explored in greater detail in Chapter 7.

## Conclusion

This chapter has identified traditional forms of authority in many aspects of the contemporary football manager's role. Drawing on the work of Weber, it has illustrated how, despite the professionalisation and bureaucratisation of many aspects of football clubs, the role of the manager has proved remarkably resistant to these processes. A picture emerges of an industry managed largely in isolation from external management influences by those who are ill-prepared, insular in outlook and drawn from a narrow segment of society. Back in 2003, John Barnwell, the LMA Chief Executive, suggested that 'the appointment procedure is flawed' (Taylor, 2003) and that managers lose their jobs 'because they are ill-prepared and the appointments, in many cases, shouldn't have been made' (Green, 2002: 89). In professional football, despite clubs' and owners' ability to obtain an exceptional amount of information on managerial performance, the fundamental uncertainty of the labour market is such that managerial recruitment and appointment, like player recruitment, is still strongly influenced by informal personal contacts (McGovern, 2002: 39).

# Chapter 3

# Previous playing experience and formal education

## Introduction

> The process to appoint a new First Team Manager has been diligent and meticulous. In order to ensure we appointed a manager who would meet our needs as a club, feedback from the dressing room, as well as taking account of our culture, vision and values, was critical in drawing up our criteria for the appointment. ... The development of our young Academy players and delivering a pathway to the first team is key to the role. We were keen to appoint a coaching team who would also work closely with Martin Hunter and Radhi Jaïdi in accelerating the development of our youngsters, as well as developing our current first-team squad as individuals and as a team.
>
> (LMA, 2016)

Implicit in the above statement from Les Reed, the current Southampton Executive Director of Football, is how the task of selecting a suitable managerial candidate involved matching the appropriate skills associated with the technical requirements of a particular role (Cohen & Pfeffer, 1986). Moreover, hiring standards and criteria are not only dictated by the particular nature of the work to be done and the skills required to perform such work but also reflect the interplay of organisational and institutional interests (Cohen & Pfeffer, 1986) and the culture of a particular club. In professional football, managerial recruitment strategies tend to reflect a general policy set at the boardroom level, and thus managerial selection criteria will tend to vary from club to club. For example, the appointment of a particular manager may reflect that the immediate objective is survival, while other clubs may adopt a more long-term strategic view taking account of youth development. While older, more experienced football managers tend to perform better than younger managers (Bridgewater, 2010), one trend in professional football is the tendency to appoint high-profile players as managers. However, it is often the case that these players do not possess the necessary qualifications and their suitability for the task is questionable

(Murphy, 2002). Their ability to draw star players to the club, as well as capturing the imagination of key stakeholders, are obvious influences in the appointment process. However, there are mixed views, with some clubs considering that ex-players have insufficient experience, while others feel that managers should work their way to top positions by a series of gradual appointments (Perry, 2000a).

This chapter develops points explored briefly in the previous chapter and examines the role of previous playing experience and coaching qualifications in the recruitment and appointment of managers. In addition, the chapter explores the views of players and managers regarding the skills, competencies and qualifications necessary for football managers to possess. The final section explores the impact of formal education on managerial success and performance and how it may assist managers in dealing with the many problems they face. This is important because, in addition to identifying the knowledge and skills that managers need to develop, we also need to understand how this knowledge is applied in the football management process.

## Previous playing experience

While there are numerous routes into club management, there is a widely held belief that previous playing experience is the main qualification (Pawson, 1973; Allera & Nobay, 1966; Carter, 2006; Wilders, 1976; Dawson & Dobson, 2002; Perry, 2000a). However, while more successful players tend to remain in professional football as coaches or assistant managers, for the majority of retired players the option of moving into football management is unattainable (Morris, 1981; Gearing, 1999; Houlston, 1982; Giulianotti, 1999). Within professional football in the UK, playing experience remains a key quality. Kenny Hibbitt, a former Wolverhampton Wanderers player with considerable managerial experience, expressed the widely held view that 'it doesn't matter what qualifications you have got, you have to have been in situations to know what it's about . . . Players respect ex-players and they find out if you've never played' (Green, 2002: 114). This is in stark contrast to the Dutch approach of appointing club managers. For example, Murphy (2002: 47) noted that the view that ex-players make good managers is not widely held in the Netherlands, where there is a 'developing appreciation of the need to gradually induct successful footballers into the skills of coaching, rather than simply throw them in at the deep end'. More recently, John Barnwell, the former LMA Chief Executive, expressed the growing view that 'players appointed to run clubs need time to develop a good understanding of the pressures involved in management' (Bridgewater, 2010: 10).

In this research, players and managers were asked to describe attributes or qualities they deemed important for a successful manager to possess. One recurring theme in all of the interviews with managers concerned the importance of previous playing experience. One experienced manager, whose comment is representative of many others, said: 'I felt that probably with the career as a footballer that you would have walked into a job in management'. Another manager, with considerable managerial experience in both the UK and Ireland, described the importance of previous playing experience as follows:

> When you . . . stand up or say something to a player's face, you've got to be able to back it up, and I suppose I was fortunate . . . from playing . . . you didn't point fingers at players if you're not able to do it yourself.

This point was borne out by the research of Taylor and colleagues (1997) who noted that, until recently, managerial appointments within professional football remained the almost exclusive preserve of former players. In 1907, Herbert Chapman's appointment as player/manager of Northampton Town was 'casually fixed in the dressing-room' (Pawson, 1973: 30). There is evidence to suggest this practice still exists today. The former manager of an English League Two side described his first managerial appointment:

> My first managerial experience was as a player at xxxx [English League Two club]. I was 33 years of age and I had come off the field at the end of the game. The vice-chairman approached me and said that the manager had resigned just before the game and that I was the senior player at the club and would I fancy taking on the job as manager. I said, "No problem".

One considerably experienced English Premier League manager described his first managerial appointment in professional football:

> I was quite lucky. I was playing at xxxx [English Championship club] and the manager got sacked. At the time I was the club captain. So they [boardroom members] asked me would I step in. So I did.

The quality of a football manager's previous playing experience is one important determinant of a manager's performance (Dawson & Dobson, 2002), while the impact of coaching staff characteristics such as previous playing and coaching experience experience all seem to impact positively on team performance (Lear & Palmer, 2007; Cunningham & Sagas, 2004). A former English Championship manager provided an insight into both qualifications and previous playing experience. In describing the importance of his previous involvement as a player in European competition, he said:

> It's invaluable, of course it is . . . You say to me, like, you're playing xxxx [German Bundesliga club] in the European Cup next week. How are you going to approach it if you haven't got that wealth of experience

in European football? How are you going to deal with it? You need to be able to say, "Look this is how we are going to play".

More recently, Les Reed, the Southampton Executive Director of Football, described the importance of previous experience in European competition in the club's recent appointment of Claude Puel:

> Claude has a fantastic platform to work from and is aware that our ambition is to repeat and improve on our performances in the Premier League over the past three seasons. His Champions League and European experience will be valuable in our Europa League challenge this coming season and with the support of our excellent staff at the club I am sure he will do well.
>
> (LMA, 2016)

There is evidence from the research data and also from the autobiographies of professional players to support the idea that it is the manager's previous playing experience that is seen as of central importance, particularly at the highest levels of the game. For example, the Dutch international player Jaap Stam, in discussing his views on managers, stressed the importance of being someone who has played 'at the highest level and understands modern football'. He described how Frank Rijkaard's

> knowledge of the game was excellent and the squad respected his international record as a player. He had quit playing only recently so he knew how difficult it was out on the pitch and could relate to the problems we had.
>
> (Stam, 2001: 125)

A similar theme emerged from the interviews with players, all of whom identified the importance of a manager possessing previous playing experience. The following two examples from players with experience in the English Premier League were typical of players' views:

> I think that it's very, very important – if you have somebody that has played the game at a high level and can get it across, then they can be very, very good.

> Some fellows [managers] who haven't played the game, they will have pencils and red arrows for this and blue pencils for that, but when you get out there and cross the white line, you need to have played, and it is a help.

Perry and Davies (1997: 11) noted that in 1995, '95% of all managers were ex-professionals, with knowledge of the game and empathy with the players being seen as crucial', with the implication that unless a manager is an ex-professional player, he is unlikely to have this empathy and knowledge of the game. A recurring theme that emerged from the interviews with players was how empathy and knowledge of the game were considerably important attributes for a manager to possess. The possession of 'knowledge of the game' is important because, while sources of codified knowledge such as formal education and books 'can impart knowledge relevant to managerial tasks' (Castanias & Helfat, 2001: 662), effective football management also requires learning by doing and demands practice. Thus, as we shall see in the next section, while playing experience does provide managers with considerable tacit knowledge, the knowledge gained from managing is considered even more valuable by players.

## Knowledge of the game

While both players and managers identified the importance of previous playing experience, one interesting theme emerged from interviews with players. They were asked to describe attributes or qualities they deemed important – in addition to previous playing experience – for a successful manager to possess. When players were questioned further, they all identified knowledge of the game as being extremely important. In describing in more detail what he meant by 'knowledge of the game', one former English Premier League player stated:

PLAYER: Well, you definitely need knowledge of the game. I think that's huge.
SK: Having played the game? What do you mean?
PLAYER: No, not being able to play the game – to have knowledge of the game. There are people out there who weren't great players, but they would be good managers. You have to have knowledge of the game and you have to get across to your players that you know what you are doing. Like, I had a manager before where he wouldn't have a clue. I've had one or two like that. Maybe a reserve team manager I've had like that – again, he didn't play, and everything was out of a coaching manual.
SK: Really?
PLAYER: And it's f****** stupid, like – a coaching manual is there for guidelines. At the end of the day, it's playing football that players want to do, it's not being coached all the time. You need to get a balance and I think the good ones have it. I don't think everyone has it. In terms of your manager, you need to have respect for your manager, you need to have faith that if a problem comes up he is able to deal with that. If he doesn't have this, then at the time you may be going "What the f*** is he doing?"

In a similar manner, one former youth international player with considerable playing experience at a number of clubs in all four divisions in the UK was probed further on what he viewed as important attributes for success in management. In particular, this player described what 'knowledge and experience of the game' entailed. He said:

PLAYER: It's knowledge of the game but being able to tell your players and get your ideas into your players that you know what you're on about. I think there is nothing worse than a manager who thinks he knows everything but his players don't have faith in him. The players *KNOW* he doesn't have a clue what he is doing.

SK: Have you experienced this kind of situation in football?

PLAYER: I will give you an example of a game [a Champions League qualifier] we played against an opposition that were far better than us. Technically, physically, they were streets ahead of us, miles ahead of us. But he went out with this formation that we knew wouldn't work – we knew it but he stuck to this formation. But this was at home. So we went away and played them [in the return leg] at a stadium that they hadn't lost in for four years or something and he stayed with this 4–4–2 formation and we got battered 4–0. Even at 3–0 down, he was saying, "Stick to the system – we will get one back", and the players were saying, "Just play 4–5–1 or 5–4–1" – you know what I mean – and I found that the players were going, "He doesn't have a f****** clue".

The message conveyed both by managers and players is unambiguous: previous playing experience and knowledge of the game are key attributes for a manager to possess. More specifically, based on the data gathered from players, both knowledge of the game and an ability to 'get this across' to players was deemed critical. This latter theme concerned a manager's ability to communicate his knowledge to his players. This is not surprising because it is well known that, 'regardless of the level of knowledge and skill of the coach, it is the application of that knowledge and skill which separates the excellent practitioner from the average' (Cushion & Jones, 2001: 355). Moreover, the ability to communicate sport-specific content that is both understandable and tailored to individuals is a form of pedagogical content knowledge (Cassidy et al., 2015; Metzler, 2005; Shulman, 1986). This is important for managers in general and new managers in particular because 'if you don't know what you're doing at professional level the players will let you know' (Lear & Palmer, 2017: 26) or, in football parlance, 'you will get found out'. Therefore, football managers, like coaches, need to know when, why and how to adopt a particular coaching method best suited to each athlete's specific needs (Cassidy et al., 2015). Implicit here is also a manager's self-awareness of his particular set of skills and the importance of recruiting appropriate backroom staff to complement and enhance his skill set and knowledge base, which should alleviate any of his perceived shortcomings.

More worrying, though, is the widely held belief by football managers that previous playing experience is sufficient on its own for entry into management. This seems to arise from an assumption by managers that the skills of a professional football player are interchangeable with those of management. However, previous playing experience is no guarantee of success in football management and many of the difficulties experienced in club management are the result of managers' assumptions about this interchangeability of skills. However, this approach to management training and the valuation of playing experience over managerial experience is not universal. For example, in Germany, aspiring football managers require 'a qualification to gain a licence to work in the Bundesliga' (Carter, 2006: 127) and need to gain at least two years of managerial experience in the lower divisions, as a form of apprenticeship, before they can manage a club in the Bundesliga (Murphy, 1998; Carter, 2006).

## Learning by doing

A key element of football management, and one clearly indicative of the resistance to professionalisation, is its traditional practical orientation, with an emphasis on learning on the job, rather than on formal training and qualifications (Carter, 2006). In addition, the practice of 'learning as you go along' also extends to coaching in professional football (Jones *et al.*, 2003: 222). As noted in Chapter 1, several studies have drawn attention to the fact that few managers have any preparatory training for club management or managerial expertise outside football itself (Wilders, 1976; Perry & Davies, 1997; Perry, 2000b; Penn, 2002; Carter, 2006). All of the managers interviewed described how, as players, they learned from, and were influenced by, their previous managers. For example, one former English Premier League manager described how he 'picked up bits and pieces from all the managers [he] had'. In addition, a number of managers identified how they learned from previous managers in relation to issues such as training sessions, match tactics and preparation. The former Everton manager David Moyes described how, as a player, he took notes on any training drills or sessions that he enjoyed, many of which he still uses today (LMA, 2009). Similarly, Roy Keane, 'spent a long time watching from the other side' towards the end of his playing career (Buckley, 2008). In his autobiography, Bryan Robson described moving as a player from Manchester United to the position of player/manager at an English Premier League club, and identified the importance of previous playing experience and his approach to learning the skills of football management:

> It was a big step, from being a player to being the player-boss, with all the responsibility that carries, but when you have been in the game as long as

I had been, at club and international level, you learn what it's about. Over the previous couple of years I'd spent a lot of time with the [Manchester] United coaching staff, watching and listening as they prepared for training sessions. In those last few weeks, when I knew I was going to Middlesbrough, I took an even closer interest in their work.

(Robson, 2006: 222)

While Robson had no formal coaching or management training prior to his appointment at Middlesbrough, implicit in his comments is how his approach to 'learning the skills of management' incorporated modelling and the observing of other people's behaviour, which seemed to serve as a guide for future action (Bandura, 1977). Moreover, it is worth noting that informal and unmediated learning sources such as interactions with other coaches (Lear & Palmer, 2007), watching other teams' training practices, modelling and the use of peer mentors (Jones et al., 2009; Carter & Bloom, 2009; Gilbert & Trudel, 2005; Gould et al., 1990; Bloom et al., 1998) considerably influence the development of coaching knowledge. For football managers such as Roy Keane, Bryan Robson, Mark Hughes and Steve Bruce, the experience of having played under Sir Alex Ferguson may assist in dealing with problems. In particular, back in 2008, Keane reflected on how his previous managers such as Brian Clough and Sir Alex Ferguson assisted him with aspects of management and stated:

When I'm dealing with a player, I often think, "How would they have dealt with the player?" I saw how they handled the big players with the big egos. The experience of playing under Clough and Ferguson, you can't buy that.

(Buckley, 2008: 12)

All of the managers interviewed were asked to describe their first managerial experience in professional football and all identified the lack of preparation and failure to comprehend fully what the role of the manager entailed. One experienced manager described management in professional football as 'a learning curve, where you learn every day how to deal with different situations'. Another manager referred to his first managerial appointment as 'a complete surprise' and went on to say that he 'wasn't particularly prepared or ready for it'. Another manager, who was managing in the English Championship, described his first managerial experience after retiring as a player:

It was a bit of an eye-opener to be honest . . . It just came out of the blue getting the job. It came to the first league match and all of a sudden I turned up pretty much as if I was a player before the game and there were just a million things to do that I didn't realise. Handing in the team sheet, getting the tactics done, getting all the set pieces written up and all these bits and pieces. I got through it, but it was a bit of an eye-opener and from then onwards I really sort of get in front of myself and get there [the ground] really early [on match days], whether it is 11 or half 11 in the morning so everything's done.

During the course of an interview, one manager described his lack of understanding of what the manager's role entailed, even though he had had considerable experience in the lower leagues as an assistant manager in the UK. In particular, he described his first 'full' managerial appointment in professional football:

> [It was] different to what I thought it would be – more intense than what I thought it would be. I found there was a lot more work with the media, a lot more work to do with individual players, a lot more to do with members of the board and with members of staff at the club, so there was a lot more to the job than I first envisaged. When I was assistant manager, I would have said, "Listen, that job is a piece of piss".

Implicit in the above manager's comments is his lack of preparation, the demanding nature of the job and the difficulty in comprehending fully what the role of the manager specifically entailed. As noted earlier, chronic job insecurity is a prominent feature of management in professional football. While this job insecurity cannot be explained simply in terms of the lack of training of managers, it may be the case that some of the initial strains involved in managing may be reduced by undertaking some form of managerial training (Bridgewater, 2006b). This is important because we know that poor education (Wilders, 1976) and inadequate formal training (Perry, 2000a; Carter, 2006) are common and traditional aspects of football management. As noted in Chapter 1, the English FA's attempts to professionalise football management by introducing formal management training courses in the 1970s and 1980s faced considerable managerial resistance and these courses were discontinued due to inadequate numbers (Carter, 2006). Since its inception, the LMA has created and developed a number of management training courses designed to assist football managers in the development of their management skills. These programmes include the Certificate of Applied Management at the University of Warwick and the Certificate in Professional Football Management and Administration at the University of Southampton. More recently, the LMA's Diploma in Football Management, in partnership with the University of Liverpool, is designed specifically to assist current and aspirant managers survive many of the problems managers face. However, it remains to be seen what impact these courses will have on football management in general and on managerial success and/or turnover in particular. I will return to this point later.

Based on the data collected in this research, professional football club managers, in general, are still ill-prepared to deal with the demands of management. Considering the increased turnover rates, high levels of insecurity and the obvious lack of preparation, one question arises: why do most professional football managers in the UK not undertake any systematic training leading to formal qualifications? Before attempting to answer this question, it is important to understand managers' views on formal management training and coaching qualifications.

## Coaching qualifications

In professional football in the UK, undertaking formal coaching and management training is seen as a desirable, although unnecessary, job requirement. Traditionally, most football managers were ex-professional players, with the majority completing their limited formal education at a relatively young age. It is worth noting that it has only been since 2003 that there has been a requirement for anyone who aspires to manage a club in the English Premier League to hold the Professional Licence of the Union of European Football Associations (UEFA), while managers outside the English Premier League are still not required to hold any formal qualifications. All of the managers interviewed saw the attainment of coaching qualifications as desirable. However, one experienced manager expressed the widely held view that while it was important to have them, considerably more value is placed on previous playing experience. The level of importance placed on coaching qualifications varied considerably from manager to manager. For example, one recently appointed manager of an English League Two side described qualifications as 'part and parcel of the game' and went on to say that, 'I think nowadays you have to have them, and that's the bottom line'. Another older, more experienced manager, with considerable managerial and playing experience in the lower tiers of English football, was sceptical of the value of coaching qualifications. He said:

> I think, yeah, it's important, but I also think it's very, very heavy stuff as well. I think particularly if you are not books-orientated and stuff like that, there is a lot of theory and I mean, OK, if you are used to it, then OK. But I didn't really go to college and I wasn't really book-orientated.

Several managers were critical of the recent emphasis on obtaining coaching qualifications. One manager, with managerial experience at club level in the UK and at full senior international level, said:

> I think it's important. But I think there's an over-emphasis on it at the moment. I'm in the process of doing the UEFA A badge. I think it's over-hyped and overrated to be honest . . . It has to be done, there's a lot of

good knowledge in it as well but you don't go and take everything out of a book. I think the biggest one that I say is that if you're 2–0 down and ten minutes to go, you don't go and look at a [coaching] manual.

Throughout football's history, qualified coaches have been regularly stigmatised as 'schoolteachers' and, for many in the game, practical experience of playing professional football has remained the key quality. Traditionally, there has been a deep suspicion of the value of education and training that does not appear to have an immediate practical basis. In this regard, one experienced manager, with considerable playing experience in the old English First Division, was more critical of coaching qualifications. He stated:

> People go on about coaching qualifications, and your UEFA badges and what not. It's crap – you can set out grids and set out sessions, your right back goes here and your left back goes there and you look at the personnel that you have got and you go, "Well, he is not capable of doing it". So coaching to me is giving something to a group of players . . . for you [as a coach] to identify their weaknesses and for you to utilise them as a player and a team unit and that's what I think about coaching.

Most managers saw the importance of possessing coaching qualifications as deriving from the perception that they were helpful – although not necessary – in getting a job, rather than in terms of the added value they bring to the job. For example, several managers expressed the view that obtaining coaching qualifications was seen as a sorting device (Bynner & Parsons, 2001) and purely as a 'marker' or 'signalling of their intention' to football clubs of their desire to manage. It could also be argued that managerial hostility towards formal coaching education programmes concerns their failure to provide adequate practical knowledge for current and aspirant managers (Bloom *et al.*, 1998; Cushion *et al.*, 2003; Gilbert & Trudel, 2005). I will return to this point later.

The relatively low value placed on formal training is also shared by other key personnel in football. For example, Carter (2006: 107) noted that club directors 'did not regard professional qualifications for management as necessary' and 'did not want to be forced to choose managers from a list of qualified candidates'. In 2006, following his appointment at Middlesbrough, Gareth Southgate stated, 'I've been given an opportunity – the chairman believes in me and he feels he should be able to appoint who he wants as manager' (Southgate, 2006). Southgate possessed no formal coaching or management training prior to his appointment. The bottom line is that clubs and directors have in mind a list of candidates from among whom they wish to select their club manager. Quite often in professional football, managerial candidates possess no formal qualifications and English Premier League clubs who have appointed managers such as Glenn Roeder and Gareth

Southgate have had to obtain dispensations from the league's governing body prior to their appointment.

Similar views emerged from the players who were interviewed; a commonly expressed view was that, in the last few years, an over-emphasis on coaching has pervaded professional football. One player with considerable experience in the English Premier League said:

> Like, I had a manager before where he wouldn't have a clue. I've had one or two like that. Maybe a reserve team manager I've had like that – again, he didn't play, and everything was out of a coaching manual. ... And it's f****** stupid, like – a coaching manual is there for guidelines. At the end of the day, it's playing football that players want to do, it's not being coached all the time.

Based on the data gathered from managers, it appears that inadequate preparation and poor levels of training and qualifications are common features of football management. Moreover, it is argued that many of the difficulties experienced in football management are a result of managers' assumptions about the interchangeability of skills between playing and managing. The following section provides a preliminary insight into why some managers place such a low priority on formal management training and coaching qualifications.

### The basis of hostility towards education and coaching qualifications

In order to understand football managers' attitudes towards education and qualifications, it is important to identify some of the central aspects of the culture of professional football. Critcher (1979: 161) identified core values in professional football as 'masculinity, aggression, physical emphasis'. These core values are reflected in the workplace behaviour and in the socialisation of young players and, it is argued, they downgrade the value of formal education as a marker of success in the game. This has important implications for players' and managers' attitudes towards training, education and coaching qualifications. Historically, within professional football there was long-standing resistance to the idea of formal educational qualifications. Carter (2006: 128) suggested that the working-class background of players with few educational qualifications engendered a distrust of people with professional qualifications and argued that 'this mistrust of the intellectual is rooted in the history of Britain's social relations'. Moreover, Carter (2006: 84) suggested that not only do 'working-class players distrust anything theoretical, but coaching challenged firmly held beliefs that English football was based on individual skill and masculine toughness'.

Gearing (1999) suggested that football clubs are sites of anti-intellectualism, reinforced in the everyday working practices of training, travelling and internal communication. Several studies have identified unfavourable attitudes towards the attainment of education and qualifications in professional football (Holt, 2002; Houlston, 1982; McGillivray et al., 2005; Pain & Harwood, 2004; Carter, 2006; Parker, 1996, 2001). Research currently underway attempts to investigate recent claims that there is a slight incremental shift in engagement by players towards the role and importance of educational and vocational qualifications (Richardson et al., 2012). Elsewhere, it has been argued that 'young players are solely focused on sporting performances and are engulfed in the social world of football which can cultivate a one-dimensional identity thus resulting in diminished involvement in academic and social activities' (Brown & Potrac, 2009: 112). Moreover, it appears that interest in, or engagement with, educational discourse is viewed as having little, if any, relationship with the process of attaining a professional football identity (Cushion & Jones, 2006). It is worth noting that in Germany, Holland and Spain a more holistic player development philosophy is adopted that encompasses educational and vocational skills (Jonker et al., 2010; Mitchell et al., 2014; Brown & Potrac, 2009; Christensen & Sorensen, 2009). In particular, McGillivray and McIntosh (2006) utilised Bourdieu's formula of habitus, capital and field to frame professional football players' social practices, with specific emphasis on their engagement (or lack of engagement) with educational discourses. More specifically, McGillivray and McIntosh (2006: 377) exposed 'the prevailing anti-intellectualism found within the professional football industry' and identified 'contestation over the relative value of physical and cultural capital within the professional football field and its deleterious impact on early educational experiences'. Thus, while 'possessing the desired cultural capital', conferred by the educational field, normally enhances individuals' opportunities for distinction (McGillivray et al., 2005: 104), the legitimate and valued ways of 'knowing' in the professional football field are invariably associated with physical performance and expressions of hyper-masculine identities rather than with academic achievement. Moreover, because 'the different goods, resources and values' that denote capital are not equally distributed within each field, 'the cultural capital ascribed to academic qualifications is of little value' (McGillivray et al., 2005: 104). Moreover, possession of such cultural capital is often deemed unwelcome and threatening in an industry that is viewed as anti-intellectual (McGillivray et al., 2005; McGillivray & McIntosh, 2006). What this means is that in professional football, the adoption of physical, aggressive and masculine attitudes and behaviours takes precedence over academic achievement. Therefore, in Bourdieu's (1986) terms, physical, or embodied, capital (speed, skill, strength or practical labour) is the dominant currency tradable within professional football and is accorded greater value than the cultural capital associated with formal educational discourses. While not always explicit, it is evident that the value of formal educational theory is downgraded as a marker for success in the game. Thus, it is argued that, historically, professional football is a sport in which educational cultural capital is devalued and in which young men tend to disassociate themselves from formal education. In addition, it may be the case that those players who do exhibit a wish for further training or qualifications may be ostracised or ridiculed by their fellow players. While the studies cited above suggest that the majority of professional players devalue the attainment of education, the data reported in this chapter suggest that a similar view is held by professional football managers. This provides a useful starting point in examining how this traditional pattern of management persisted in professional soccer when it has long been superseded in industrial relations more generally.

While traditional authority is based on respect for the sanctity of age-old rules and customs, traditional social action is a reflex action, an automatic response to a habitualised stimulus. Subsequently, a person obeys 'cultural reflexes' that have become entrenched, or in Weber's terms a 'settled orientation' exists, whereby one does something merely because it has always been done this way (Weber, 1964: 75). One traditional element of football management – and one clearly indicative of the resistance to the professionalisation of the manager's role – is something that has been a central characteristic of football management from its nineteenth-century origins: its traditional practical orientation, with an emphasis on learning on the job, rather than formal training and qualifications (Carter, 2006). As Weber noted, traditional leaders are not 'professionals' in the modern sense, since their claim to authority does not rest upon training and the possession of formal qualifications. The traditional leader exercises 'personal authority ... which he enjoys by virtue of his traditional status' (Weber, 1964: 341–5). In this regard, it is important to note that few football managers have any formal training in management or, indeed, any managerial experience outside football. Those who manage professional clubs outside the English Premier League are still not required to hold any formal qualifications. This long-standing tradition of 'learning by doing' lays emphasis not on the formal qualifications of a manager, which can be assessed in a relatively detached way, but on the personal experience of each individual manager, the value of which is more difficult to assess. This is important because the more difficult it is to appraise an organisation's product, the more difficult it is to gain legitimacy through task-related activity and, thus, the more likely it is that the organisation will adopt institutionalised practices to obtain legitimacy (Meyer & Rowan, 1977; DiMaggio & Powell, 1983). Also implicit in this traditional emphasis on 'learning by doing' is an ideology that asserts that, while the principles and techniques of management in industry can be classified, codified and taught – for example, in the form of degrees in business or management – football management is so different from management in other industries that it is not possible to classify, codify and teach the principles of good practice; rather, each manager must develop his own individual approach and style based on his personal experiences in football. One consequence of this is that it is difficult to challenge the managerial style of a particular manager by claiming that it represents 'bad practice', since there is nothing that can serve as an agreed measuring rod. In the world of professional football, there is no attempt to identify and disseminate good practice. Rather, each individual manager defines 'good practice' as *his* good practice, based on his own experience. While there is no one specific style of football management (Bridgewater, 2006b), a small but growing body of literature has recently examined styles of football management in Ireland (Molan *et al.*, 2016), England (Mills *et al.*, 2016) and Denmark (Nissen, 2016). Research currently underway attempts to develop an appropriate leadership framework that professional managers may adopt.

While this chapter argues that the majority of professional managers devalue the attainment of formal coaching qualification and management training, it would be a mistake to assume that all managers lack an engagement in learning about aspects of football management. As discussed, managers regularly meet up socially and discuss managerial problems, which constitutes a form of peer-to-peer learning (Winter, 2007; Buckley, 2008). Managers often seek out assistance from fellow managers, while the supportive role of Sir Alex Ferguson as a mentor was a recurring theme in a number of manager interviews. It is argued that managers should 'consider the philosophical assumptions and practical applications of pertinent learning theory' (Roberts & Potrac, 2014: 180), which will assist them in developing expert management knowledge (Jones *et al.*, 2004). Learning is a broad, complex concept involving many different perceptions, theoretical frameworks and assumptions and refers to a relatively enduring change in a person's knowledge or behaviour or in the capacity to behave in a given manner. In this regard, there is evidence to suggest awareness by some managers of the importance of adopting a growth mindset in which they are open to, and accepting of, change. For example, Sam Allardyce is widely regarded for his openness to change and the adoption of sport psychology, while considerable evidence exists concerning Sir Alex Ferguson's openness and willingness to embrace change regarding new coaching and managerial practices (Ferguson, 2013; Elberse, 2013). It is worth noting that Ferguson's style of management and openness to change was a recurring theme during the action research workshop with 14 current/former English Premier League players. In addition, evidence supporting the recent importance of formal football management training exists. Stuart Pearce stated, 'I appreciate that the most important thing is to get good results but to me the bottom line is that the more education you can give yourself, and the more preparation you can do, the less chance you have of failing' (LMA, 2009: 20). More recently, Chris Hughton endorsed the PFA's Diploma in Football Management and stated that 'it helped me to make the step up and has been of immense value to me' (LMA, 2016). Roy Keane has argued that the Pro

Licence is 'a great source of information and way of meeting different people' and qualifications 'are very, very valuable, but they don't necessarily make or break you as a manager' (Winter, 2007; Buckley, 2008).

The provision of tailored football management courses reflects attempts to professionalise the post of the football manager. This is important because Bridgewater (2006b) identified a significant change in the fortunes of managers who have undertaken coaching and management qualifications. More specifically, 'managers with no qualifications, or only the limited B Licence, achieved lower percentage wins than those with the Pro Licence' (Bridgewater, 2006b: 8). Richard Bevan, Chief Executive of the LMA, stated that 'historically, there has been a significant lack of investment in the provision of management support and training programmes for the development of young coaches and managers' (Scott, 2010). In 2002, 60 of the 72 managers in the Football League had gained an advanced coaching licence, while by 2006 a UEFA census identified that there were 45 coaches with Pro Licences in England and this figure rose to 115 by 2009. However, the ratio of available Pro-Licensed coaches to players shows an alarming gulf between England and Spain: 1:190 in Spain and 1:19,565 in England, with 2,140 Pro-Licensed coaches in Spain (Scott, 2010).

In 2006, PFA Chief Executive Gordon Taylor stated, 'The role of the modern football club manager has changed considerably . . . The high-profile nature of the industry now requires that players considering a career in football management need high-quality management training' (Bridgewater, 2006b). It is argued that formal management education programmes might perhaps focus more on specific aspects of the manager's role rather than scientific methods to promote player development. This is important because the pressures and demands placed on managers are quite different from those placed on coaches and is perhaps one reason for managerial resistance towards coaching qualifications. Building on existing research (Bridgewater, 2010), further research on the content, delivery and assessment of formal management training is required in order to develop appropriate football management skills and competencies. Based on the data gathered from the research workshops, we know that critical thinking and self-reflection assists managers in dealing with many of the daily problems they face. It is well known that Sam Allardyce, Aidy Boothroyd, Brendan Rodgers, Eddie Howe, Rafa Benitez and Sir Alex Ferguson are keen endorsers of reflection as part of their coaching and management practice. It might also be a worthwhile exercise to examine the observation methods employed by Sir Alex Ferguson (Elberse, 2013). This is important because we know that a specific type of observation, and being 'sensitised or primed to notice certain things, often distinguishes the ordinary coaches from the really good ones' (Jones et al., 2013: 276). In addition, the utilisation of problem-based scenarios, divergent and convergent questions and feedback helps managers in the assessment and development of players' perceptual cognitive skills (Kelly, 2016).

## Conclusion

The findings highlight a lack of formal management training, hostility towards education and coaching qualifications, and mistaken assumptions by managers that previous playing experience is sufficient preparation for entry into football management. While mandatory qualifications have recently been introduced for those who aspire to manage in the Premier League, traditional aspects of management culture still dominate in the appointment of football managers. Professional football clubs regularly appoint big-name ex-players because it pleases fans and creates excitement, yet this appears to be an inappropriate method for appointing managers. However, some clubs, such as Liverpool, Southampton and Swansea, are beginning to adopt more sophisticated and objective criteria in the selection of prospective managers.

# Chapter 4

# The assessment and recruitment of players

## Introduction

When a football manager is appointed, one of the first and arguably most important tasks that is undertaken concerns an assessment of the club's registered players. Following this assessment, a decision is made as to whether new players need to be recruited to complement and enhance the existing squad of players. For professional football managers, the recruitment of playing talent is the subject of considerable scrutiny from the media and fans (Bridgewater, 2010). In addition, the ability of a football manager to identify and recruit 'true talent is a much sought-after quality that enables clubs not to waste time and money by investing in the wrong players' (Christensen, 2009: 366). Moreover, player assessment and recruitment decisions are considered a prime measure of managerial acumen and one of managers' most important yet difficult tasks. Some managers, such as Sir Alex Ferguson, Arsène Wenger and Dario Gradi, have gained reputations for their expertise in the assessment and recruitment of players. Considering the increased inflow of migrant players, the escalation in transfer fees and FFP restrictions, it is imperative that clubs optimise their financial resources and ensure their player recruitment decisions are wisely informed and are not labelled as 'bad'. These developments place a number of additional constraints on a manager's ability to assess, recruit and manage players in general and foreign players in particular. Moreover, inherent in this process of player assessment and recruitment is subjectivity and risk. In this regard, Christensen (2009: 371) challenged the assumption that this is a rational or objective process, arguing instead that coaches and managers utilise 'intuition and gut feeling' in the selection and recruitment of elite football players. Moreover, professional football 'is a sport in which the "right" and "wrong" qualities are identified not through a few single factors but through a multifaceted set of characteristics' (Christensen, 2009: 366). This raises a number of obvious questions: what are the 'right' and 'wrong' qualities and how are they assessed? In addition, what process do managers utilise when assessing and evaluating players and who do managers consult in making such crucial decisions? Before examining these issues, the following section will discuss the various player recruitment methods in professional football.

## Player recruitment in professional football

A number of academic studies have examined the recruitment strategies of professional football clubs in England (Sutherland, 1986; Szymanski & Kuypers, 1999; Bourke, 2001, 2002; McGovern, 2002; Littlewood & Richardson, 2006). Players may be recruited internally via the trainee system or externally via the transfer system. The transfer or market system is based on two elements: registration and contract. In addition to signing a contract of employment, every professional football player must be registered with the Football League and FA. Players may move between clubs when their registration is transferred from one club to another. Quite often, this is subject to a transfer fee paid to the club holding the player's registration. Football clubs may also recruit 'free agents' or players not currently under contract with another club. Alternatively, clubs may recruit players internally via their youth trainee systems. Most professional clubs in the UK have replaced their former two-year youth training scheme with a three-year modern apprenticeship scheme, referred to as the 'scholarship system'. Professional football clubs' youth development and apprenticeship schemes have attracted considerable academic attention (Parker, 2001; Holt, 2002; Monk, 2000; Monk & Russell, 2000; Monk & Olsen, 2006; Stewart & Sutherland, 1996; Waddington, 2001). While most professional football clubs remain focused on youth development (Walters & Rossi, 2009), some clubs have placed a greater emphasis on the recruitment of cheaper, more experienced players from abroad (Walters & Rossi, 2009; Stead & Maguire, 2000; Gilmore & Gilson, 2007). This may be a reflection of the difficulties that young indigenous players face in trying to make the grade in professional football today (Conn, 2009). More specifically, only 15 per cent of football trainees in the UK will be earning their living as professional footballers by the time they are 21 (Brown & Potrac, 2009; Gerrard, 2009). Given the insecure nature of the manager's position, and the pressure for immediate results, relying on long-term youth development strategies for playing talent is a luxury few managers can afford (Gilmore & Gilson, 2007) and appears to be leading managers to bring high-profile players into the club (Relvas et al., 2010).

A useful starting point in understanding the recruitment strategies adopted by professional football clubs in the UK and by managers in particular would involve an examination of player migration patterns in professional football. This is important because, as noted in Chapter 1, structural, financial and legislative changes have acted as a lubricant, easing and accelerating the international movement of football players. This recent inflow places a number of additional constraints on managers' ability to assess, recruit and manage foreign players. For players in general and migrant players in particular, the sociocultural problems of adjustment and dislocation need to be taken into consideration, which means that managers need to acknowledge cultural dimensions of both the host country and the club as both may have a considerable effect on the potential success of player recruitment decisions (Roderick, 2006; Maguire & Pearton, 2000: 762; Williams & Reilly, 2000). This is important because, in comparison to other leagues across Europe, English clubs employ the highest proportion of foreign players (Besson et al., 2011; Walters & Rossi, 2009; Madichie, 2009) and are by far the most re-exporting national association (Besson et al., 2011). For example, in 2010, 241 (111 from the Premier League) foreign footballers moved away from the UK (Besson et al., 2011), which may, in part, reflect the inability of foreign players to fit in and adapt to the culture of both the club and the host country (Maguire & Pearton, 2000; Brady et al., 2008; Besson et al., 2011). Unfortunately, the ability of foreign players to settle in the host national culture is an important yet often overlooked aspect of the recruitment and assessment of professional football players (Richardson et al., 2012).

## Player mobility and migration

The migration of professional football players has attracted considerable academic attention (McGovern, 2002; Bale & Maguire, 1994; Maguire & Pearton, 2000; Maguire & Stead, 1998; Magee & Sugden, 2002). More specifically, academic studies have examined the migration of professional football players from Ireland (Bourke, 2001, 2003; McGovern, 2000), Africa (Darby et al., 2007; Poli, 2006), Brazil (De Vasconcellos Ribeiro & Dimeo, 2009), Hungary (Molnar & Maguire, 2008), Scotland (Moorhouse, 1994) and the Nordic/Scandinavian countries (Stead & Maguire, 2000). More recently, professional football in the UK has witnessed a considerable influx of foreign players (Walters & Rossi, 2009; Madichie, 2009) and a notable decrease in the recruitment of both UK- and Irish-born players (Littlewood & Richardson, 2006; Curran, 2015). A recurring theme in all of the manager interviews concerned the importance of establishing international football academies and scouting networks in their search for new playing talent (Walters & Rossi, 2009). For example, one current English Premier League manager described how one of his main priorities, following his arrival at a particular club, involved the establishment of a football academy and scouting networks in China. Another English Premier League manager described how he was currently in the process of establishing a football academy in Africa. While such formal recruitment networks are particularly evident at English Premier League clubs, all of the managers interviewed identified the role of informal networks, such as scouts and agents, in the domestic and international search for playing talent. While most UK-based clubs – particularly those in the lower leagues – still rely on domestic scouting networks, it seems clubs are adopting a more international emphasis in their player recruitment strategies. For example, Steve Bruce, speaking while manager of Sunderland, described how he 'scours the globe for fresh talent' and some of his more recent signings had come from Albania, Paraguay and Ghana (Taylor, 2009). Historically, when recruiting foreign players, English football managers have tended 'to draw heavily on those foreign sources that most resemble local sources in terms of climate, culture, language and style of football' (McGovern, 2002: 23), which is viewed by managers as a means of reducing the uncertainty involved in the recruitment of players in general and foreign players in particular.

Social ties and recruitment networks are not unusual in determining how, and where, migrant players find employment (McGovern, 2002; Maguire & Stead, 1998; Maguire & Pearton, 2000). Critically, once such links are established, they are likely to sustain themselves (Tilly & Tilly, 1998; Portes, 1995). For example, the transfer of Kolo Touré from the Ivory Coast to Arsenal was because of the personal links existing between the manager of the English club, Arsène Wenger, and Jean-Marc Guillou, who owned the football academy at which Touré had been trained. Furthermore, the difficulty of reliably predicting how any player will perform, especially a foreign footballer, means that it is entirely rational for employers to adhere to the local conception of what makes a good professional. Consequently, managers often hire those who most resemble themselves since they believe they can be trusted to act in the expected manner. Such homosocial reproduction, Kanter (1977: 63) argued, provides 'an important form of reassurance in the face of uncertainty about performance management in high-reward, high-prestige positions'. This phenomenon is reinforced by two related factors. First, a tradition of recruiting, for example, African-born players produces a 'demonstration effect' that is likely to attract other African hopefuls. Newcomers may be comforted by the knowledge that other (young) African footballers have already been given the opportunity to play first-team football at the club. From the manager's perspective, he may be somewhat reassured in the knowledge that players from similar backgrounds have proved successful in the past. Second, the presence of other African players could make it easier for such players to adapt and settle into their new surroundings.

In addition to formal recruitment networks, managers may also rely on informal contact networks.

## Informal contact networks

In addition to providing and accessing information about potential job opportunities, football managers also utilise informal contact networks in the recruitment of players. The informal sharing of information within a manager's network of contacts considerably influences player mobility and recruitment (McGovern 2002; Stead & Maguire, 2000; Roderick, 2006). None of the data collected in this research would disagree with this statement. One relatively inexperienced English Championship manager described how personal contacts influence the recruitment of players:

> Although I mightn't have the contacts that some of the other managers have, you know I think there are probably a few people that are good contacts. I would speak to xxxx [manager], because he is the international manager. I would often ring him up and ask him about a player. I think you need these contacts. I would also keep my ear to the ground, and you'd often hear through word of mouth that a player is available, and so you would keep your ear to the ground. But I would also keep my eye in further afield, whether it was abroad or wherever.

Another manager, with considerable managerial experience in both the UK and Ireland, described the importance of personal contacts:

> I would have a network of personal friends. I have brought some decent players in from the UK. Having spent 17 years in the UK, I have a lot of friends who are now coaches and who are now agents and who know the scene.

Implicit in the above managers' comments is the importance of contact networks in the recruitment of players. Personal contacts may also provide a manager with support, in terms of a second opinion, when recruiting players. As noted in Chapter 2, trust plays an important role in the context of whom a manager appoints as part of his backroom staff. In the context of player recruitment, a recurring theme in the manager interviews concerned the importance of maintaining personal contacts with those whom they could trust. In this regard, one current English Premier League manager described the importance of using a particular scout whom he trusted:

> I've got this scout I use and, you know, it's almost a case that I nearly don't have to go and see the player [he recommends]. I've worked with him for so long and he is always spot on. I trust his judgement. He doesn't ring me with bullshit players they [other clubs] are chasing. Now he might not ring me for a while, but when he does ring me with a player, I always listen to him. I can always rely on xxxx [scout's name].

Implicit in the above manager's comments is the importance of both interpersonal and competence trust, the latter relating to his knowledge and skill in assessing prospective recruits. The importance of 'trustworthy contacts' was particularly evident during the course of an interview with a former English Championship manager:

MANAGER: The more contacts you know, the better. You know there may be a rumour that you're going to sign a player and you might just get a phone call saying, "Don't go near him".

SK: Really. Just out of the blue?

MANAGER: Yeah, definitely, and it is someone that you might know quite well and trust. They might say, "He's a wrong 'un, don't go near him". You're not always going to buy that – obviously you'd find out why would that be – but that does happen quite a bit. It's a small business.

When a manager is interested in signing a particular player, the normal procedure is to formally approach the player's club. Unless permission is granted, clubs are prohibited from approaching players while they are contracted to another club (Holt et al., 2006). However, in professional football informal or illegal practices such as 'tapping up' are common features of player recruitment (Magee, 1998; Roderick, 2006; Holt et al., 2006). This practice – an informal 'testing of the water' (Roderick, 2006: 182) – is widespread in professional football and usually involves contacting prospective recruits as a means of gauging their interest in a potential move or in facilitating a potential transfer. Quite often, football managers and clubs use agents and current or former players and coaches to informally contact prospective recruits. A recurring theme in all of the player interviews concerned the prevalence of tapping up in professional football. One current English Championship player stated that 'tapping up players goes on all the time – it's part and parcel of the game'. When asked whether tapping up was widespread, another former English Premier League player stated: 'Absolutely, sure – how else do you instigate a move?' A similar theme emerged in the manager interviews, with the majority of managers agreeing that 'tapping up does go on' in professional football. For example, one current English League Two manager described how he would look for certain qualities when assessing a prospective recruit. He also stated how he would tap up such players:

MANAGER: I think for a player coming into the team, you are looking to see if he has got what you are looking for, and that's the way you would sign him. And looking at it first, like, the way you sign them is you tap them up.

SK: Does that happen a lot in the game?

MANAGER: Course it does.

Similarly, one experienced manager stated how he would do everything he could to secure a 'signature signing' or someone he considered to be a 'key player'. When asked about the process he adopts in signing players, he said:

Yeah, I mean if I thought I'd get a player, I would do anything in my power to get him. I'd try [contacting] him, and then I'd get someone else to try him and bend his ear. If he has to be tapped up, then fair enough – it's part of the game. Sure, they are all at it. Just do it in the right way, though. If they are awkward, then fair enough – I might let them sweat for a little while.

Implicit in the above comments from players and managers is the prevalence of tapping up in professional football. Moreover, the practice of tapping up a player 'in the right way', as described in the above extract, quite often involves a manager utilising informal personal contacts to 'bend his ear' in an attempt to recruit prospective signings.

Contacting a player, either formally or informally, usually follows a process whereby managers draw up a list of prospective players that they wish to sign. The key question, then, is: how do managers assess both current players and prospective recruits in professional football? The following section attempts to answer this question.

## Player assessment in professional football

Assessment is an ongoing process of evaluating players – current and prospective – who demonstrate appropriate levels of performance for inclusion in the team. This is a multi-faceted approach and considerable academic attention has focused on the assessment of elite football players with regard to anthropometric, physiological, technical, tactical, social and psychological characteristics (Richardson et al., 2004; Williams, 2013) and from sociological perspectives (Williams & Reilly, 2000). Factors such as a player's willingness to learn, mental strength, resilience, professional attitude, dedication and work ethic influence the recruitment and assessment process (Mills et al., 2012; Holt & Dunn, 2004; Christensen, 2009; Bourke, 2002, 2003; Roderick, 2006; Stead & Maguire, 2000; Maguire & Pearton, 2000; Cushion & Jones, 2006). Considerable significance is also placed on players' ability to cope with the physical demands of the game (Carling, 2010), the sociocultural problems of adjustment (Roderick, 2006; Maguire & Pearton, 2000; Weedon, 2011), the quality and provision of coaching (Partington & Cushion, 2013; Cushion et al., 2012), and the level of support from players' families, agents and existing migrant players (Nesti, 2010; Richardson et al., 2012; Williams, 2013). While 'no unique characteristics can be isolated with confidence' (Williams & Reilly, 2000: 657), the analysis of players' physical, physiological and psychological characteristics impact their success in the game (Williams, 2013). In this regard, the adoption of sport science techniques may play a significant role in the recruitment, assessment and development of players. For example, Sam Allardyce – with limited financial resources to attract and retain the most talented players at Bolton Wanderers

– adopted and developed 'sport science techniques that were designed to improve the day-to-day capabilities and capacity of their existing squad' (Gilmore & Gilson, 2007: 418). While financial restrictions may prevent some clubs from adopting the above-mentioned techniques, hostility exists within professional football towards the use, application and perceived value of some of these techniques in general and of sports psychology in particular (Pain & Hardwood, 2004; Nesti, 2010).

Professional football is a unique industry in which the observation of a player's performance is unusually transparent. Football managers can observe individual performances during games and obtain a wide range of statistics on players' strengths and weaknesses. For example, computerised systems such as Computer Coach value both current and potential players along a list of 'qualities or functional requirements' (Boon & Sierksma, 2003: 278). In addition, individual player and/or team quality may be assessed from player performance (Gerrard, 2005) and financial expenditure perspectives (Szymanski & Kuypers, 1999). In their attempt to incorporate more rational and scientific player recruitment and assessment decisions, managers may utilise player quality indexes based on observable player characteristics (Gerrard, 2001) and computer-based player tracking software applications incorporating game statistics, such as Opta and Prozone (Carmichael et al., 2000, 2001). These systems may assist managers in combining both their rational and intuitive assessment of players, leading to more optimal spending of money, thus reducing the possibility of making poor recruitment decisions. Moreover, scientific observations may complement intuitive judgements and assist a manager in confirming his initial perception of a player's strengths and weaknesses.

However, while such systems and statistics may provide reliable information on previous player performances, the quality of any future performances cannot be predicted with certainty (McGovern, 2002). It is argued that currently there is an overemphasis on the appropriate adoption and use of performance analysis (PA) utilising optics and analytics in professional football. PA is firmly embedded within the coaching process (McGarry et al., 2013; Carling et al., 2014; Groom et al., 2011) and can facilitate the process of improving player performance (Bampouras et al., 2012). However, despite a significant growth in PA research, a number of issues and questions remain concerning the progress of the field and the assumptions underpinning such research. For example, Mackenzie and Cushion (2013) argued that the adoption of a reductionist approach has resulted in PA research consistently reducing the complexity of performance by portraying it as a series of steps to be followed in an overly descriptive, systematic and unproblematic process with little regard for how this knowledge is transmitted from coach to athlete. They also argued that PA research has been driven to establish causal relationships between isolated performance variables in an attempt to predict outcomes. Isolated performance variables are independent variables that are directly associated with match outcomes in isolation without acknowledging potentially confounding variables or providing sufficient context to the variable itself. Moreover, Mackenzie and Cushion (2013) argued that variables have been measured as a result of availability with little attention paid to the applicability of performance variables in the context of complex sporting performances. Patton (2002: 574) was also sceptical of objective approaches such as notational analysis and suggested that 'numbers do not protect against bias, they merely disguise it'. This is important because 'all statistical data are based on someone's definition of what to measure and how to measure it' (Patton, 2002: 574). Despite the considerable range of sources of data now available to managers, recruitment decisions may omit important aspects of performance not captured by statistics. For example, even Sir Alex Ferguson stated that his decision to replace Jaap Stam, which he later identified as being mistaken, was based solely on his assessment of the player's match statistics.

Based on the data collected from players, managers and agents, it is argued that additional personal qualities exist that are deemed important and that may not be fully evident from statistics. It is important to note that there are many aspects of a player's performance and behaviour that are difficult to measure. Traditionally, scouts and managers have subjectively assessed playing talent based on their intuition (Richardson et al., 2004; Thomas & Thomas, 1999). Because talent identification is a rational or objective process, many coaches and managers utilise 'intuition and gut feeling' in the selection and recruitment of elite football players (Christensen, 2009: 371). Taylor (2009) noted how gut feeling and instinct influenced the then Sunderland manager Steve Bruce's decision to sign Lorik Cana (Albania), Paulo da Silva (Paraguay) and John Mensah (Ghana) and how these players complemented existing UK-born players such as Lee Cattermole, Darren Bent and Andy Reid. This is an important point and arguably a key aspect of the process of assessing and recruiting players. More specifically, when recruiting players, managers need to understand and be cognisant of the importance of both natural and contextual talent. The former relates to talent that is owned by the player while contextual talent refers to 'that component of talent that is a function of the player operating in a particular environment' (Brady et al., 2008: 63). Moreover, contextual talent concerns how a player 'fits in with the team ethos and style of play' and in what way the role of 'inherent talent is deployed' (Brady et al., 2008: 63). For example, consider the ability of Sam Allardyce to utilise players who have experienced success in their own settings (such as Ivan Campo, Fernando Hierro and Youri Djorkaeff) and exploit their capabilities within the context of the English Premier League (Gilmore & Gilson, 2007). This is important, as

> some players who "fit" a particular team's style or culture will perform up to and even in excess of what their intrinsic talent would suggest is

possible, while others, who do not fit, will generate negative contextual talent and fail to reach expected levels of performance.

(Brady et al., 2008: 63)

While PA can certainly assist in the assessment of players, data gathered in this study suggest that football managers place considerable importance of the role of intuition and gut feeling in their assessment of players. The difficulty in assessing players was particularly evident during the course of an interview with a former professional player, now employed as an agent. During the interview, we discussed how a number of the players, agents and managers that were interviewed suggested that some managers have a unique ability to identify prospective recruits:

> I think it's a massive skill to look at a player and spot him, you know. You can go around and watch games – like, I do a lot of it with work – and watch a lot of games and, like, it mightn't be the best player, it mightn't be the one player that stands out, but there is always something there, particularly the younger [players] you look at them, you have to look beyond the player who, like, goes around four or five players – kind of look beyond that, and it can be very difficult to pick that player out, you know. It's easier when they get to 18 or 19 – well, they're there and you can see if they are going to progress on, but, like, looking at someone when they are 14 or 15 – it can be difficult, but particularly xxxx [current English Premier League manager], he is very good at it.

One experienced manager described the process of how he assessed playing talent. In addition, he described how he assessed the squad and identified which players he deemed as being suitable or unsuitable:

> You look at the player who you're getting rid of first, if you like. First and foremost, you have to say, "Have I as a manager exhausted all avenues to extract more from this player?" "With this player, have I got as much as I can out of him?" "Is there more in the bag"? I would question myself first. "Am I doing the right thing?" I would seek critical support from others, from my two colleagues who run the team with me. If I have an opinion, by and large the others may agree. They might say, "No, he is not good enough – he's too short, he is shorter than we want". OK so, we are letting him go then. So, who are we going to bring in, who's coming in behind him? Have we got anyone here at the club? No, so we need to look elsewhere.

Having identified that suitable players are not presently at the club, a manager must then recruit players elsewhere. All of the managers interviewed identified how they were constantly evaluating and looking to improve their existing squad. One current English Premier League manager described how he was always 'looking at weaknesses in the squad' in addition to 'keeping a constant eye out for replacements'. Another manager, with considerable managerial experience in the UK and Ireland, gave a description of the assessment process he adopted when recruiting and assessing players:

> Well, I have a self-assessment procedure that I use on players and that I would have learnt when I was in the UK. You would have my assistant manager watch him home and away, I would watch him home and away, and my chief scout would watch him home and away. You would look to see between six and ten games. What I would always do is that I would like to get them in [training] for a week, and get about eight [training] sessions in and get a proper match in. Then a decision would be made.

However, it may not be possible for a football manager to bring in prospective signings for training sessions and/or matches. All of the agents interviewed were questioned about the process that managers adopt in the assessment of players and in particular what specific qualities they look for when recruiting potential players. For example, one agent stated:

AGENT: Depends on what player they are looking for at the time, you know. You would be surprised how many managers look to the player's personality. What are their circumstances? Are they married? Do they have kids? Things like that. Especially if a player is going from Ireland to England. You know, if they are a young player, they want to see where they have come from, what is their background, you know, so they can get them into a similar environment. You know, if they come from a family in a home, they will put them into digs with a family. Little things like that. In terms of older players, I think it's more of an issue because they want to make sure that someone wants it enough, particularly if there is big money involved. Like, have they got a good attitude? So they do look into that as well as whatever qualities on the pitch they are looking for at the time. But, em, fitness, you would be amazed, is such a major factor. It is such an issue now. I know one particular club, no matter how good a player is, like, on Day 1 of a trial they will have a fitness test, and if you don't pass it, off you go.

SK: So basically what you are saying is that it depends on what the manager is looking for?

AGENT: This is for now ... like, players who would be ready for the first team. That particular manager wants players who are ready to go into his first team, and if you're not fit enough, they won't even look at him. Because he is not going to be ready for at least another six months, and so they wouldn't be interested. Which in some ways is wrong, as you could have a good player who is not fit because of injury.

In addition, quite often the signing of a player will involve a transfer fee. In this regard, a number of managers identified how financial restrictions often influence their player recruitment process. In terms of placing a value on a prospective recruit, Lawrie Sanchez stated that you value a player according to 'how much you need that player, how badly the player's club needs to sell and whether you have the money to pay' for that particular player (Hoare, 2006: 38). A former English League Two manager, currently employed as an assistant manager with an English Championship club, described the process of assessing a player's 'worth':

> At the moment we're looking for a midfielder. I watched a game last season and one midfielder stood out and I recommended him [to the manager]. I've been to watch him now three, four, five times with different people. The manager was the last one to come watch him and then it goes down to opinions. I've said "Yes" and another coach said "No", while others have said a definite "Yes". So the manager took a final look and said "No". So that's the process of actually looking to sign a player. So we decided it wasn't just a no because he wasn't good enough, it was because of the money the club were asking. He's not worth it and he's not miles better than what we've got. So that would be the process of signing someone. It would also involve researching him quite a lot to see what kind of person [he is].

When probed further, this manager explained that 'researching him quite a lot' involved 'looking into the background' of a potential signing. Similarly, the former Charlton Athletic and West Ham United manager Alan Curbishley identified the importance of 'doing your homework' on prospective signings. In the context of signing players in general and foreign players in particular, he said:

> I don't buy players from watching videos sent by scouts or from agents I've never met. I'll watch the player myself five, six times – maybe more – before making a decision. With foreign players, I make sure that they've already played a full season here with someone else. I'll talk to people who know them and find out about their character.
>
> (Wylie, 2004: 61)

There is considerable evidence to suggest that other factors appear to play a significant role in the assessment and recruitment of players. For example, implicit in the latter two managers' comments is the importance of gathering information about a player's background. More specifically, the following section identifies the importance of a player's off-field behaviour in the assessment and recruitment process.

## Off-field behaviour and player recruitment

Because statistics fail to gather all relevant data, managers may also have a 'shopping list' (Williams & Reilly, 2000) of desirable characteristics when recruiting or assessing players. For example, we know that a player's willingness to learn, mental strength, dedication (Christensen, 2009; Cushion & Jones, 2006), professional attitude and work ethic (Bourke, 2002, 2003; Roderick, 2006; Stead & Maguire, 2000) influence the recruitment and assessment process. We also know that 'ascribed' factors, in addition to 'achieved' factors, appear to play a significant role in the judgement made about the qualities of players (Maguire & Pearton, 2000: 766). What this means is that, in addition to players' on-field performance, their lifestyle, work ethic and professional attitude may also play a significant role in their assessment and recruitment. Regarding the latter, the importance of players' attitude and character extends not only to how they approach training sessions and competitive fixtures, but also what they do 'in their own time' (Christensen, 2009: 376). Cushion and Jones (2006) identified how the attitude of youth players, both on and off the field, was quite often deemed more important than any innate talent possessed by the players. In addition, Holt and Dunn (2004: 217) noted the impact that an 'overly active social life away from the competitive environment may have upon their readiness to compete or train'. In particular, Christensen (2009: 376) also noted the significance of a player's 'character and attitude toward training and games' as a 'dominant category in the classificatory scheme that distinguishes one highly skilled soccer player from another'.

The off-field activities and secret lives of professional footballers have always been the subject of considerable media attention, much of which has focused on players' drinking, gambling, ill-discipline, smoking and alleged extramarital affairs (Redhead, 1997). Such media attention may detract from the performance and cohesion of a team, influence fans' and managers' perception of these players and contribute to managerial dismissals (O'Leary, 2002). Media coverage of English Premier League players' off-field behaviour has highlighted what many would consider an unsavoury, yet traditional, aspect of professional footballers' private lives. This is important because quite often players gain reputations in relation to their playing styles, playing ability and overall professionalism (Maguire & Pearton, 2000). For example, Stead and Maguire (2000) noted English managers' enthusiasm for signing players from Nordic/Scandinavian countries. While these players may be a low-cost option in terms of transfer fee, it was their disciplined approach, professional attitude and physical attributes that were deemed important. In the context of player recruitment, Harry Redknapp stated: 'Scandinavians are safer' (Stead & Maguire, 2000: 51). With particular reference to Norwegians, George Graham stated that 'their approach to the game is superior. The way they live their lives away from the stadium is exemplary. Their diet is first class and very few are big alcohol drinkers' (Stead & Maguire, 2000: 51).

### The 'good professional'

A recurring theme in the manager interviews concerned how a player's lifestyle and off-field behaviour were significant factors in the recruitment and assessment process. One former English Championship manager stated: 'I definitely think that looking into the character of the player is of massive importance, as important as his ability . . . It's a huge part of it.' Another former English Premier League manager described how a player's attitude would significantly influence the recruitment process. In describing what he would look for in a prospective recruit, he said:

MANAGER: I would look for clean-living fellows that don't act the bollox. Like xxxx [player], he would be the perfect example, and xxxx [player] . . . like, these fellows are the business.
SK: Good professionals?
MANAGER: Yeah, good pros. You can tell by their appearance, their fitness levels. Like, if you are messing outside of football you will be found out sooner or later. Your performances, and even your appearance, and physical condition, will suffer.
SK: Have you experienced instances where players don't take care of themselves?
MANAGER: Yes, of course. Players have got to look after themselves . . . If you have to keep on to a player, well, then you are wasting your time, and the next thing is: "Out you go". Because you're wasting your time [with these players].

Implicit in the above managers' comments is the importance of a professional attitude 'outside of football'. One former Scottish Premier League manager developed this point further and identified the relationship between a player's on-field performances and off-field behaviour:

MANAGER: It's important to know that they're good professionals and they'll live their lives the right way and they won't be a bad influence. As long as they conduct themselves properly and do the job on the field. But to do the job on the field they have to live right off the field as well. I think that's right, it is only right. I definitely think that's right and it's sort of checking people's life, because you are putting a lot of faith in these with three- or

|  | four-year contracts. You are taking your chances with them, and why have that baggage? |
|---|---|
| SK: | Because you could sign another player for the same money? |
| MANAGER: | Yes. You could get someone else for the same price and do the same job and you know he isn't coming up to you and saying, "I have a problem at home". Or missing training because he had a rough night, or something like that. |

Quite often, football players may develop reputations or stereotypes concerning their association with alcohol and/or possession of an unprofessional attitude, resulting in them being labelled as being 'a bad influence' and/or 'disruptive'. During the course of an interview with a former player, with considerable playing experience in all four divisions, the topic of drinking was discussed. In addition, this player gave an insight into how managers tend to keep a close eye on players to see if there is was any evidence of drinking:

> You are going to get clubs . . . where there might be a drinking culture. You can't say everything changed because you're going towards greater emphasis on diet and fitness. Obviously, if a manager thinks there is an issue, then he needs to suss it out and address it. But I just think, particularly in England, it's so intense over there and fitness is such an issue, that you just can't get away with it [drinking]. But at this stage I don't think managers even think about it. It shouldn't be an issue . . . I don't know a team in England, particularly in the Premiership, or any player who just isn't fit enough. You know, so it shouldn't be an issue.

Professional football players' association with drinking, infidelity and gambling are well documented in a number of player autobiographies (Adams, 1998; Keane, 2002; McGrath, 2006; Gascoigne, 2006; Merson, 2011; Carlisle, 2013) and a number of academic publications (Redhead, 1997; Brown, 2005; Kimmage, 2005). While such reputations may seem harmless, they may have a number of unintended consequences for players. The networks of relationships in which players are bound up at their workplace involve not only associations with supporters and the media, but what, for them, are more central interdependencies – that is, relationships with managers and coaches (Roderick, 2006). It seems reasonable to suggest, therefore, that managers may have a number of fears concerning certain players' lifestyles and, as a result, may decline the opportunity to (re)sign such players. This point was borne out by a former senior international manager who described a situation in which he had to deal with a so-called 'problem player':

> These people are no use to you, and are no use to the team. I think no matter who he is, and supporters might think, like, he is the best player, but, like, if he doesn't want to be here, well then, that's fine – he has to

go. Like, outside the game he wasn't prepared to conduct himself properly. So he had to go.

## 'Baggage'

Richardson *et al.* (2004) explored how certain mitigating factors can be seen to limit technically gifted academy players' development and progression opportunities. For example, for some players, adherence to the academy's guidelines on discipline, behaviour and attendance proved troublesome. The general view from the coaches' perspective was that some players were 'adjudged to be' burdened with emotional baggage while others would 'find trouble or trouble would find them' (Richardson *et al.*, 2004: 207). A number of managers interviewed described how players' 'baggage' would influence their decision to (re)sign certain players. More specifically, a number of managers described how players' baggage might relate to how players deal with issues such as being dropped and/or injured. For example, one current English Premier League manager noted how a recent signing had what this manager termed 'a bit of baggage', which in this case referred to the player's recent separation from his wife. The majority of the managers interviewed associated baggage with trouble. In addition, a number of managers identified how some players are stereotyped as 'troublemakers'. How football managers deal with such issues in general and problem players in particular is a crucial aspect of management and will be considered shortly.

It became evident from the interviews with managers that it was the manager's responsibility to identify the type of baggage that a player possessed. One current English Premier League manager described how, before signing a player, he would always perform background checks on him. This was an attempt to identify information concerning, as this manager put it, 'the kind of person he was'. He stated:

MANAGER: There's always baggage, but it depends on what kind of baggage. Is it family or private baggage? But you can go through all the players that I have taken in. You take xxxx [player], who was absolutely nuts, like, but you had to pick him.
SK: Why was that?
MANAGER: On the field, you know he would do the business. And OK, he would give you problems, but if he wins you games, then you're entitled to pick him. But some players will go out and give you everything, and yet they can't win you games.

During the course of an interview with an agent, discussions focused on how a player's off-field behaviour may influence some managers' assessment of the player and influence their decision to sign him. In particular, this agent was asked if he thought off-field behaviour was a factor in the recruitment of players in professional football:

AGENT: Yeah, but I wouldn't say just that. It depends.
SK: What do you mean?
AGENT: I wouldn't say that. I'd say some would, some wouldn't. Some managers would sign players purely on ability. If they [players] have a reputation for trouble or for drinking or whatever, they [managers] say, "That doesn't matter as long as they do the business on the field and I'll sort them out and get them into line". Other managers will think, "He has got a reputation for drinking or whatever and I wouldn't touch him with a barge pole". It's different.
SK: So are you saying that for some managers it comes down to performances on the pitch?
AGENT: Yeah, I think ultimately it does, because that's what wins you games. And once you're winning games, they don't care what you are doing off the pitch.

While most football managers said they were careful not to sign what they referred to as 'problem players', implicit in the above comments are two important points. First, the above manager's willingness to put up with a so-called 'problem player' and his decision to select this particular player may be, in part, a reflection of the obvious pressure for immediate results. It may also be the case that some football managers feel that their style of management may curb the behaviour of such problem players. For example, the ability of both Harry Redknapp and Sir Alex Ferguson to manage and control allegedly 'problem' or 'difficult-to-manage' players such as Paolo di Canio and Eric Cantona is well known. More recently, the former Manchester City manager Roberto Mancini was able to manage Mario Balotelli, a player whom many would could consider troublesome and whom José Mourinho argued was 'unmanageable'. The second point concerns the possible influence problem players may have on squad cohesion, which may place considerable pressure on the football manager's authority, and raises questions about the ability of a manager to maintain control over players in general and problem players in particular. While Chapter 5 deals with discipline and man management in greater detail, the following interview with a considerably experienced former English Premier League player provides a preliminary insight into how some football managers deal with problem players. During the interview, the player commented on the importance of really 'knowing your players' and how one particular manager possessed an ability to manage troublesome players. He stated:

> Yes, of course – if a player is not happy in his own life, he is not going to be able to perform. Like xxxx [Premier League manager] knows so many people around Europe and the world that when he signs someone I think he knows quite a lot about the people – yeah, he gets so much information about a player and it may not be all about football, you know. The big

thing with him, though, I think if there is someone a tiny bit off the rails, then he is the kind of manager who can straighten them out.

Moreover, the following interview with a considerably experienced former English Championship manager provides considerable insight into how some football managers deal with problem players. During the course of the interview, he described how he faced stern opposition from the club chairman in his attempts to sign a player who was considered by many as being 'troublesome'. The player in question had considerable previous playing experience with two English Premier League clubs. During the course of the interview, the manager identified how contacts influenced the recruitment of this player, how he managed to control and discipline the player and the importance of a player's attitude in the recruitment process. He said:

MANAGER: Yeah, definitely, like, the general character of a player is important as well. So sometimes the first thing you'll say is, "What kind of a lad is he?" And someone might say, "He's a total wrong 'un, don't go near him – he will cause you problems at your club".

SK: And have you experienced this as a manager?

MANAGER: Yeah – for example, I went and signed xxxx [player]. And I took a lot of stick for taking him, because he was a bit wayward, but he turned out to be a smashing lad, and never let me down.

SK: How did you go about signing him?

MANAGER: I knew him as a kid, and he was a very, very good player, a young kid and I watched him when he went to xxxx [English Premier League club]. Then he moved to xxxx [another Premier League club]. The manager at that club was my previous manager at xxxx [English Premier League club] when I was a player there. I spoke to him [English Premier League manager] about signing the player and he said he was an absolute cracko, "Don't touch him". But I knew he would have something to offer. He showed great ability but he started to miss training regularly – once a week, then twice a week. Then he got released at xxxx [English Premier League club] but they took him back. I then rang xxxx [English Premier League player], who was playing there at the time, and he would get into his ear. So I invited him up to pre-season training on a six-week deal – no money involved in it. Part of the deal was that he had to be at the training ground first and he had to be the last to leave the training ground. If he missed training because of nights out . . . or whatever, then it [contract] was over. And to be fair he had been brilliant for those six weeks. So I gave him a one-year contract, and in the middle of that contract he improved, and I gave him an extra year.

| | |
|---|---|
| SK: | That's amazing – like, one manager says, "Don't touch him" and yet you managed to get him right. Was that down to your approach, to your man management? |
| MANAGER: | Yeah, it is all down to man management. Because loads of managers might say, "Don't touch him". But any player that I was taking, I would have thought I would have done my homework. But some of the referrals you get from managers, after having them as players, would be like, "F*** me, he was miles off the mark". Then other managers will give you referrals of players and, like, you'd go, "How close they would be". |

Implicit in the above comments is the subjective nature of player assessment, the role of gut feeling and intuition and the importance of man management. Regarding the latter, we know that while some behaviours or leadership styles are more effective than others in particular contexts (Renshaw et al., 2009), more 'athlete-centred' approaches may facilitate greater connections with an athlete's needs (Barić & Bucik, 2009). In addition, implicit in the above comments is how the manager–player relationship not only influenced this player's motivation (Barić & Bucik, 2009) but also his continued participation in professional football. One point is clear: each player is unique and knowing every aspect of a player's background considerably improves a manager's ability to manage him.

## *Surveillance and questionable management practices*

In addition to personal contacts, quite often managers utilise alternative methods in trying to elicit information concerning a player's off-field behaviour. One former Premier League academy player was asked to describe the positive qualities of one of his former managers. He stated:

| | |
|---|---|
| PLAYER: | The good side of him is the fact that he is so meticulous. I mean, he just knows everything about everyone – he knows everything about the team that he is playing, their tactics, and every player, and he remembers everything. I mean, he would be in the office at six in the morning. |
| SK: | Are you serious? |
| PLAYER: | Yes, he would be, like, in there every morning – I mean, the youth team would be in at eight o' clock and he would be there every morning before us, and every single day he would always be the last to leave – I mean, he would be leaving at five at night. I mean, he just constantly works, he has a great work ethic . . . I mean, I think that comes from his background and the way he was brought up, but, I mean, you have to respect someone like that. I think that's one of the main things that stands out – he just knows everything |

about everyone. Like, even if you go out on a night out in xxxx [city centre], he would know exactly where you were the next day, like – he would know.
SK: Really? Would he?
PLAYER: Yes, he would know the next morning if you were out in town.

In this regard, it has been alleged that Sir Alex Ferguson employed 'a network of spies' to monitor his players (Carter, 2006: 136). Similarly, one former Irish-based manager described how he formed relationships with local nightclub bouncers in an attempt to monitor his players' off-field activities. As regards managers' attempts to elicit information concerning players' off-field behaviour, a recurring theme in the player interviews was how managers closely supervised them during training sessions. For example, one former English Premier League player described how his manager would withdraw players from the warm-up and ask them questions about previous games:

> Like, he would call you out from training and he'd walk right up to you. He'd be right in your face and, like, he would be, like, smelling your breath. He'd wait until you'd talk and try and see if you were out drinking.

In not too dissimilar fashion, one current English Championship player described how his former manager would closely monitor players in training sessions. More worryingly, he described how, following training sessions, the manager would 'stare' at his players in the showers:

PLAYER: Like, this fella was a nutter. You would be in the shower after training and chatting with the lads and you'd look out [towards the dressing room] and he'd be staring in at you.
SK: What?
PLAYER: Yeah, like, he was crazy, he'd be sitting down and just looking in at us – like, we were totally starkers. We used to think it was great craic – like, we would be making jokes about it and stuff. Ah sure, he was f****** nuts, mate.

## Conclusion

This chapter has highlighted the importance of personal contacts in the assessment and recruitment of professional football players. The chapter has also explored how managers adopt scientifically proven methods in addition to intuition and gut feeling in the assessment and recruitment process. What is particularly evident is how a player's off-field behaviour influences the process. Moreover, the chapter has shed light on the investigative and in some cases questionable practices employed by some managers in trying to elicit information concerning players' off-field behaviour.

# Chapter 5

# Maintaining discipline and control

## Introduction

This chapter examines aspects of the relationship between professional football managers and their players, with particular emphasis on the ways in which managers maintain control over players at professional football clubs. More specifically, the chapter focuses on the ways in which disciplinary codes are established by managers and the sanctions that are imposed on players for breaches of club discipline. The chapter highlights the arbitrary character of these codes and the central part played by intimidation and abuse, both verbal and physical, as aspects of managerial control within clubs. It is argued that these techniques of managerial control reflect the origins of professional football in late Victorian England, when professional football players were the equivalent of workers within industry and, like industrial workers, were seen as requiring authoritarian regulation and control. This pattern of management has persisted in professional football long after it has been superseded in industrial relations more generally because, while the management of football clubs has involved increasing professionalisation and bureaucratisation, the role of the manager has proved remarkably resistant to these processes and, as a consequence, the authority of the team manager continues to be based on traditional forms of authoritarianism. This has allowed managers an unusually high degree of autonomy in defining their own role, while placing relatively few constraints on their authority in relation to players. What, then, are the rules of conduct at professional football clubs and how are they formulated? How do managers discipline their players? Does this treatment vary from club to club and from manager to manager? And what are players' views of the rules and sanctions imposed by their managers?

## Establishing rules of conduct

It is important to recognise that, although there are some common themes found at most professional football clubs, club rules are characterised by important arbitrary elements. The rules are normally drawn up and imposed on players by the manager without any discussion with the players or the PFA representative. Thus, both the rules and the ways in which they are enforced are left almost entirely to the discretion – or the whim – of the manager and therefore reflect, to some extent, each manager's preferences, experiences and 'pet hates'. There is in this area, as in others (Waddington *et al.*, 1999), no attempt to identify and disseminate the elements of a good practice model in professional football. As a consequence, both the rules themselves and, perhaps more importantly, the ways in which they are enforced vary from club to club; indeed, within a club both the rules and the methods of enforcement may change when there is a change of manager.

All of the managers interviewed saw the establishment of club rules as a key method of controlling the behaviour of players. One current English Championship manager described how he established the code of discipline:

> When I took over . . . we had rules of conduct at the club. There was one [set of rules] previously, but I got the lads to sign up to it . . . If players were late, they got fined. I would never fine players for bookings. You know, for verbals [e.g. remonstrating with a referee], maybe. We had little funny fines, like [for not wearing] flip flops [in the shower] . . . which went into a fund for a drink at the end of the season.

All of the players interviewed described how each club had its own particular mechanisms for controlling players' behaviour, based largely on the idiosyncrasies of the manager. However, central to all rules was the imposition of fines on players who breached those rules. One former English Premier League player said:

> Every club has it – it's a discipline thing. When you go into football – as soon as you go into football – you know what the done thing is so you don't complain about it. You know, you're one minute late [for training] and you're fined a fiver.

Players generally felt that managers see financial penalties as the most effective means of punishment. However, several players pointed out that in the higher leagues, where players' incomes may be very high, the effect is limited. One former English Championship player said:

> Obviously, when players step out of line, what the managers do is fine the players, because they feel that that's what hurts them most: hit their pocket. But there is so much money now . . . If you look in the Premiership, and the top teams and you're fining players – the big, big names – it's like nothing to them.

However, for players in the lower leagues, many of whom receive relatively modest wages that may amount to no more than a few hundred pounds or euros a week, the imposition of fines has a greater impact, particularly when a player is fined one or two weeks wages.

Different managers lay particular stress on different aspects of players' behaviour, and it is perhaps here that the arbitrary elements of club discipline are most evident. For example, several players stated that some managers have what players regard as a fixation with punctuality, while others have very strict guidelines pertaining to off-field behaviour. I will return to this point later. Several players commented on what they saw as the obsession of some managers with players' weight and diet. For example, one manager weighed his players every Monday morning in an attempt to identify those players who had had what the player described as 'a good weekend'. Another current League Two player added:

> It was crazy – like, some of us would starve ourselves on a Sunday in case we were overweight. Sometimes he would run us into the ground. Other times he would just fine us. We actually had a "fat squad" for all those players who the manager reckoned needed to lose weight. They used to be run into the ground.

The rules of conduct are accepted by players whether or not they agree with them or consider them to be reasonable. The reasons for this acceptance – even when they contain elements that players may consider 'crazy' – are considered later.

## Socialisation of apprentices and young professionals

The induction period for a young trainee can be intimidating. In his ethnographic study of youth trainees at a professional football club in the 1990s, Parker (1996: 199) noted that 'a dominant masculinity presides at all times'. Critcher (1979: 161) described the core values of the game as 'masculinity, aggression, physical emphasis'. Thus, professional football is an aggressive, tough, masculine and at times violent 'industry', and these values are reflected in workplace behaviours and in the socialisation and social control of young players.

When a young football player signs a contract with a professional club, he is socialised into what in professional football are considered appropriate values, attitudes and behaviours (Gearing, 1999). These include increased levels of commitment, sacrifice, dedication, discipline and an ever-increasing affinity with the role of a professional football player (Brown & Potrac, 2009). Historically, the cultural practices and behaviours that young aspirant professionals are socialised into include dressing-room banter, gambling, drinking and promiscuity (Gearing, 1999; Parker, 1996), most of which are still prevalent today. Appropriate work-based values and attitudes include obedience, the ability to conform and the adoption of 'good habits', which pertains to such things as punctuality and mental and physical preparation for training and matches (Parker, 1996). These attitudes become ingrained over time and constitute a normative form of control that attempts 'to shape work culture and workers' subjectivity in order to ensure compliance' (Ezzy, 2001: 632). It is certainly the case that when a young player is 'seen to comply with appropriate attitudes and values, this quite often will generate increased favour in terms of managerial preference' (Parker, 1996: 111) and demonstrates to club coaches signs of the player's progress and personal maturity (Parker, 1996, 2001). Moreover, failure to develop a healthy professional attitude or accept such values may generate unfavourable reactions from coaches and teammates, which can result in players being ostracised. This latter point is important because, as we shall see later, many young players are unaware of the culture of professional football in general and football clubs in particular, as both have their own specific cultural environment, subculture, tradition, values and working practices (Potrac et al., 2002; Parker, 1996; Brady et al., 2008).

Cushion and Jones (2006: 149) noted how the style of coaching at one particular English Premier League academy involved 'a combination of abusive language, direct personal castigation, and threats of physical exercise'. Roderick (2003: 81) noted the advice of a coach at an English Premier League club: 'Smile, be happy in your life, but when you cross that line, whether it be for training or a match, you've got to become a bastard. You've got to be a hard, tough bastard.' All of the players interviewed were asked to describe their experiences with their first manager in professional football. The responses were strikingly similar, with a recurring theme being their fear of the manager, and the manager's use of verbal and physical abuse to intimidate young players and to induce fear. One player, with considerable experience in all four divisions, recounted his experiences as a young professional at a Premier League club in England:

PLAYER: I remember [the manager] was under a bit of pressure at the time. It's not an easy world to live in. I mean, the youngsters used to get assaulted all the time. They are just trying to toughen you up, I think, and [there was violence] from senior pros as well. And the manager especially – there would be a fear there, you know.
SK: So were you afraid of the manager?
PLAYER: Yeah, I think especially when you are younger and just getting started. As you get older, the fear goes away a bit and you'd stand up for yourself a bit.

All of the players recalled their fear of their managers and coaches when they were young players. Another player recounted his experiences as a young professional at an English Premier League club:

> Oh God, it was frightening. He was totally the hardest manager I have ever come across. He f****** didn't take any shit at all. Sort of old school in terms of behaviour . . . But you pretty much got the drift of it [his approach] after an hour with him. He was very strict. There was a fear factor with him – total fear factor. There was a fear factor that if you didn't perform, you were out. He'd hammer you. He would verbally abuse you if you didn't do it.

The physical and verbal abuse administered to apprentices and young professionals was a recurring theme in the players' responses. Another noted:

> He would hurl abuse at you all the time. In front of other players, in the office, on your own, or in the office in front of the coach and staff. Now, it brought out the best in me. It did bring out the best in me. But I know not all players could hack it – they just couldn't hack it. I know I asked once what his policy on being late was – how much were we fined, you know. You weren't late – that was his policy. I think that all players know it. If you are a young lad just coming in, then a manager will just take their frustration out on young players generally.

The use of physical violence as a means of intimidating young players does not appear to be unusual. One interviewee spoke about his experiences as a youth team player at an English Premier League club. The manager, he said, would 'frighten the life out of you – he would use bully tactics . . . Sure, he used to hit players':

> I remember [the manager] smacked us all in the head with a cricket bat once. We had training and I remember I was a youth team player at the time, and we used to get kitted in the morning and then get changed, put on fresh kit, go up [for food], but we were meant to put the old kit in the wash bags for the wash man to wash, but I think xxxx [the manager] walked by and saw the kit on the ground, went up to his office and got the cricket bat out. He lined us all up, turned the cricket bat to one side . . . and smacked us all on the head. Yeah, and it was a good hard smack as well.

In describing in more detail this manager's technique for controlling players, the interviewee said:

> He would square up to you and everything. Oh, he would have no problems in giving you a clip, and it hurt . . . He didn't really care. I mean, he was so successful with all the players that he worked with. I mean, everyone respected him because he knew what he was doing, everyone was afraid of not doing [what he wanted] . . . I mean, off the

pitch he was a lovely guy – I mean, a really nice guy – but everyone was afraid not to do what he said when you got on the pitch. I think because people respected him so much was one reason why he got away with it. I mean, if you speak to him off the pitch or go into his office and have a chat with him, I mean, he is great, like, he would be like a father figure to players off the pitch, but on the pitch it would be bully tactics all the way. I mean, if you crossed him, then it's the worst – he is the worst person ever to cross. It's like the end of the world. Players would be so afraid of him – that's how he got players to do what he said. Players would just do exactly what he said.

Before examining the central part played by intimidation and abuse as aspects of managerial control within clubs, the following section will explore themes discussed in Chapter 4 concerning the management of a player's baggage and off-field behaviour.

## Baggage, 'bomb squads' and beer

As discussed in Chapter 4, a recurring theme in the manager interviews concerned how a player's lifestyle and off-field behaviour were significant factors in the recruitment and assessment process. In professional football, the arrival of a new manager or coach considerably heightens players' feelings of insecurity – especially, as one current English League One player stated, 'if your face doesn't fit and you're not seen as part of their plans'. Current Ireland international Stephen Ward recounted his arrival at pre-season training and his subsequent relegation to the 'bomb squad' at Wolverhampton Wanderers. Ward stated: 'The exiles were separated from the rest of the first-team group and left to do their own training together as the Molineux hierarchy waited for an acceptable offer' (McDonnell, 2014).

Gareth Southgate (2010: 106) recently stated that 'we are breeding players that look for excuses, that don't want to take responsibility. Selfishness within the game – that is awful for team spirit. A generation with an aversion to learning from the coaches, or from senior players.' In particular, Southgate (2010: 106) stated that in 'speaking to other managers, the same themes crop up: young players who earn too much too soon; players who care less about improving their game and more about becoming celebrities; players who talk about cars and girls rather than the game'. Implicit in Southgate's comments is the possible influence that problem players may have on squad cohesion. This places considerable pressure on the football manager's authority and raises questions about his ability to maintain control over problem academy players in particular (Mills *et al.*, 2012; Mills *et al.*, 2014). This raises an important question: how do managers deal with problem players at senior level? Some managers may relegate certain players to bomb squads or force them to train separately or with the youth team. Other managers may adopt more subtle styles of management in their attempt to manage senior players (Mills & Boardley, 2016). For example, the allocation of training kit in general and in pre-season in particular can also have more implicit connotations. In terms of the (re)allocation of squad numbers, some managers like to play mind games with both senior and youth players. For example, being allocated number 24 on your kit in pre-season training, having worn number 9 the previous season, has obvious implications in terms of signifying your current standing within the squad. This can be viewed by players as their manager challenging them to perform well in the forthcoming pre-season training. One current English Championship player stated:

PLAYER: Yeah, like, I remember coming into pre-season one year and having the craic with the lads, then going and getting me kit off the kit man and, like, he's only gone and given me kit with the f****** number 24 on it, and I'm like, "What the f***? I was 9 last year!" And he just says, like, "Don't shoot the messenger – speak to the gaffer".
SK: And why was that?
PLAYER: They do that shit sometimes, especially if you had a good season and the gaffer might think you're smelling yourself a bit. Normally they change the numbers for the start of the season, though. Looking back, it was quite funny really, but the lads *absolutely* ripped me to bits over that.

While a number of studies have noted that aspects of professional football culture incorporate hyper-masculine workplaces epitomised by authoritarian styles of management and coaching (Cushion & Jones, 2006; Potrac & Jones, 2009; Roderick, 2006), some studies (Richardson et al., 2012; Mills et al., 2014) have argued that this style of managerial control at youth level in particular has been replaced with a more participative style of management. In this regard, one player was questioned about his recent experiences of the style of management and coaching at an English Premier League club:

> I think especially last year the staff were always mean to the young players and that kind of annoyed me because I remember when I was younger, growing up in the job, that that kind of aspect was gone out of apprenticeships when I was working. To be fair, walking in on your first day, there is nothing more nervous going into a work environment with lads that have been there for years, laughing and joking, all knowing each other. Then suddenly you are the new fellow walking in. It's very tough. So I knew what it was like for these young lads of 16 and 17 to be walking in and having men of 45 to 50 – grown men, say coaches – picking on them. It was something that I didn't like, some lads found it funny but I didn't.

In addition, one former Premier League academy player described his recent experience of professional football in England and his coaches' attitudes at that club in particular. He stated: 'It's just a meat market . . . A lot of the time you are just a product – I mean, it's such a big business . . . They don't really care about you.'

Dunning and Waddington (2003: 359) noted that the 'culture of many sports in modern Britain involves an association with heavy drinking'. This has been, and to some extent remains, true in relation to professional football. In particular, as discussed in Chapter 1, even as far back as the 1890s, alcohol was described as the 'curse of the team' (Dixon & Garnham, 2005: 378). At all professional clubs, alcohol consumption is prohibited 48 hours prior to a match day. One player admitted that professional players do indeed enjoy having a drink, but stressed 'at the right time'. The players generally agreed that alcohol consumption has a detrimental effect on performance levels. Several of the players stated that they would only drink in situations where they were not training the next day. However, although most players accepted the need to drink sensibly and in moderation, the consumption of alcohol remains a key issue for many managers. Several managers interviewed stated that players who 'abuse' themselves and fail to 'look after themselves' would be 'found out in the end'. One manager spoke about disciplining a player who turned up in a 'dishevelled state':

> I disciplined a player when he came in one day and I think that he wasn't in a physical enough state to train, you know, and when I went to the player, you know, I can be very aggressive, and I can be quite nasty in my own way, but I have another side to me in that I try to get on with as many players as I can. But if they let me down, it's one chance and it's over . . . So I pulled him in and I said, and it was in pre-season training, and I said, "You weren't able to train this morning, you're stinking of alcohol", and, you know, he denied it. And I said, "If you deny it the next time, then it's over between you and me". And I said, "Because we do section times on the training pitch and you're ten seconds outside your section time", and then he went, "Yeah, well, I was out". So I said, "Well, that's all right – so you were out yesterday, you will be fined two weeks' wages. It's the maximum I can fine you for, and it's over. So what I'm saying to you now, what I'm saying in this office now, is between you and me. It doesn't go outside the room but I am telling you, *IF YOU EVER* come in again in that state, then it's over between you and me". And that was fine – we shook hands and then moved on, end of story.

In his autobiography, Sir Alex Ferguson described how he disciplined experienced players such as Jonny Evans, Darron Gibson and Wayne Rooney by suspending them for having a big night out and 'turning up for training dishevelled' (Ferguson, 2013: 142).

There is evidence to suggest why managers deem heavy or inappropriate consumption of alcohol a very serious matter. One player spoke about his views on drinking in general and an incident that occurred at an English Premier League club in particular:

PLAYER: There's no harm in going and letting off some steam every now and again. I wouldn't, like, be every week going and getting hammered, like. I don't think it's right. Look at the situation at xxxx [former club] with players getting into trouble. I was at a club when there was this incident and it ended up with players getting charged with stuff. It ruined the club. It ruined it. It really did. That night ended up in a fight and two lads charged with it. Personally, with some of the managers I've had, you wouldn't drink, you wouldn't come in with drink on you. Other managers, you could get away with it.

SK: And just one question relating to that. As a manager, how do you think they should deal with that sort of behaviour?

PLAYER: As a manager, I think it is one of the hardest things. But as a manager you shouldn't let that happen because I think that could be stopped in terms of your players don't go out like that. If they do go out, you tell them. It comes back to how we started off. Discipline as a child in football and how you are brought up. As a manager, it is hard. I feel sorry for managers, but players have to go out in terms of their lifestyle. They are entitled to go out and there is no harm in going out in terms of a golf day with a group and a few drinks afterwards, but allowing your team to start at eleven o'clock and twelve o'clock in the morning drinking . . . That's scandalous, I think – that wouldn't happen in an office job, you know what I mean? If you want to get a bit of team bonding, which is good, go-karting, game of bowls, something like that, and then go for a meal afterwards and players have eaten, then go for a few drinks. But it all comes down to individuals as well, doesn't it? It's very hard for a manager.

## Abuse, intimidation and violence as means of managerial control

Parker has suggested that professional football is a 'distinctively working-class occupational domain [which] resolves primarily around a strict diet of authoritarianism, ruthlessness and hyper-masculine work-place practice' (1996: 1). Similarly, Magee has suggested that players need to be able to 'look after themselves' (1998: 129). None of the data collected in this research would contradict these comments. Verbal abuse and intimidation, and sometimes the use, or threat, of physical violence, are all aspects of this ruthless and hyper-masculine work culture, and not just with respect to young players. Although young players are particularly vulnerable to abuse and intimidation, there is evidence, both from the data collected and the autobiographies of professional players, that these techniques are also routinely used against more established players. For example, one former English Championship player described how players were punished for defensive errors (even in training) and for losing matches, by being made to do additional running:

> When we trained, if someone got a clear shot at goal, then he would stop training and make us run for 20 minutes. [For] any mistakes at all. We were terrified to make mistakes. It was entirely based on fear. We were scared. After matches that we lost, he would have us in at six in the morning running.

Even senior and established players may be verbally abused and even physically assaulted. In his autobiography, the former professional footballer Mick Quinn, who had a very successful playing career with several clubs including Coventry City, Portsmouth and Newcastle United, described professional football 'as a sport full of bullies and lunatics' (2003: 50). With the arrival of a new manager, Larry Lloyd, at Wigan Athletic, the squad was directed to the players' lounge to be introduced to him. Quinn described what happened:

> Larry slammed the door open, nearly taking it off its hinges, strode in and bellowed "Hello, I'm Larry Lloyd. If you don't like what I'm going to say, then I'm going to head-butt you". Everyone looked at one another in amazement.
>
> (Quinn, 2003: 50)

Quinn also provided a good illustration of the abuse and violence to which even senior players may be subjected:

> On one occasion we came in at half-time after what was admittedly a poor performance to Larry [the manager] going bananas. He smashed all the teacups against the wall above our heads as we sat on the benches, and ranted, "You were a f****** disgusting shower of s*** out there!" He pointed to my fellow Scouser Tony Quinn and screamed, "You f****** stank out there, get in the f****** shower!" Tony, who was sitting next to me, got up and left. I was frowning at the weird sight of Larry having virtual convulsions, so he turned to me. "What's the f****** matter with you, Quinn?" "Well", I replied, "if you got off our backs, we might be able to play." "Get in that f****** shower! You're off!" he screamed. So I joined Tony in the baths.
>
> (Quinn, 2003: 51)

The message conveyed to players was unambiguous: no matter how abusive or violent the manager's behaviour may be, his authority was not to be questioned and those who did question it were punished, in this case by being withdrawn from the game. Other senior professional players have recorded not just the threat but the actual use of violence by managers against them. For example, in his autobiography, Roy Keane described how the Nottingham Forest manager, Brian Clough – who is regarded by many people as one of the greatest of English managers – reacted to an error by Keane in an important FA Cup match:

> When I walked into the dressing room after the game, Clough punched me straight in the face. "Don't pass the ball back to the goalkeeper", he screamed as I lay on the floor, him standing over me. I was hurt and shocked, too shocked to do anything but nod my head in agreement. My honeymoon with Clough and professional football was over. Dressing rooms can be hard, unforgiving places. Being knocked down by Clough was part of my learning curve. Knowing the pressure he was under, I didn't hold the incident against him. He never said sorry.
>
> (Keane, 2002: 38)

In his autobiography, Steve Claridge also described being assaulted by his manager, John Beck, when he was a player at Cambridge United:

> At half time I was in the medical room when he [Beck] came in, obviously ready for a showdown, and told me to get into the dressing room. "I'm not doing an effing thing you say any more", I told him. "Just stick it up your arse." He flew at me, trying to head-butt me . . . He came at me again, swinging his fists, but I connected first and punched him in the eye . . . Anyway, he then took a run at me but I gripped him in a headlock and started punching him . . . He was kicking and punching back at me. His assistant, Gary Peters . . . came round the blindside and I was also trying to fend him off. It was pandemonium. At this point Liam Daish [another player] arrived and grabbed Beck, while Peters grabbed me and held us apart. We were pulled apart. "I'll see you after the game", Beck spat at me.
>
> (Claridge, 2000: 135–6)

Claridge commented that it 'did surprise me, but then in football people lose their tempers all the time and say and do silly things'. It is difficult to imagine any other modern Western industry in which abuse, intimidation and violence of this kind would be regarded as legitimate instruments of managerial control; indeed, outside the relatively closed social world of professional football, these techniques would almost universally be regarded not just as bad management practice, but would almost certainly result in cases being brought to industrial tribunals and might also result in criminal prosecutions.

There is some evidence to suggest that the use of various forms of managerial intimidation is so commonplace in professional football that not only do most players accept it, but that some players may even have difficulty in adapting to less authoritarian, less intimidatory and more open and democratic styles of management. This was certainly the view of one experienced manager who was interviewed. He had been appointed to an English Premier League club where the previous manager used abusive and violent tactics similar to those described by Quinn. The manager described how some players at the club had had difficulty in adapting to his quiet and more thoughtful style of management:

MANAGER: It was my style of leadership, which maybe was unusual for them.
INTERVIEWER: Yes, tell me about your style of leadership.
MANAGER: I am quiet and I am very analytical. When they lost a game under their previous manager, he would kick in the door and kick players, and lift them up to the wall and say various things . . . He was very angry. He was furious after he lost a match. He was managing through fear, he was scaring the players. Then I came in and was very quiet, and I would say that we would watch the match [on video] tomorrow.

## The basis of managerial authority

Abuse, intimidation and violence are routinely used by football managers to impose their authority on players. However, within professional football, players generally appear to accept this pattern of arbitrary and authoritarian management, and the use of abuse and violence. For example, Steve Claridge dismissed being assaulted by his manager by saying that 'in football people lose their tempers all the time and say and do silly things'. Similarly, Roy Keane simply regarded Brian Clough's assault on him as part of his 'learning curve'. Perhaps significantly, Clough appears not to have felt any obligation to apologise.

This acceptance of arbitrary discipline and abuse was also evident in the interviews with players. For example, the interviewee who said that his first manager 'would hurl abuse at you all the time' went on to say that 'it did bring out the best in me'. Implicit in this player's comments is an apparent acceptance of the ruthless and hyper-masculine character of professional football (Parker, 1996) and, coupled with this, an acceptance of the idea that, though it was unpleasant at the time, the abuse he experienced as an apprentice was an effective way of preparing him for a career in professional football. Several interviewees expressed the same idea, suggesting that if apprentices and young players can learn to handle the abuse, and negotiate what one player called the 'not so nice stuff', then they were prepared for anything in football. These comments seem to suggest that professional football players not only accept the use of intimidation and violence by managers, but that many of them even see it as an appropriate way of socialising young players into the football industry. Both the arbitrary nature of managerial authority and its acceptance by players have been noted by Perry, who in his study of football managers noted that 'the position of "boss" was maintained through the use of sanctions of various kinds including financial and emotional'. He added that discipline 'can be draconian and bullying was tolerated by the players themselves' (Perry, 2000b: 9). The following is a preliminary attempt to account for this arbitrary and authoritarian style of management and its general acceptance by players. Parker's (1996: 48) study of football apprentices suggested that one of the central tasks of club officials is to promote attitudes of 'acceptance, obedience and collective loyalty' among apprentices. He went on to say that the essential characteristics that apprentice-professionals must demonstrate to club managers as signs of their progress and personal maturity include 'an acceptance of workplace subservience, an ability to conform' (1996: 200). He suggested that the central values of football culture are akin to those of 'a working-class shop-floor culture' (1996: 67).

There is one aspect of football culture that, though arguably trivial in itself, is perhaps particularly symbolic not just of working-class shop-floor culture but also of a particularly traditional form of shop-floor culture: the almost universal imposition of fines at football clubs for late arrival for training and for other minor offences. Although there is a general expectation in all occupations that people will arrive at work on time, in most occupations people who occasionally arrive at work late are not subject to fines. Nor are they subject to fines for other minor offences. This has probably never been part of the occupational culture in most middle-class and professional occupations. However, a system of fines for lateness was, as Engels (1845: 201–4) noted, a key instrument for controlling workers' behaviour in the factory system in the nineteenth century. Although some shop-floor manual workers – unlike most of their middle-class and professional counterparts – may still be required to 'clock in', the use of fines for late arrival is rare in industrial relations today; other, and less arbitrary, measures, such as a system of informal or formal warnings, which has often been agreed with the relevant trade union, are more normally used to deal with workers who are persistently late. However, professional football retains a disciplinary system for dealing with lateness and other minor offences that is modelled on the system that was introduced in the nineteenth century to deal with workers unused to the discipline and the time constraints associated with the new factory system. In this respect, it might be said that professional football not only has some of the characteristics of working-class shop-floor culture, but that it also has the characteristics of a *traditional* nineteenth-century form of shop-floor culture. The values of football culture identified by Parker – obedience, and acceptance of workplace subservience – are also part of this traditional shop-floor culture, which would be seen as outmoded and inappropriate, and which would not be accepted by most workers, in most modern factories and workshops. How, then, does one account for the persistence of this arbitrary and authoritarian style of management at football clubs? In order to answer this question, it is necessary to examine briefly the origins of football management, as it is not possible adequately to understand contemporary structures without reference to the ways in which those structures have developed (Elias, 1987).

Carter suggested that, within modern football, 'it is still possible to detect the influence of the football manager's Victorian roots' (Carter, 2004: 45). More specifically, he drew attention to the fact that management–worker relations within early professional football clubs 'echoed the strict hierarchy of Victorian class society' (Carter, 2006: 5). While almost all professional football players were drawn from the working classes, directors were usually local businessmen or professionals (Carter, 2006: 38). Within the clubs, the professional players were, in status terms, the equivalent of workers within industry and, like industrial workers, were seen as requiring regulation and control. The style of management that emerged within this situation was, like that in industry, highly authoritarian. The management of players, Carter suggested, 'largely mirrored attitudes towards the handling of young, working-class men in general' (Carter, 2006: 2) and was based on 'a clear hierarchical structure, autocratic tendencies, traditional notions of masculinity and the need for discipline' (Carter, 2006: 5). A 'management of fear', he suggested, 'quickly became institutionalized throughout much of British professional football and in some ways it was admired because it appealed to some of the masculine sensibilities of working-class players and fans' (Carter, 2006: 6).

This provides a useful starting point, but no more than this. This authoritarian style of management was not unusual at the time, for it reflected the general pattern of management in industry in the late nineteenth and early twentieth centuries. The key question, then, is why, and how, has this traditional pattern of arbitrary and authoritarian management persisted in professional football when it has long been superseded in industrial relations more generally?

### Traditional authoritarianism as the basis of football management

A fruitful avenue for exploration is to be found in Penn's suggestion, noted previously, that there is an inherent contradiction within modern professional football clubs between 'the rational forms of organization within the management of the club as a business and the non-rational, charismatic form of organization inherent in team management' (2002: 45). Penn argued that there has been a

> systematic bifurcation of management within the core of contemporary football clubs. On the one hand is the management of the team, which is essentially charismatic ... On the other is the increasingly complex management of the club which is subject to a triad of forces – professionalization, differentiation and an increasing application of rational modes of co-ordination and control.
> (Penn, 2002: 40)

However, the role of the manager remains largely untouched by this 'triad of forces'; the manager's authority, Penn argued, remains 'essentially charismatic: his personality and the mythology that surrounds him is what gives him authority' (2002: 44–5). Penn was correct to draw attention to two very different kinds of authority to be found in professional football clubs. However, it is argued that Penn was using the term 'charisma' in the very loose sense in which it has increasingly come to be used in everyday life; in terms of Weber's (1964: 358) classic and more precise analysis of authority, there are very few managers whose authority could properly be described as 'charismatic'.[1] In this regard, it is argued that the contradiction within modern professional football clubs is not between rational-legal authority and charismatic authority, as Penn suggested, but between rational-legal authority and traditional, authoritarian domination. In the following section, Weber's work on bureaucracy and on types of domination will be revisited to explore these ideas further. As noted in the introduction, Weber's types of domination are, of course, 'pure types' and, as Weber (cited in Bendix, 1962: 329) pointed out, all forms of domination occurring empirically are 'combinations, mixtures, adaptations, or modifications' of the charismatic, the traditional and the rational-legal type.

Penn noted that football clubs have recently developed an increasingly complex management structure which involves greater professionalisation and differentiation and an increasing application of rational modes of coordination and control; as a result, clubs have increasingly taken on the characteristics of modern rational-legal, bureaucratic organisations (Penn, 2002). As noted in the Introduction, one major characteristic of rational-legal bureaucracies, as defined by Weber, is that each managerial position has a defined sphere of competence in the legal sense, which is ordered by rules or administrative regulations. This means that the regular activities that are carried out by the holder of a given position are assigned as official duties (for example, in a job description) and, of particular importance in the context of this chapter, the authority to give orders to subordinates is, as Weber (1948: 196) noted, 'distributed in a stable way and is strictly delimited by rules concerning the coercive means, physical, sacerdotal, or otherwise, which may be placed at the disposal of officials'. Thus, a critical aspect of rational-legal authority is that authority is not exercised in an arbitrary manner and that the limits of authority are clearly defined and rule-bound; one aspect of this rule-bound character is that, while managers have authority over their subordinates, that authority is limited and regulated and, as Weber noted, formal provision is also made for appealing against the decisions of superiors.[2]

It is clear that, although the professionalisation and bureaucratisation of football clubs in recent years have involved the increasing application of rational modes of coordination and control to areas such as ticket sales, marketing club merchandise, sponsorship and public relations, the role of the football manager has remained remarkably resistant to these processes. Even a cursory glance at the role of the football manager is sufficient to indicate how little it has in common with managerial posts in most modern organisations. Traditional elements of the football manager's authority are evident in many aspects of his role. As noted in Chapters 2 and 3, very few football managers have a clear job description, or any formal management training or managerial experience outside football.

However, in the context of this chapter, one of the most commonly used sanctions in football clubs – the imposition of fines – is a traditional sanction that has now been almost universally abolished in every other modern industry. A central characteristic of traditional authority is that it is not rule-bound and regulated in a stable and systematic way, as is rational-legal bureaucratic authority. In this regard, Weber pointed out first that traditional authority is based on traditions that partly define the content of commands and the objects and extent of authority – witness the traditional use of fines in this regard – but second that tradition leaves a certain 'sphere of action' open for the leader's 'free personal decision'. This means that traditional authority is characterised by what Weber called a 'double sphere': 'on the one hand, of action which is bound to specific tradition; on the other hand, of that which is free of any specific rules' (1964: 342). As Weber noted, this means that the person who exercises traditional authority 'is free to confer "grace" on the basis of his personal pleasure or displeasure, his personal likes and dislikes, quite arbitrarily' (Weber, 1964: 342). This latter point is of major importance; it means that, in the exercise of traditional authority – unlike in the exercise of legal-rational authority – the extent of the leader's authority is not clearly specified and delimited. On the contrary, there is scope for the arbitrary exercise of power.

The relevance of Weber's work for understanding the position of the football manager is clear. The limits of the football manager's authority, unlike that of most managers in other modern industries, are not clearly defined or limited by formal rules or regulations, but are left largely for each manager to define for himself. The fact that the limits of managerial authority are not clearly defined means that scope exists for the arbitrary exercise of power. It is this that explains why club disciplinary codes include important arbitrary elements. They are based on and reflect the personal experiences and individual style of each manager rather than an established body of knowledge that defines 'good practice'. It also explains why these codes, and the manner in which they are enforced, vary from club to club, as well as the fact that they can change radically within a club when there is a change of manager.

One question still remains: why do players generally accept the arbitrary exercise of authority by managers? In this regard, it is important to note that young players enter a workplace in which the arbitrary exercise of managerial authority has been long established, and in which abuse, intimidation and violence have long been part of the armoury of managerial control over players. When an apprentice player signs a contract with a football club, he learns, as part of a process of occupational socialisation, to accept what, in the context of the ruthless and hyper-masculine culture of professional football, are considered appropriate values and attitudes. Young players, in particular, are vulnerable and relatively powerless in relation to the manager and they quickly learn that it is important for them to develop a 'good professional attitude', not least because this will affect the way in which they are perceived and evaluated by their manager, upon whom they are heavily dependent for career advancement. In this regard, the manager is a very powerful figure. He is the gatekeeper who controls access to desired goals: for young apprentices, the offer of a full-time professional contract; for older players, the offer of a new contract at the expiry of their existing contract; and for both, team selection. The idea of the 'good professional attitude' is central to the way that players are evaluated by managers and, although this point was mentioned in Chapter 4, it merits further exploration.

Parker's ethnographic study of football apprentices was replete with references to 'attitude' and, as noted previously, he suggested that among the immediate tasks of club officials is the promotion of attitudes of 'acceptance, obedience and club loyalty' and 'an acceptance of workplace subservience, an ability to conform' (Parker, 1996: 200). These values are deeply embedded in the traditional shop-floor culture of professional football and learned and internalised by players from a young age. Roderick (2006: 49) similarly noted that the 'importance of developing a "good attitude" is impressed on younger players from the moment they have contact with the coaching staff at clubs'. But the importance of a 'good attitude' is not confined to younger professionals; Roderick noted that even older and established professionals in his study spoke similarly of having regularly to '(re)prove themselves to new managers . . . and that one way in which this can be achieved is by demonstrating a good professional attitude' (Roderick, 2006: 37–8). As Parker (1996: 111) noted, the acceptance of these attitudes by young players is seen as a sign of their progress, which may generate 'increased favour in terms of managerial preference'. However, players who do not accept and behave in terms of these values are likely to be perceived by their managers as 'troublemakers', as people who do not have the 'right attitude', and their careers are likely to suffer as a consequence. In this regard, as Roderick (2006: 43) correctly noted, 'one of the central aspects of the "good attitude" ... [is] ... that it can be thought of as a powerful form of social control in the context of professional football'.

## Conclusion

Abuse, intimidation and violence are aspects of managerial control in professional football. It is argued that the roots of this arbitrary exercise of power are to be found in the fact that managerial power relies on the exercise of a form of traditional authority that is not clearly defined, regulated and circumscribed in the manner of rational-legal authority.

It may the case that these traditional styles of management are in the process of changing, perhaps partly as a result of the significant increase, during the last two decades in particular, in the number of foreign players and coaches/managers in football in England, many of whom appear – though there are no systematic data on this – to be better educated than their English counterparts.[3] In this regard, the former Arsenal player Ian Wright said that Arsène Wenger, the French manager of Arsenal, 'doesn't bully his players into performing for him' but that he 'treats people like adults' (Carter, 1999: 51); the implicit contrast with other managers under whom Wright played seems clear. However, it is wrong to assume that all managers from continental Europe necessarily eschew what might be described as more traditional ways of controlling players. For example, in a recent book on Chelsea, the former assistant manager Steve Clarke described events in the Chelsea dressing room at half-time in a game that Chelsea were losing to Arsenal. Clarke said that Chelsea's then manager, the Portuguese José Mourinho, 'wasn't happy':

> He was working himself up into a little bit of a frenzy. He picked up a plastic cup and assumed it was empty but it had some Lucozade in it. So the players ... and the staff are standing behind him – and he dropped it and volleyed it back towards the staff. The Lucozade came flying out right into my face. Carlo Cudicini [the reserve goalkeeper] was next to me and it's gone all over Carlo's clothes. And the boss is ranting and raving and then he's picked up a tub of Vaseline and he's heaved that as well, and it's bounced off the wall in the dressing room and there's a big blob of Vaseline stuck on the wall but slowly falling down towards the fitness coach's clothes. And I'm thinking, "What can I do? I can't tell the manager to f*** off." He just drowned me in Lucozade; it was running down my face. No one really noticed because the players were focused on the manager, but all the staff were looking at this Vaseline

dripping down the wall. He was in the middle of his talk, so no one wanted to interrupt him because it was crucial. So I'm trying to grab a towel to wipe the Lucozade off my face and Carlo's trying to wipe the stuff off his gear and the fitness coach is trying to make sure the Vaseline doesn't fall on his clothes.

(Glanvill, 2005: 26)

However, even here there is evidence of one small divergence from the behaviour of English managers: Clarke recorded that after the game Mourinho, unlike his English counterparts, apologised for his behaviour!

## Notes

1  'The term "charisma" will be applied to a certain quality of an individual personality by virtue of which he is set apart from ordinary men and treated as endowed with supernatural, superhuman, or at least specifically exceptional powers or qualities' (Weber, 1964: 358). The concept of charisma might apply to a professional football manager in its more common meaning. For example, few managers are heroic in the sense of the real political drama of history. However, as celebrities, their accomplishments may be turned into quasi-heroic deeds by the media. This is referred to as 'pseudo-charisma' (Cantelon & Ingham, 2002: 71).

2  The authoritarian style of management in professional football has led some observers to point to similarities between football and the military (see, for example, Carter, 2006). Although there are some superficial similarities, this comparison is in most respects misleading. As previously identified, a striking feature of football management is the degree to which it has proved resistant to bureaucratisation; this is a key source of the arbitrary power of managers. By contrast, and as Weber (1964: 334–5) pointed out, 'the modern army is essentially a bureaucratic organization', which is ordered by general rules and administrative regulations and in which the duties and powers of officers are clearly defined and limited. Of course, these powers may on occasions be exceeded, for example in cases of bullying of junior soldiers, but where this occurs it represents a clear breach of army regulations and those responsible may be subject to disciplinary procedures. This is not the case in professional football.

3  There is a widely held view that managers/coaches from Western continental Europe tend to be more 'progressive' and less authoritarian in their relationships with players. If this is indeed the case, these differences may be related to different patterns of industrialisation and associated differences in patterns of worker–management relations. However, the view that Western European coaches are less authoritarian is largely impressionistic, and is not based on any systematic data. Nor is this an area that was probed in this study. There is clearly a need for comparative studies in this area, which would enable the exploration of similarities and differences – and the reasons for them – between UK management styles and those of continental coaches.

# Chapter 6

# Agents

## Introduction

For a number of reasons, an understanding of the agent representation business is crucial for managers and young or aspirant managers in particular. First, agents play a central role in facilitating the transfer of players both domestically and internationally and in their contract (re)negotiations. Second, FIFA's introduction and subsequent updating of its regulations and legal frameworks governing the activity of agents in professional football (Rossi *et al.*, 2016) has important implications for the role of the manager. Third, managers need to be aware of the dynamics of the agent industry because, throughout football's history, the role of agents in English professional football has been the subject of considerable media attention, much of which has concerned their informal and questionable business practices. In this regard, FIFA's decision to deregulate the industry is perhaps a reflection of its inability to govern the behaviour of agents and the alleged bribery, exploitation and trafficking of young players in what is, as we shall see later, an extremely complex industry that is characterised by unethical and deceitful conduct. While most professional football managers will have an understanding of agents' involvement in player transfers, it is only through media exposure (for instance, BBC *Panorama* special investigations), commentary on the Lord Stevens inquiries (Scott, 2007), agent revelations (Ashton, 2011) and a number of high-profile court cases that the general public has been made aware of their questionable practices.

In general, the role of a football agent typically involves contract (re)negotiations for players and managers, the scouting of players for clubs, managing players' and managers' image rights and providing financial, counselling and support services. While non-academic studies have identified the unethical and in some cases illegal business practices adopted by some agents (Stevens, 2006; Bower, 2003), a number of academic studies have identified the different types of agents and their role in professional football[1] (Roderick, 2006; Holt *et al.*, 2006; Magee, 1998, 2002; Poli, 2010; Siekmann *et al.*, 2007; Demazière & Jouvenet, 2013). However, few academic studies have utilised semi-structured tape-recorded interviews with agents in examining how they impact on the role of the professional football manager. This chapter attempts to redress this gap in our knowledge by examining the industry from the perspectives of players, managers and agents. In particular, the chapter focuses on three key aspects of the agent industry which influence the role of the contemporary football manager. First, the chapter explores the central role that agents play in professional football in general and in player contract (re)negotiations in particular. Second, it examines the considerable hostility that exists towards agents, much of which concerns their alleged unethical behaviour. Despite such hostility, we examine why managers still utilise the services of agents when recruiting players. The final section explores what is arguably a crucial development in professional football, the considerable shift in power away from clubs and managers towards players and their agents. Before these issues are examined, however, the following section will briefly examine the emergence of agents in professional football.

## The emergence of agents in professional football

Professional football agents are not a new phenomenon, as they played an important role in scouting and recruiting players on clubs' behalf following the legalisation of professional football in 1885 (Roderick, 2006). The entrepreneurial agents of the early professional days tended to represent football clubs and not players (Taylor, 1999) and 'it was not until the mid-1970s that players began to turn to people "outside" the game for professional advice on contract and transfer negotiations' (Roderick, 2006: 127). It has been in the post-Bosman era of professional football, with greater-value contracts on offer, as well as more out-of-contract footballers seeking to maximise their career potential, that there has been a significant increase in the number of players using agents in contract negotiations (Horne et al., 1999). For example, in 2001, there were '179 FIFA-registered agents in England, compared to 88 in France, 80 in Germany . . . and 54 in Italy' (Banks, 2002: 167). By 2007, there were 325 registered agents in England (Poli, 2010) and by 2015 this figure had increased to 550 (Rossi et al., 2016). In recent years, a number of solo agents have merged to form their own player representative companies, while media companies such as Proactive Sports Management, IMG, First Artist Sport and SFX provide services traditionally associated with the solo agent. Unsurprisingly, all of the players and seven of the managers interviewed for this research utilised the services of a registered agent.

The escalation in the number of agents now operating in professional football can be attributed to three principal factors. First, from the mid-1990s, professional football 'underwent an unprecedented boom, making the game more popular and affluent than at any other time in its long history'

(Magee, 2002: 218). As a result of clubs' improved financial status, many invested heavily in the acquisition of players in the hope of improving their on-field performance. This resulted in an upward spiralling of players' wages. For example, in the 2013–14 season, the total wage costs for English Premier League clubs was £1.9 billion, while the total wage costs for Championship clubs exceeded £500 million (Deloitte, 2015). It is argued that the primary benefactors of football's increased wealth have been the players, a development that has not been lost on football agents (Szczepanik, 2009). The fee that agents charge for their services is capped at 3 per cent of the player's basic gross income or transfer compensation (FIFA, 2014), having previously varied between 5 and 10 per cent of the player's salary (Poli, 2010). While detailed information relating to payments made by players to agents is difficult to attain, in recent years many clubs have made public any payments made by them to agents. For example, English Premier League clubs paid out £66 million in agent fees in the 2007–08 season (Kelso, 2009), with this figure rising to £115 million in the 2013–14 season. In the 2003–04 season, Manchester United paid out £5.5 million to agents involved in the acquisition of nine players; this figure had grown to over £7.9 million in 2014, with Chelsea paying over £16.7 million in the same year. In particular, the Portuguese agency Gestifute received '£1.129 million for negotiating Cristiano Ronaldo's transfer to Manchester United' (Poli, 2010: 203), while in 2009 Jorge Mendes reportedly earned €3.6 million of the €9 million Manchester United paid for Bébé, gazumping the player's former agent in the process (Conn, 2012).

Second, and more important, was Jean-Marc Bosman's success at the European Court of Justice in 1995, which rendered the then transfer system illegal. As noted in Chapter 1, the Bosman ruling opened up the British market for professional footballers beyond the UK, and players at the end of their contract were able to move freely across Europe. This ruling also provided English clubs with the opportunity to compete with European clubs for their top players. As noted in Chapter 4, football agents' close collaboration with club officials and managers has in many ways replaced the traditional role of the club scout in the recruitment of football talent (Magee, 2002; Poli, 2010). Many agents are now in a position to provide reliable information on the availability of playing talent globally, which has considerably influenced the growth in the number of agents and reinforced their power in professional football in particular (Poli, 2010). Moreover, as we shall see later, agents' access to privileged and sensitive information concerning players' salaries and their level of satisfaction at their current clubs considerably influences agents' power. The internationalisation of the labour market for professional players and the emergence of new talent pipelines in particular (Poli, 2010; Commission of the European Communities, 2007), combined with the Bosman ruling, has had a perceptible effect of shifting power away from football clubs towards players and their agents (Whitehead, 1998;

O'Leary & Caiger, 2000; Lonsdale, 2004). Thus, players and their agents in particular are now in a considerable stronger position to negotiate better contracts and more lucrative options both at home and abroad. This is an important point that will be explored in greater detail later.

Finally, it is important to identify the relative ease with which an individual can obtain an agent's licence. The process for becoming a licensed players' agent is relatively straightforward[2] and begins with an application to the individual's national football association. Back in 2006, the English FA required all candidates to pass an agent examination and sign a 'Code of Professional Conduct' in which they 'pledge[d], without fail, to abide by the basic principles described therein when acting as a players' agent' (FA, 2006: 13). In 2008, FIFA updated its regulations and introduced a legal framework that governed the activity of agents in professional football (FIFA, 2008). However, following FIFA's decision to deregulate agents' activities in 2015, applicants are no longer required to sit the players' agent examination, provide police verification letters or have professional indemnity insurance. In theory, anybody in England can become an agent or intermediary provided he or she has an impeccable reputation and no criminal record or conflicted interests and pay the English FA £500 in registration fees (Riach, 2015). Each national football association is still required to draw up a list of all of the licensed intermediaries in its territory and forward it to FIFA. Perhaps surprisingly, there are no pre-requisite educational qualifications or experience required to secure a registered agent's licence.

The considerable influx of money into professional football combined with the expanded opportunities to recruit players, both at home and abroad, has had a direct effect in increasing the number of agents now operating in professional football. Out-of-contract players in general and more successful players in particular provide lucrative opportunities for agents to get involved in football, and they now occupy key roles in contract negotiations. Back in 1998, Maguire and Stead (1998: 61) astutely argued that 'the appearance of agents as part of soccer's economic relations is likely to have a growing impact on the form and extent of international player movements, and the range and complexity of transfer activities are likely to increase'. More recently, attracted by the large commissions available and the increased levels of power (Poli, 2010), agents have now become central figures in the football transfer market (Cashmore, 2000; Magee, 2002). However, as we shall see in the next section, professional football was 'unprepared for the increased involvement of agents, their business approach, and their rapid centralisation in the transfer and contract negotiating processes' (Magee, 2002: 230).

## Hostility towards agents

There is a view held by many people in professional football that agents are damaging the game. Data gathered from managers, players and, surprisingly, even some agents identify considerable hostility towards football agents and their business practices in particular. Many of the football managers interviewed described agents as 'parasites' and 'con-men', while players viewed them as 'scumbags' and 'cowboys'. During the course of one interview, a manager with considerable experience in Ireland and England became very animated when the issue of agents arose. Shifting uncomfortably in his seat, he described agents in the following terms:

> They are a disaster, an absolute disaster. I just have no time for them, and I've dealt with quite a few. I've dealt with so many of them in England, not so many here [Ireland]. I've met many of them in England, and I have yet to meet a good one, a genuine one. They're parasites.

Several managers expressed the view that players do not need agents. One manager said: 'Now, I am not saying that a player shouldn't be represented, but I feel that their union should represent them. There are representatives in the union and they are qualified to do so.' In this regard, the English FA argues against the need for players to employ agents, and that, rather than being 'ripped off', players would be better advised to use their own union, the PFA, a role for which it is better equipped and could provide at a fraction of the cost (Magee, 2002; Roderick, 2001). The data reported in this research reinforce the views held by the English FA that 'players do not need agents' (O'Leary & Caiger, 2000: 272). The following two examples from managers with experience in the English Premier League were typical of managers' views:

> To be honest with you, the view I'd have is, I wouldn't have a problem if a player has an agent, as I said, but I think they are foolish to have agents. That's my view.

> They are in the game, they are part of the game and they have to be dealt with. You have to deal with them professionally. The nature of the game is that everyone knows everyone so there is possibly not a need, from a manager's point of view, to go through an agent. From a player's point of view, he is protecting his own interest during negotiations, maybe to strengthen his negotiations – then I don't have a problem.

Roderick (2003: 272) suggested that agents' 'close association with their clients, in terms of negotiating on their behalf and often in their absence, leaves open the possibility for shady maneuvering in relation to the way in which the players' agents conduct their business'. A recurring theme that emerged from the interviews with managers concerned their distrustful attitudes towards agents. For example, one former English Championship manager said:

> I've used xxxx [agent's name] a few times. Yeah, you come across them from time to time. I find that if there is an agent involved, there is a

motive. And I'm not saying that is negative or positive, but there is a motive there in some way. I've taken my chances with them and I've dealt with them and some of them are absolute chancers and I've signed a few dummies in my time.

Personal contact networks and trust are crucial assets 'in the player transfer and representation business' (Poli & Rossi, 2012: 60). More specifically, current agent and former Danish international Mikkel Beck stated: 'Despite all the money that is involved, and how much importance people place on it, the only way you can be successful is to build up trust with your client. I have always had excellent relationships with my clients' families' (Evans, 2013: 37). A similar theme emerged from the interviews with players, who identified the importance of securing the services of an agent whom they could trust. The following two examples from players with experience in the English Premier League were typical of players' views:

> I mean, there is always going to be a bad cloud hanging over agents. But I think if you can get the right one and someone who is legitimate, from a player's point of view, like, it's great . . . It takes so much pressure off you. I think the trust factor is very important.

> Oh yes . . . like, trust is a massive factor, like, that is the main thing. If you don't trust whoever is looking after you, well . . . then you're in trouble.

Implicit in the above comments is the importance of trust between players and agents (Demaziere & Jouvenet, 2013). However, the data collected from players and managers suggest that agents have acquired a poor reputation, which may, in part, impact on their ability to do business in professional football. In this regard, some clubs and managers refuse to deal with certain agents. This point was developed further during the course of an interview with an agent who was working with a prominent English-based sports agency:

> Yeah, like, there are a lot of managers who will not deal with certain agents. I mean, that's why in this business it's all about reputation and trust. If you're working in a company . . . the company's reputation is so important, and you would never do anything to jeopardise that – I mean, not even one thing wrong, because word spreads very quickly. You know it takes a long time to build up a good reputation, and it's very easy to get a bad reputation.

In the context of player contract (re)negotiations, there is some evidence to suggest that it is not just agents who have acquired poor reputations. As noted in Chapter 4, some managers adopt tactics such as 'tapping up' in their attempts to sign prospective recruits. All of the agents interviewed were asked to describe their experiences of negotiating player contracts with managers. One licensed agent described some of the difficulties that he had experienced when negotiating with managers on players' behalf:

AGENT: Yeah, sometimes it can be difficult. Yeah, well, actually it is a nightmare at times. I mean, people lie through their teeth to get players – like, blatant lies.
SK: Really, like who?
AGENT: Managers. Yeah, I mean . . . like, you are talking to managers and they are blatantly lying to you and you know it. Like, they are trying to play cute and be dull – it's just unbelievable what is going on.

Similarly, one former English Premier League player described how he used an agent to negotiate a move to a Championship club. The agent had previously negotiated the player's contract with the Championship club's manager. The final step involved the signing of the contract by the player. The player described how, prior to signing the contract, he wanted to meet with the manager to discuss a few 'minor footballing issues'. The player then described how the manager tried to change the terms and conditions of his contract:

PLAYER: When I was moving to xxxx [English Championship club], xxxx [agent's name] dealt with the money side of it. So he had met the manager and gone through all the details and told me what was on the table.
SK: So, what happened then?
PLAYER: Then I went to meet the manager and I knew what my situation [proposed deal] was. I was told by the agent that the manager would try and talk about money. So the agent said to me, "It's up to you what you do, but you're better off not talking about it". So I said to the agent, "I don't want to talk about money" and the agent said that basically he [the manager] would probably try and offer me less. I was told I was getting x amount [per week] and when I spoke to the manager, the money situation changed. He said to me, "We'll start you off on x amount", which was less than what he told the agent. Because I was one-on-one with the manager . . . and all managers do this . . . I felt I was in a corner. Like, you're trying to sign for this fellow and he is offering you this money and you are not going to tell him "No", so it isn't a very good start, is it?

Implicit in the above comments is how this manager, in the absence of the player's agent, managed to alter the agreed contract terms and assume a greater level of control in the negotiation process. A recurring theme, discussed later, concerns how the balance of power shifts towards the manager and away from the player and his agent during contract negotiations between managers and players. Currently, there are many agents operating in professional football and, considering the level of competition among agents, acquiring a client base is a crucial strategy for agents. The PFA representative Mick McGuire noted that 'there are a few top agents who have grabbed the market and . . . eighty per cent are fighting over the crumbs' (Magee, 2002: 232). This strong competition between agents for players may encourage some agents to engage in illegal or ethically dubious practices (Poli, 2010). One licensed agent, who at the time of the interview was working for a leading UK-based sports agency, described the nature of the player representation industry and the level of competition that exists within the industry. In particular, he described some of the dubious practices adopted by some agents:

AGENT: You know, there are a lot of people in the business who are backstabbers and who lie. Like, some people would say things about the company [agency], or me, which aren't true, you know. I mean, I could easily turn round and bad-mouth other agents or companies, but it's not in my nature to do that. I mean, people who know me know what I do. I think they trust me and respect me, and I would hope that people would have a good impression of me and wouldn't listen to what other people say about me. Like, you wouldn't believe what goes on out there . . . and, like, there are five or six other companies, and you wouldn't believe the things they are saying about me and the company. *LIKE, THEY HAVE NEVER EVEN MET ME* and the things they are saying about me and the company, and they wouldn't know me from Adam – like, they wouldn't even know me if they saw me walking down the street.

SK: Really? So it seems quite competitive and cut-throat. Is there a lot of that type of behaviour, like bad-mouthing or backstabbing etc, going on in the industry?

AGENT: It's unbelievable, really . . . You can get caught up in it. But you get nowhere with it, so you are better off to just keep your dignity. I mean, I just lay my cards on the table. You would just say to the player that you're trying to sign, "Listen – this is us, this is our company and this is what we do", you know, and I would say [to the player], "Go and listen to other companies if you want".

The above comments support the view that professional football is an industry characterised by endemic distrust (Deutsch, 1958; Fein & Hilton, 1994; Sztompka, 1998). The specific distrust of agents has arisen largely due to the alleged unethical and questionable practices adopted by some of their number.

## Unethical and questionable practices

Numerous concerns have been publicly expressed in relation to the alleged unethical and illegal practices adopted by some agents. For example, serious ethical concerns have been raised about the treatment of young African playing talent during the 1990s by unscrupulous agents and speculators (Broere & van der Drift, 1997; Darby et al., 2007), who 'recognized in the trade in African talent an opportunity for personal financial gain' (Darby et al., 2007: 147). As noted in Chapter 1, illegal payments have been a feature of English football since its professionalisation in 1885. The testimonies collected by Taylor and Ward (1995) suggested that under-the-counter payments, or 'backhanders', to players were common ways of circumventing the wage restrictions in the 1950s.

One recurring theme from the data gathered from players, managers and agents concerned how backhanders and 'dodgy' payments are still common aspects of professional football. For example, one former English League One manager interviewed described a situation in which, following his appointment, he was looking to sign prospective recruits to enhance his squad. In order to do so, he needed to raise money by selling players within his existing squad, which would also assist in reducing the club's wage bill. The manager discussed with the club chairman, who also part-owned another club, several players whom he was considering selling in order to generate the required money. The chairman then offered to buy for his other club two players who had a combined market value of £80,000. This would have left the manager in a situation in which he would have received £80,000 for the two players and a wage bill reduced by £4,000 per week. The manager described how, during the conversation with his chairman, he was offered money to facilitate the deal. In short, this proposed deal would have saved the chairman £15,000 and given the manager a 'bung' of £5,000. He said:

> The chairman says to me, "Listen, I'll sort you out in the morning. So we've agreed that it's 80 grand". "Yes", I replied. The chairman then says to me, "I'll give you 60 grand for the players, and I'll give you five grand for yourself", and I said, "No, no way – I don't want money, I want success. I'm not in it for the dough."

One former English Premier League manager described, during the course of an interview, the role of agents in professional football as 'a load of bollocks, a shitty business – they are greedy and are full of f****** hookery'. More specifically, raising his arms in the air, he described a discussion he had had with an agent concerning a prospective player that he wanted to sign:

MANAGER: We were talking about doing a deal with a player and then some other [Championship] player's name came up. The Championship

|||
|---|---|
| | manager is my pal, and he [agent] wanted to get this player a move to a Premiership club. Now, I also knew the Premiership manager and he [agent] knew this. He says to me, "Look, I have a player and I want to get him to a Premiership club". The agent then asked me if I could set up a chat with the Premiership manager. The agent then says to me, "Listen, I know that the Premiership manager likes to take a brown envelope, but maybe if you have a chat with him, we might be able to do it through you, and get you a few bob and get this kid a good contract". |
| SK: | What? Really? Is this common practice in professional football? |
| MANAGER: | It's worse than that . . . believe me. |
| SK: | Tell me, how do you deal with this? How do you manage in that kind of an industry and in such an environment? |
| MANAGER: | [Leaning forward in his chair and pointing his finger at me] Well, I'll tell you how you manage, and how you can stay the distance. You've got to be so streetwise, and you've got to be so f****** sharp, because it's stinking, it's absolutely stinking. |

Implicit in the above comments is how in professional football it is not unusual for managers and/or players to be contacted by agents to broker or facilitate a deal. I will return to this point later. Moreover, implicit in this manager's comments are the questionable tactics that some agents will adopt in facilitating a move for their players and the nature of the industry in general. In this regard, the 2007 court case involving Stewart Downing shed light on how some agents may abuse the player–agent relationship and siphon money from players' personal bank accounts (Collins, 2011). Similarly, a number of players identified that they were distrustful of agents, with several players describing situations in which they had been 'messed around' by agents. For example, one former senior international player with considerable English Premier League experience described a situation in which a fellow player received a massive sum of money when he signed for a particular club. However, it transpired that the money he received from the agent was only a loan to the player. He said:

> There was this one player, who didn't realise and who got a massive amount of money – I think it was £50,000 – and he had to pay it back to xxxx [the agent]. The agent said to the player, "Like, you didn't read the small print – that the money was only a loan". You know, that's the kind of stuff that goes on and you know it's an absolute disgrace, so you just have to be very, very careful.

Given the levels of hostility and distrust towards agents, one obvious question arises: why are agents so widely utilised by managers and players? The following section attempts to answer this question.

## Why do managers and players use agents?

One reason why players are keen to be represented by an agent is 'that it takes them away from the possibility of negotiating with the very person – the manager – who will be selecting them to play in the first team, and with whom they will have to develop a working relationship' (Roderick, 2003: 272). Agents, therefore, can be seen as a means of relieving players of the difficult and sensitive burden of contract negotiations with football managers. This point was borne out during the course of an interview with a former English Premier League player. More specifically, shaking his head from side to side, he stated: 'I dealt with one manager with a contract when I came over here [English Premier League club] first and it is a nightmare. I don't think it should be done.' Similarly, one current English Championship player described how he would always use an agent to negotiate 'money matters' with the manager. This would then allow the player to discuss purely football-related matters, such as training methods and first-team opportunities, with his prospective manager:

> I think the big thing is that when you are signing for a club . . . as a player you want to talk about football. You don't want to go into a manager and start demanding x, y and z, because it looks bad on you, whereas if you have a representative going in for you, then obviously they are the ones who are looking greedy. Then the club thinks, "Well, it's an agent, that's an agent's job, that's what they are there for, they are greedy". So they are getting the best deal for you and you're still not looking greedy from it. Plus, from a business point of view, not many players know enough about the business side to justify going in on their own and dealing with them [managers].

Another former English Premier League player stated:

> Yeah, I would use a third party. The last thing you want to do with a manager is to get into a row about money. A manager should look after the football side of things. I'm a footballer, I want to play football. I don't want to get involved in that side of things and if I can help it, I would get an agent in to help me. Just so he can go to the meetings, he can discuss things, he can do the dirty work and I can concentrate on playing football and training.

Quite often, professional footballers feel intimidated and pressurised when it comes to personally negotiating a contract with a prospective manager. For example, one young player described the process of negotiating with a prominent English Premier League manager without the assistance of an agent. He said:

> When I first went to xxxx [English Premiership club], my dad and myself went in to talk to him and to be honest we felt we would have got eaten alive. We didn't know anything – like, it was a huge Premiership club. I mean, looking back, we should have got advice at that stage. I was obviously very nervous, it was the first time I'd done it, plus the manager was one of those sorts of fellas with a very forceful personality, very charismatic sort of fella, and you know he'd twist you round his little finger. So I ended up signing for whatever he wanted to give me.

Implicit in the above player's comments is his perceived lack of knowledge in the context of how contracts are negotiated and ultimately agreed. Moreover, it seems that when an agent is not present during contract negotiations, players in general and young players in particular are in a less powerful position due in part to their lack of knowledge concerning the contract negotiation process. More specifically, agents bring with them to the negotiations a body of knowledge concerning the prospective manager's intentions, budgets and motivations.

A common theme that emerged from player interviews concerned how the balance of power can shift dramatically during contract negotiations between a manager and a player in the absence of the player's agent. For example, one player described how, following his release from an English Premier League club, he went on trial at an English Championship club. In addition, this player described how he negotiated directly with the manager:

> I remember at xxxx [English Championship club] . . . I went for a week and at the end of the week they offered me a contract and he [manager] basically said, "Listen, we know other clubs are looking at you" and "If you go to any other clubs on trial, then we are not giving you a contract". Well, you know, that's why I took the contract, but you never know when they are bluffing or not and I wasn't willing to take the chance.

One former English Premier League player, currently employed as an agent, argued that players use the services of agents because, without them, they are often unable to negotiate effectively and the balance of power is skewed strongly in favour of the club. When asked his views on why players employ agents, he said:

> You have parents going in with kids and the parents don't have a clue about the business side of things and you see managers and youth development officers and chief scouts and they lie through their teeth, big time. I have seen contracts from players that are shocking and I'm not talking about money, I'm talking about the way the contract is drawn down and it's just disgraceful and players are thinking they are getting this and they are not getting it and you can't blame the player

> ... because they just don't know themselves. You know, you blame the clubs, in that sense, so I think it's important that someone knows the business side of things and understands what the market is as well and what players are entitled to obviously so the player doesn't look greedy coz, like, agents have bad reputations and they always will so if you go in greedy on your player's behalf, you know, it's no skin off your arse.

Based on the data collected in this research, players employ agents to alleviate any potential pressure and intimidation during contract negotiations, while managers employ agents for the level of knowledge that they possess. For example, possessing knowledge to which a manager or player is not privy can enhance an agent's position of power in contract negotiations. Roderick (2003: 273) noted, in the context of negotiations between players and managers, that 'it's not a level playing field when they [players] go talking to managers about contracts. The manager has all the information, a player doesn't – it's an unequal struggle.' The level of knowledge that an agent possesses is crucial in terms of his ability to negotiate, and one reason why agents spend considerable time networking is in order to gain access to such crucial information. In this regard, there is evidence to suggest that managers may also benefit from the level of knowledge that agents possess. For example, one former English Championship manager became quite animated in describing how an agent could provide him with useful information concerning a player's wages and whether or not the player was happy at a particular club. He said:

> Now, I've got this agent, which I use. I deal with him all the time. Now, the only reason why I deal with him is because he is a little jewel for me. Now, he knows everything, f****** everything. If I want to know what a player is on [wages], he knows, or if he doesn't, he will find out. The agent will come back to me and say to me, "This is what he is earning, this is what he is at, and the player is not happy". He's a little squirrel, he is – he is brilliant.

Implicit in the above manager's comments is how agents' access to sensitive information – such as a player's wages and current employment status – may be used to tap up potential recruits in general and those perceived to be unhappy at their current club in particular. In addition, many agents operate as brokers or facilitators due to their knowledge of potential transfers that could be negotiated concerning out-of-favour players or players perceived to be unhappy at a particular club. Agents thrive on such valuable sources of data, which quite often create a potential opportunity for them to facilitate a potential deal with interested parties and considerably enhance contract negotiation strategies should an opportunity arise. Moreover, agents are notorious for unsettling players by providing them with information concerning a potentially interested club. However, it is not uncommon for managers to provide agents with information concerning players surplus to requirements or on high wages that they wish to transfer. Moreover, because such agents are not identified as the player's licensed agent, these individuals are quite often utilised to tap up potential recruits. One former manager interviewed, with over ten years of managerial experience in professional football in England, gave an overview of how many transfers are facilitated. He said:

> It's simple. If you know xxxx [Premier League club] are looking for players, then find out what players are on their list. Then find out who represents the players. If you don't know the agent who represents the player or someone who knows the player, then find someone who knows the player and use him. You get a cut, the player's agent gets a cut and we are all happy. The key thing is . . . as long as the club gets the player they want, then we're all happy.

Implicit in this manager's comments is how deals are completed in professional football in terms of tapping up players and the role informal personal contacts play. Moreover, of central importance is agents' access to information regarding rumours concerning dissatisfied players or potential transfers. This point was particularly evident during the course of an interview with a current English Championship manager:

> You see, agents – I've used them myself, and they can find out about a player. Like, they might know a player – "Is he happy?", "Does he want a move?" – and get in their ear or know someone who plays in the same team, etc, and bend their ear a bit. I have no time for them at all. They are a scourge. And one thing, Seamus: they are always there when you or their player is doing well. You never see them when the shit's hitting the fan.

Based on the data collected in this study, an interesting dichotomy exists. On the one hand, some managers have stated that they will not utilise the services of an agent. On the other hand, some managers have stated they will not utilise an agent unless he can gain direct access to a prospective signing. This may be, in part, a reflection of the insecure nature of their position and the considerable pressure for immediate results in general and at key moments in the season in particular. Success for a manager, in terms of results, is quite often dependent on the securing of players in general and the more successful players in particular. The following section explores these issues and the shifting balances of power between managers, agents and players.

## Shifting balances of power

Stead (1999: 24) argued that 'player power has increased disproportionately at the very highest levels of English football', while Magee (2002: 234) highlighted the difficulties of working with agents and the increased power that they now possess in relation to clubs. Therefore, and despite doubts over their motives and their actions, it has become almost impossible for managers not to deal with certain agents. This is because failure to do so may result in a manager not securing the services of particular players whom he wishes to sign.

Based on the data collected in this research, there is considerable evidence to illustrate the power of some agents in general and football clubs' dependence on agents in particular. For example, one former English Premier League player described how the arrival of a prominent international player at the club was clouded in scandal. Two weeks after the arrival of the international star, a second unknown player was signed. The player described how his fellow players at the club responded to this second signing with considerable scepticism. The player, raising his eyes to the ceiling, stated that 'all hell broke loose' when it transpired that the second player had been signed simply to provide a large fee for the agent. Raising his voice, the player said, 'It was a f****** disgrace' and explained exactly what had happened:

> What happened was that the international player wanted to use his own agent, while the club insisted that the player use the Premiership club's agent. When the player and his agent refused the club's request, the club were forced to use the player's agent. When the club's agent found out about this, he was furious and threatened to withdraw his services from the club. To sort the whole thing out, the club asked the agent to select a player [from his portfolio of players, who had signed up with the agent], which the club would sign and the agent would then get his commission [having lost out on his commission from the international player's deal]. The players at the club went ballistic that this player had been signed, even though no one had any knowledge of the player. I mean, I BURST MY B******* to get a full contract . . . and this chap just gets one off the back of that'. It was a f****** joke.

Implicit in the above player's comments are the power some agents have assumed. Furthermore, this club's insistence that the player use the club's agent breached the then English FA's regulations governing agent practices. More specifically, conflicts of interest are prohibited and occur when an agent represents both a player and a club. The issue arises where you have a duty to act in the best interests of two or more different parties and your duties conflict, or there is a risk that they may conflict. This point was particularly evident when questions were raised following the arrival of

José Mourinho at Chelsea in 2004. Jorge Mendes acted for both club and players in the same transfer involving a number of Mourinho's former Porto players. However, despite an apparent breach of FIFA regulations, these transfers were allowed by the English FA at the time (Conn, 2012). It seems that if players are happy with this arrangement, then it is allowed.

In recent years, players in general and those players who are considered more valuable in terms of their playing talent have been able to exercise greater muscle in contract negotiations with their managers. However, the level of power that players possess varies considerably. By definition, the improved ability to sell your labour applies most to those players who are in great demand. Post-Bosman, clubs began to offer improved terms to players under contract to keep them at the clubs. As a result, players are now able to use the threat of seeing out a contract and taking a transfer-fee-free move as a lever to negotiate improved terms in their existing contract. In comparison to their pre-Bosman predecessors, players are now in a relatively powerful position, especially the top ones, as clubs cannot afford to lose players without receiving reimbursement in the form of a transfer fee. The removal of transfer fees and the potential severance notice has allowed players and their agents greater bargaining power to demand increased wages without the necessary contract commitment that was a feature of the pre-Bosman transfer system.[3] The increased power that players have assumed was a recurring theme in the interviews with players, managers and agents. More specifically, one former English Championship player stated:

> Players now can talk to other clubs long before their contracts end, so if they go into negotiations, they can say that "This club has offered this", "I've got this, that" and, you know, that they [the clubs] must basically match it. And also with more agents in the game now, the players are getting better deals. The agents are looking after the players. When they look after the players as best they can, it puts the players in a powerful position.

Similarly, one UK-based licensed agent described the shifting balance of power towards players:

> I think in the last ten years a lot of the power has shifted towards the player's side of things, with the Bosman and different things like that, you know, where before I think clubs had so much power over players and now it's kind of turned full circle. Clubs nowadays are afraid of players going on a free [transfer] and you have the ridiculous wages that they are looking for and transfer fees are crazy – like, you can see it now that clubs are struggling big time . . . but I think definitely that the players have more power at the moment.

It seems that agents have exploited this shift in players' bargaining power. Magee (2002: 230) argued that 'even though the player has gained significant control . . . it is the agent who ultimately controls and potentially exploits the player'. However, as discussed earlier, some managers may also attempt to open a rift between the player and the agent by challenging the abilities of an agent during negotiations. This point is borne out by O'Leary & Caiger (2000: 273), who describe an interview between a manager, a player and the player's agent. The manager said:

> We try to bypass agents. We signed a player. He had his agent present at the negotiation. The agent asked for an impossible salary. The agent wanted £15,000 and £500 per week. The player was on £450 per week and was not in the first team. The agent said, "My client won't accept the deal". I said to the player, "Where did you get this prat from? We want your contract – why don't you tell him to go?" The agent protested. I said to the player, "Do you want to sign for us or not?" He said, "Yes" and told the agent to leave.

This manager's reluctance to deal with agents may be in part a reflection of managers' frustration 'at the changing balance of contractual power' (O'Leary & Caiger, 2000: 273). Roderick (2003: 228) suggested that the relative power that players possess 'may depend on factors such as their age and the work-related reputations they develop'. Magee (1998) developed a useful typology and suggested players could be categorised into three broad groupings. The first group of players, the 'exploiters', are those players whose talent is sought after. Second, the 'exploited' are those players who have relatively few choices in terms of career options and choice of club and have relatively little power to determine their future. If one imagines these two groupings of players at the extremes of a continuum, then players who are referred to as the 'marketable' occupy the middle. The 'marketable' are players who are viewed as club assets and may be sold in order to generate capital and to relieve financial pressures. Such players have a value that managers may be able to exploit for their own interests. As Magee (1998) suggested, the 'exploiters' are powerful in the sense that they are in a strong bargaining position, while the 'exploited' have considerably less power. It is clear that these three ideal types of players must be considered in relational terms for players are never in, or out of, full control. More specifically, it is a question of power ratios or balances, and over time players' positions on this continuum will change. For example, players grow older or suffer serious injury, while coaches' or managers' opinions of their playing performance may also change. Thus, the degree of power that a player and his agent have in relation to a club or manager depends largely on the player's position on this continuum. In this regard, one registered agent was questioned whether he viewed players as possessing more power in recent years:

> I think the players have a lot of power now. I think it comes down to how well you are doing how much power you have individually. But if you are not doing it on the pitch, there are not too many people looking for you. So basically you have to be doing it on the pitch to have the power. You have to be putting in the performances, you know.

Agents, managers and players are all bound up in a complex process and each must take into account the actions of the others. The people who occupy central positions within these networks of relations have power insofar as they are less dependent on specific others, while those others are more dependent on them. Managers, for instance, rely on the levels of performance achieved by their players, and this in turn can be a means by which players can exercise a degree of power over their employers. Conversely, club managers can utilise the threat of rejection as a means of exercising power over prospective recruits or omitting current players from the playing squad. Thus, an examination of the dynamic balances of power among those involved in the network of relations within professional football – such as players, managers and agents – is essential to understanding adequately the role that each plays.

These balances of power form an integral element of all human relationships. To put it at its simplest, 'when one person, or a group of persons, lacks something which another person or group has the power to withhold, the latter has a function for the former' (Elias, 1998: 119). Therefore, people or groups that have functions for each other exercise constraints over each other. Their potential for withholding from the other what the other requires is usually uneven, which means that the constraining power of one side is greater than that of the other. In the overall nexus of interdependencies, individuals may question another individual's power of constraint, or their 'potential for withholding'. These, in effect, are trials of strength between two parties. At the root of these trials of strength are usually problems such as: 'Whose potential for withholding what the other requires is greater? Who accordingly is more or less dependent on the other? Who, therefore, has to submit or adapt himself more to the other's demands?' (Elias, 1998: 120). In more general terms, whoever has the higher power ratio can steer the activities of the other side to a greater extent than they can steer his activities. Put simply, who can put more pressure on whom? Agents, it can be argued, have greater power, or a higher power ratio, when representing a player who, in Magee's (1998) terms, is considered an 'exploiter'. That is not to say that the 'exploited' possess no power, but their power is more limited. These power resources and relative strengths are constantly tested. Each side tries to weaken the other by a variety of means, and both sides are involved in a continuous process of interweaving actions with each other and with other groups. The sequence of moves on either side can only be understood and explained in terms of the immanent dynamics of their interdependence.

## Conclusion

In September 2003, the English Football League broke new ground for transparency in the football industry when its clubs voted to publish, every six months, their aggregate payments to agents. These regulations came into effect on 1 January 2004 and required clubs to disclose to the Football League any payments made to agents. The regulations represented a significant step forwards in the governance of agents' activities by introducing measures to improve transparency and increase the level of protection offered to young players. Since 2001, rules relating to the conduct of agents have been regulated by the Players' Agent Regulations of FIFA (Stevens, 2006). Historically, in terms of agent regulations, one of the major problems concerned the discrepancy between FIFA and national governing bodies' regulations (Siekmann et al., 2007). In response, in January 2008, FIFA updated its regulations and introduced a legal framework that governed the activity of agents in professional football (FIFA, 2008). While FIFA's recent deregulation is a reflection of its inability to govern the behaviour of agents, Scott (2009) has argued that 'such a move could turn the global transfer market into a free-for-all'. Agents have secured a considerably powerful position in professional football. The lack of quality control over the granting of agent's licences has raised issues concerning the ethical and legal aspects of their behaviour, as well as raising questions about the commitment of the football authorities to controlling transfer dealings.

The new FIFA Regulations on Working with Intermediaries came into effect from April 2015. The English FA has issued a set of notes and guidelines on working with intermediaries in line with FIFA's new regulations and has worked with the Association of Football Agents on their application (FA, 2015).[4] It is questionable what impact, if any, FIFA's deregulation of the industry and delegation of responsibilities to national football associations will have on the industry. What is clear is that the power that some agents have assumed in general and over clubs and managers in particular will facilitate their continued engagement in unprofessional business practices.

## Notes

1. There are at least four types of agent operating in professional football. First, the most popular type are solo agent. These are licensed agents who deal mainly with transfers and contracts. Second, sports agents provide a wider support service beyond contract negotiations and also have agent's licences. Third, solicitors provide legal services and may not have agent's licences. Finally, promotions agents provide advice on career management and promotion opportunities but do not have agent's licences.
2. Prior to deregulation, in order to undertake the work of a players' agent, an individual had to be one of the following: a licensed players' agent; a solicitor or barrister in possession of a current practising certificate; or the parent, spouse or sibling of the particular player in question. Players may still represent themselves.

3 Under FIFA regulations, a player is allowed to commence negotiations with other clubs six months from the end of a contract. From a player's perspective, it seems only reasonable that a player should be allowed to negotiate during what is in effect his notice period. However, players who have already negotiated and signed contracts with rival clubs for the next season are placed in a position in which, should the teams meet, a conflict of interest may arise.
4 The English FA has published a Standard Player/Intermediary Representation Contract and a Standard Club/Intermediary Representation Contract which must contain the entire agreement between the parties in relation to the intermediary Activity and contain all Obligatory Terms of the relevant Standard Representation Contract. Parties may add other terms so long as they are consistent with the Obligatory Terms of the Standard Representation Contract and the requirements of the English FA regulations and the FIFA Regulations on Working with Intermediaries.

Chapter 7

# Directors and owners

## Introduction

Throughout this book, trust has been an underlying theme within the networks of interdependent relationships in professional football. For example, Chapter 2 noted how trust plays an important role in the context of whom a manager appointments as part of his backroom staff. In addition, Chapter 4 identified how a manager's trustworthy contacts are critical in gathering information about prospective recruits and in securing information in relation to potential employment opportunities. The lack of trust and general feelings of distrust towards agents was particularly evident in Chapter 6. While distrust and suspicion are common and recurring problems within many organisations (Fox, 1974; Sitkin & Roth, 1993), Sztompka (1998) argued that some occupations develop robust cultures of distrust or are pervaded with endemic distrust. The professional football industry has been identified with distrust, and as one in which employees struggle to forge friendships that are characterised by high levels of trust (Magee, 1998; Roderick, 2006; Gilmore & Gilson, 2007; Morrow & Howieson, 2014), while professional player autobiographies also note the lack of trust in a range of contexts (Adams, 1998; Fowler, 2005). Former Republic of Ireland international Johnny Giles (2008) noted that trust in professional football was a scarce commodity, while the former Manchester United and Republic of Ireland captain Roy Keane (2002: 181) described professional football as 'a bad movie, full of spivs, bluffers, bullshitters, hangers-on, where players screwed managers, managers screwed players, and were in turn screwed by directors'.

The point of drawing attention to the previous chapters and the above academic studies is important. Rather than taking a purely reductionist approach that focuses solely on micro-level trust-building processes, it is important to be cognisant of how 'the constitutive embeddedness of actors' behaviour and interactions in institutional environments' impacts the trust development process (Bachmann, 2011; Bachmann & Inkpen, 2011). What this means is that reductionist approaches that ignore the environment in which socio-economic relationships are embedded (Granovetter, 1985) quite often fail to explain fully why individual actors trust one another in certain environments but not in others. Because trust is a deeply contextualised phenomenon (Granovetter, 1985), this research is cognisant of the contextual factors and institutional arrangements that constitute the business environment in which individual relationships are nested. Certainly, institutional-based trust may generally be seen as a weaker form of trust compared to interaction-based trust. Therefore, despite the fact that institutions apparently play a relatively insignificant role in trust-building processes (Bachmann & Inkpen, 2011), an appreciation of the relevance of institutions is important to understand the development of trust between two actors (Kramer & Tyler, 1996). Thus, the central question at the heart of this chapter concerns how micro strategies of social action conducive to the development of trust are developed and sustained in an industry characterised by endemic paranoia and distrust.

The growing influence of directors and owners of professional football clubs in England is currently attracting considerable media attention. In recent years, the considerable influx of foreign owners has had important implications for both the role and security of the football manager. In 2015, 28 English clubs were owned by overseas owners (Conn, 2015). With experience of the (non-football) business world and a new attitude to the financing of the game, some wealthy club owners are seeking to make many of the critical decisions at football clubs (Malcolm, 2000). Quite often, this involves decisions concerning the playing side of the business and, more worryingly from the managers' perspective, interference in their role. As we saw in Chapter 1, most managers began to assume total responsibility for player recruitment and team selection in the 1960s. More recently, foreign owners have sought to abolish relegation from the Premier League. Recent developments at a number of English Premier League clubs have highlighted the growing involvement by directors and owners in transfer policies and decisions related to the playing side of the business. Some English Premiership clubs have moved towards a more 'European' style of management. Within this European-style management structure, it is common practice for directors and owners of football clubs to sign and release players without much input from the manager. However, considerable hostility exists towards this perceived European style of management from more traditionally minded managers in the UK, who have always deemed player trading to be a central aspect of their role. The relationship between club owners, directors and the manager is one of the most important at a professional football club (Green, 2002; Pawson, 1973), yet little is really understood about this relationship. Despite limited academic research on directors and owners, a few journalistic (Ridsdale, 2007; Mallinger, 2007; Tomas, 1996) and academic studies (Gilmore, 2001; Molan *et al.*, 2016; Nissen, 2014) exist. This chapter examines the relationship between the managers and directors/owners of professional football clubs and attempts to provide an understanding of this relationship from the managers' perspective. As we shall see, hostility and distrust is a common feature of the relationship. More specifically, this chapter explores how football managers' hostility towards and distrust of directors and owners emanates from both managers' perceptions concerning the limited football knowledge at boardroom level and directors' and owners' interference in the manager's role.

## Hostility towards directors and owners

Since 2000, the influx of overseas owners has been particularly evident at English Premier League clubs, but is a trend that has spread throughout the lower leagues (Hope, 2003). Hamil *et al.* (2000) raised concerns about the increased numbers of foreign-owned clubs, threats of hostile takeover bids and the lack of transparency in clubs' ownership structures.[1] More specifically, there have been accusations of fraud by senior club officials (Emery & Weed, 2006), dishonesty and corruption at boardroom level (Green, 2002; Holt, 2003) and illegal payments by directors (Mason, 1980; Russell, 1997). In addition, numerous concerns surround wealth extraction and asset stripping (Emery & Weed, 2006) and poor management practices at boardroom level (Ozawa *et al.*, 2004; Hamil *et al.*, 1999, 2000; Carter, 2006). Conn (1997) concluded that the practice of many Football League directors was deeply disturbing, while others have argued that greater accountability needs to be adopted in the recruitment and appointment of directors (Cannon & Hamil, 2000; Green, 2002). More recently, Conn (2015) has raised concerns over the 'ownership of football club shares via offshore companies' with regard to the potential tax avoidance implications when clubs are sold. In light of the above-mentioned concerns, it is reasonable to argue that, in general, managers may be suspicious towards directors and owners. However, it is also worth noting managers' alleged involvement in illegal (Taylor & Ward, 1995) and under-the-counter payments (Taylor, 2001). In addition, numerous accusations concerning bungs, bribes and the misappropriation of funds have been aimed at managers (Bower, 2003; Freeman, 2000). In particular, following a series of high-profile and damaging scandals surrounding transfer dealings in the 1990s, managers' involvement in transfers came under increased scrutiny. Thus, it is also reasonable to argue that directors' and owners' distrustful attitudes towards managers may be fuelled, in part, by such concerns. This may be one reason why many owners have adopted a more European-style structure in which responsibility for transfer deals and player signings is often delegated to a director of football. It is argued, considering the mutual levels of distrust and suspicion between managers and directors/owners, that a climate of presumptive distrust exists (Brewer, 1981, 1996). This may, in part, be a reflection of trust-disconfirming events in the past that may affect the willingness of both managers and directors/owners to engage in trusting behaviour with each other. The above-mentioned allegations and concerns provide a useful starting point in understanding the conditions that engender distrust between managers and directors/owners in professional football – but no more than that.

A number of academic studies have noted how category-based trust may heighten distrust and suspicion between individuals from different groups within an organisation (Brewer, 1981, 1996; Insko & Schopler, 1997). Kramer (1999) argued that distrust may emerge as a function of social categorisation processes. In this regard, the categorisation of individuals into distinct groups often results in individuals evaluating out-group members as less honest, reliable and trustworthy than members of their own group. These studies suggest that mere categorisation and perceived differentiation may create a climate of presumptive distrust between groups within an organisation. Category-based trust refers to trust predicated on information regarding an individual's membership of a particular social or organisational category. As we saw in Chapter 6, a climate of presumptive distrust exists towards agents and, as we shall see shortly, category-based trust is of central importance in helping to understand much of the hostility between football managers and club directors/owners. Brewer (1981) identified a number of reasons why membership of a salient category may provide a basis for presumptive trust or, in this case, distrust. First, shared membership of a given category can serve as a 'rule for defining the boundaries of low-risk interpersonal trust that bypasses the need for personal knowledge when interacting with members of that category' (Brewer, 1981: 356). Second, because of the cognitive consequences of categorisation and in-group bias, individuals tend to attribute positive characteristics such as honesty, cooperativeness and trustworthiness to other in-group members (Brewer, 1996). As a result, 'individuals may confer a sort of depersonalized trust to other in-group members that is predicated simply on awareness of their shared category membership' (Kramer, 1999: 577). Based on the data collected in this research, there are two further reasons for the prevalence of distrust specifically between managers and directors/owners.

## Football knowledge at boardroom level

While hostility between football club owners and fans is well documented (Brown, 1998; Redhead, 1991, 1997), hostility from players and managers towards directors/owners has also existed throughout much of football's history (Wagg, 1998; Gwyther & Saunders, 2005; Pawson, 1973). Much of this hostility and distrust has concerned directors' and owners' supposed lack of football knowledge and their limited playing experience (Carter, 2006; Pawson, 1973; Green, 2002; Wagg, 1984). In general, directors' interest in football only very rarely stems from any experience of playing the game professionally. In his autobiography, former England international Len Shackleton made reference to the average football club director's knowledge of the game by including a blank page on the subject (Malam, 2004). Over 40 years ago, Arthur Hopcraft (1968: 140) referred to the institution of the football club director as 'the sport's central contradiction' whereby the amateurs govern the professionals. Brian Clough, who is regarded by many people as one of the greatest English managers, made no secret of his contempt for directors and chairmen, considering them as little more than a nuisance (Szymanski & Kuypers, 1999). More recently, Gwyther and Saunders (2005) noted the acrimonious relationship between Sir Alex Ferguson and the Manchester United chairman Martin Edwards. None of the data collected in this study would contradict these views. Much of the conflict that informs the relationship between managers and directors/owners concerns the lack of football knowledge at boardroom level. This point was borne out during an interview with a former English Premier League manager. The manager described being summoned to a board meeting to answer questions in relation to new signings, team selection and the team's recent poor form. He described the meeting as follows:

> I went to this board meeting once. I knew what it was about. But anyway, I answered all the questions. One director asked me why xxxx [player] wasn't playing, and I said, "He was injured". Then one fella asked me, "Why did all the corners at the xxxx [opposition team] match end up at the back post?" And I said to myself, "What the f\*\*\*? Is this guy for real?" So I said, "Well, we had practised that in training because they had conceded a few goals recently in those areas". And he asked me another stupid question and I went, "F\*\*\* this". This is what you're dealing with, you know – crazy stuff. They hadn't a f\*\*\*\*\*\* clue.

One former English Championship manager stated that 'directors haven't a clue about football' and how 'they're trying to have some sort of say in the team as well'. Another manager stated that 'some chairmen would be OK, but the majority of them would be a nightmare to deal with'. One manager, in addition to describing some of the pressures of management, was generally quite dismissive of chairmen and directors:

> Pressure – yeah, the main bulk of pressure comes from yourself. You don't listen to the fans too much. You certainly don't listen to the media too much. And with all due respect to some of the chairmen and directors who I've worked for, you wouldn't be listening to them too much either.

Former Manchester United manager Tommy Docherty stated:

> The relationship between the chairman and the manager is the most important one at the club. You've got to get the players playing for you

and you've got to have the respect of the chairman. You need to know that he supports you 100 per cent in what you're doing.

(Green, 2002: 139)

More recently, David Moyes stated that 'the manager's relationship with his chairman is probably the most important of all. You need someone who can support and work with you' (LMA, 2009: 10). Similarly, when speaking about both his current and former owners, Carlo Ancelotti stated that 'the most important thing is to have the support of the owner. Nothing else matters' (Fifield, 2009). The importance of managing upwards, boardroom skills and establishing strong working relationships with owners and chairmen has been recognised by the LMA (Hoey, 2016) and the Scottish FA (Morrow & Howieson, 2014) in their new courses/programmes and are a welcome addition in terms of providing specific management training and education. The importance of support from the club chairman was particularly evident during an interview with a former English League Two manager. When questioned about the main source of pressure that he faced in professional football, he said:

> It would be definitely the chairman, because ultimately they are the ones who decide your future, you know what I mean. The pressure always comes from the people that are there to employ you – that's where the pressure comes from, you know. And when you haven't got that backing, then you're in trouble.

There is evidence to suggest that some managers attempt to generate rapport with boardroom members. This was certainly the view of one experienced manager interviewed. Interestingly, though, he described his general wariness and scepticism of directors:

> Like, I wouldn't have much time for them [directors]. But the first thing is to try and get them on your side. I know some managers who have gone into clubs and obviously you are playing shite, because you're on the bottom of the table, so there's something wrong, but that's not the right way either. When I joined xxxx [club], I think there was only 15 games to go, and we were halfway through the season, so you have to get the results. Now don't get me wrong, we ended up doing all right, like, – we stayed up and that was the main thing and built from there. But there was a bunch of them [directors] there and they might have been maybe looking to question what I was doing and how I was doing it and maybe get rid of me.

Implicit in this manager's comments is the importance of attempting to obtain support from the club's directors, which may be construed as a form of knowledge-based trust (Lewicki & Bunker, 1995). This involves the gradual development of a relationship that may facilitate the development of some level of trust. What this means is that if trust is evident, it provides the basis for a relationship and it may be deepened to provide the basis for further extending the relationship. However, as the above managers have identified, the presence of suspicious and hostile attitudes may prevent the development of relationships with those considered as 'outsiders'. In this regard, it is questionable whether such relationships could be characterised as possessing knowledge-based or thin interpersonal trust.

In trying to understand why trust remains such an elusive and ephemeral resource within many organisations, researchers have focused attention on identifying psychological and social processes that impede the development of trust. Rotter (1971, 1980) argued, in the context of people's general predisposition to trust others, that they extrapolate from their early trust-related experiences to build up general beliefs about others. Similarly, history-based models of trust (Boon & Holmes, 1991; Solomon, 1960) view trust as a function of an individual's cumulative interactions which provide information that is useful in assessing other people's dispositions, intentions and motives, whereby predictions can be made concerning their future behaviour. The emergence of trust concerning people's judgements about the trustworthiness of others is anchored, at least in part, in their prior expectations of others' behaviour. Such expectations may change in response to the extent to which subsequent experiences either validate or discredit them. Shapiro (1987) noted how social exchange relations evolve in a slow process, commencing with low-risk minor transactions in which little trust is required. In short, repeated interactions between people increase the probability that trust will emerge between them. This forms a sort of knowledge based or personalised trust (Lewicki & Bunker, 1995) that is grounded in other people's predictability and, as a result, we can anticipate and predict their behaviour. In this regard, some individuals may form a personality-based predisposition to distrust other people in general, usually based on generalising from a pattern of trust-disconfirming events in the past (Mayer *et al.*, 1995; Rotter, 1971). This was particularly evident in Chapter 6, in which a recurring theme from the interviews with managers and players concerned their hostility towards agents, which may, in part, be a result of previous trust-disconfirming events or experiences with agents. While a recurring theme in the interviews with football managers concerned directors' and owners' lack of playing experience and knowledge of the game, we have seen in Chapter 3 that a professional football manager's knowledge of the game often emanates solely from his previous playing experience, and there exists a mistaken assumption among managers that previous playing experience is sufficient preparation for entry into football management.

## Interference in the manager's role

The influx of new owners is having huge implications for both the role and tenure of the football manager. Quite often, new owners appoint prestigious and, in some cases, popular managers to appease both supporters and shareholders. While doubts exist as to whether these new owners have sufficient experience to run football clubs, it is their interference in the manager's role that generates more concern. At many football clubs, 'chairmen are notorious for their interference in all aspects of the game, from team selection and tactics to transfer decisions' (Gilmore & Gilson, 2007: 417). David Moyes recently noted how 'interference from club chairmen and owners has become a real problem for some managers'. Moyes' advice to aspiring young managers is 'to interview the chairman, rather than let him interview you' (LMA, 2009: 10). The former Charlton Athletic and West Ham United manager Alan Curbishley recently noted that overseas owners often have unrealistic expectations and a lack of empathy for the role of the manager. Daniel Taylor (2008) noted how both Curbishley and Kevin Keegan resigned as managers of their respective clubs (West Ham United and Newcastle United) following complaints that player trading decisions were taken out of their hands. In October 2008, Harry Redknapp was offered the manager's job at Tottenham Hotspur. He only accepted the position following assurances from the club chairman that he would have total control over the club's transfer policies. As we have seen, a recurring theme in the manager interviews concerned directors' and owners' lack of knowledge in football matters, but the principal bone of contention is when directors and owners interfere in matters believed by managers to fall within their jurisdiction.

While directors and owners are responsible for running a club's affairs, their responsibilities depend very much upon the individuals involved and the club structure. For example, at some clubs their role may involve addressing sponsorship issues or ground improvements, while at other clubs the directors may play a dormant role, interested only in appointing the manager. Based on the data collected in this research, some directors and owners directly interfere in aspects of the manager's role, such as team selection. This perceived interference in the manager's role is of central importance in understanding the lack of trust between managers and directors/owners within a notoriously insular and closed subculture. The game has altered markedly in the past two decades, so that traditional structures and boundaries have changed. Freeman (2000: 148), in describing the way things used to be in the game, suggested that 'everyone knew their place: directors swanked, managers ordered and players did as they were told and were sold if they did not'.

In describing their relationships with chairmen, directors and owners, a recurring theme in the manager interviews concerned how they were questioned on issues surrounding the playing side of things. One former

English Championship manager gave his views on this 'new' breed of directors and identified how the club chairman attempted to interfere in his role and to elicit information from players behind his back:

MANAGER: Well, the thing about it is . . . you have these chairmen who have loads of money, and as soon as they invest their money in football, they become experts. You know, chairmen, when they put money in. Like my experiences at xxxx [Championship club]. I met the chairman here and he went and bought the club, and suddenly he knew more than Alex Ferguson – ah, he knew everything, he knew more than me.

SK: And was he involved in any footballing matters?

MANAGER: Oh, big time – that's how it all came about, that's how the breakdown came about. The thing about it was, like, at half-time you would come into the dressing room, and he would be sitting there, and I'd have to say, "Can I have a little bit of privacy, please?" So he would leave, but he would leave the dressing-room door open and he would be listening in.

SK: Seriously?

MANAGER: Yeah, and he would go behind your back. Like, if a player was not playing [in the first team], he would be pulling them [aside], and he would sit down and chat to them and try to find out what's going on, and why they're not in the team. He would be calling me a f****** idiot, and would be saying to the player that he should be in the team. Like, he would just undermine you, and would try to find out what's going on in the background. But yeah, like – stuff like that . . . chairmen are definitely the ones to watch.

Implicit in the above manager's comments is how undesirable eventualities and harmful motives can cause the erosion of interpersonal trust between two people (Lewicki *et al.*, 1998). Distrust or suspicion is viewed as a lack of confidence in other people's behaviour where a concern exists that they may act in a hostile or harmful manner towards oneself (Deutsch, 1958). Moreover, the 'positive expectation of injurious action' (Luhmann, 1979: 72) can cause the development of high levels of distrust between two people. What this means is that high levels of distrust are characterised by feelings of paranoia whereby undesirable and harmful behaviour is actually expected (Lewicki *et al.*, 1998). Thus, the pervasive generalised climate of suspicion, characteristic of the 'syndrome of distrust' (Sztompka, 1999) or 'culture of cynicism' (Stivers, 1994), hampers the effective functioning of a social group. In this regard, there are data to support the view that the undesirable behaviour of owners fosters the prevalence of suspicion and distrust between managers and owners. One former English League Two manager described how his chairman tried to undermine him during a game. In addition, this manager spoke about how he was faced with a relegation battle with three games of the season remaining. He described how, during one game, the team were 3–0 down with a crucial match coming up the following week. He then described how, following his decision to substitute three of his best players in the first half, the chairman approached him during the game and verbally abused him. He said:

> After 30 minutes we were 3–0 down. So I took off my three best players – xxxx, xxxx and a fellow called xxxx – so I took them off. Well, the next thing, I got lambasted . . . the chairman came down from the stand, shouting and screaming: "What the f\*\*\* are you doing? We were 3–0 down and you took off our best players – what the f\*\*\*?" And I went, "I know, because we are playing xxxx [opposition team] next week and we are going to win – I was resting them". He never even thought of next week. But anyway, we won the game the following week.

In addition, there is evidence from interviews conducted with players of the power and influence directors and owners have assumed. More specifically, a number of players identified how some owners and directors directly influence team affairs. One former English Premier League player stated:

> That's the thing: you have no control over it – your career and your life is in the hands of managers and chairmen. The chairman has a big input in picking the team and whoever he wants in the club. The manager's just the puppet. He gets paid himself so it is a fine line and it's a very, very insecure job – you don't know when your contract's up, you don't know if it's going to be renewed or not, you wait till the last month of the season.

Another player described how the chairman of an English Championship club influenced the recruitment decisions at the club. Moreover, the player described how the chairman wanted to see him play before he was signed:

PLAYER: I was initially offered a very good contract but the chairman was away at the time, and he hadn't seen me play. So he [chairman] came back and obviously he is the businessman and found out about my [injury] history and he said there is not a chance that he can give me this contract until I prove my fitness.
SK: Really?
PLAYER: So I signed a year on a lesser contract with a clause in it saying once I got into the first team, then the club would bin that contract and replace it with the original contract.
SK: So did the chairman have an input, then?

PLAYER: Yeah, well, he stepped in because although the manager was very impressed with me and wanted to sign me, and the original contract was very, very good for me, and I was very happy with it, the chairman said that he hadn't really seen me play.

The following interview with an experienced English Championship player provides a good example of deception and distrust in general, and a good description of a chairman's interference in the manager's role in particular. The player described how the chairman was looking to cut the wage bill at the club. In short, the club was trying to off-load players who were on good money but were not playing in the first team. As one of these players, the interviewee described how the club was trying to force him out of the club. He explained how these players were separated from the first team, forced to train on their own in the club's gym, and described the situation as follows:

PLAYER: The manager told me it was down to him, but he pretty much said to me that although he was the manager, things were pretty much taken out of his hands and it was the chairman's decision. Then I met the chairman. Now, I'd just had a meeting with the manager, so I turned up for training the following day and again we weren't allowed to touch the footballs again and we were just sent up to the gym. I pulled the manager [aside] and he said it was pretty much the chairman and the chairman was outside and I said it to him [chairman] and he said he knew nothing about it. So I said, "Right, let's all three of us get into a room together and I'll ask you both whose idea this is about the training regime", and the chairman wouldn't do it – he wasn't man enough at the time to face up and be honest enough with me about what the situation was. You know, from then it was clear that it was the chairman's idea. It was the chairman, but at the same time the manager is still managing so he has got to accept the responsibility.

SK: That must have been quite difficult. Like, you have a reputation as being an honest player and a good professional. How did you feel about that?

PLAYER: It's not good at all, but it does happen at a lot of clubs as well. It's not good, but from the manager's point of view, I know he is the manager and the buck stops with him. You can still half understand it. If the chairman says to him [manager], "Right, you're going to lose your job unless you do this to these players", then he's going to look after his own skin and do what the chairman wants really because it's the chairman's money, so I can understand it really.

The above chairman's attempt to force these players out of the club could be construed as a form of constructive dismissal. Moreover, implicit in the above player's comments is the level of distrust within professional football clubs and the general acceptance by the player of the chairman's influence over team affairs. We know that high levels of distrust are expressed in the form of fear, scepticism, cynicism and wariness (Lewicki et al., 1998). Moreover, suspicion has been viewed as one of the central cognitive components of distrust (Deutsch, 1958) and has been characterised as a psychological state in which individuals 'actively entertain multiple, possibly rival, hypotheses about the motives or genuineness of a person's behaviour (Fein & Hilton, 1994: 168).

## Conclusion

This chapter identifies hostility and distrust as a common feature of the relationship between managers and directors/owners in professional football. More specifically, from the standpoint of managers, this hostility and distrust partially emanates from the perceived motives of owners and directors and their interference in issues traditionally seen as falling within the manager's role. It is argued that much of this obviously stems from a lack of trust that is predicated for both parties on a mutual suspicion of 'outsiders' and dealing with people who are perceived as very different. Trust is essential in the workplace for enhancing organisational performance and being competitive in what is an increasingly global game. Bases of trust can take time to develop and thick interpersonal trust is not something that may necessarily ever be a part of the relationship between many football managers and their clubs' directors/owners, given their very different backgrounds. Yet what must be accurately defined is some level of organisational trust that centres upon clearly defined roles, behavioural consistency, integrity and clear communication channels. This chapter clearly highlights how a number of these factors are not present in the eyes of many football managers.

Further engagement with the academic literature is required to assist in understanding how trust may be developed and sustained in an industry characterised by endemic paranoia and distrust. This is important because we know that processes and strategies for rebuilding trust exist (Lewicki & Bunker, 1995). A useful starting point might involve examining how recent ownership structures and management teams at clubs such as Southampton and Liverpool have assisted in developing trust between the CEO, owner and manager. Liverpool, under new owners Fenway Sports Group, developed management teams incorporating clear roles, responsibilities and open lines of communication between the CEO, owners and manager. Finally, while long-term trust repair might be unrealistic in professional football, structural solutions and strategies such as contracts and frequent interactions may assist in developing and rebuilding short-term trust (Lewicki et al., 2016).

## Note

1 In terms of the lack of transparency in clubs' ownership structures, if anything the flotation of a club on the stock market makes it more exposed to regulation and inspection than if the club is privately owned. However, when clubs are bought by foreign interests, their ownership may be difficult to trace.

# Conclusion

## Introduction

This book is the first academic study of its kind that examines the role of the contemporary professional football manager. It endeavours to present a more reality-congruent understanding of the manager's role in professional football through the application of the theoretical concepts of Max Weber and Mark Granovetter. This book has identified how professional football is an industry that involves unscrupulous activities by agent and directors, quite often including unethical and in some cases illegal recruitment practices. In addition, professional football, at all levels, is a cut-throat, ruthless and results-based industry in which chronic insecurity and vulnerability are prominent characteristics of football managers' daily lives. This vulture culture of insecurity generates a psychological fear of failure and high levels of distrust characterised by feelings of suspicion and paranoia whereby undesirable eventualities and harmful motives are expected.

In addition to reviewing the main themes, this conclusion identifies the key findings of the research and provides recommendations for football managers, clubs and football's governing bodies. The final section outlines an agenda for avenues for future research, derived from the limitations of the current study and from issues raised during the course of this study. The central academic question at the heart of this research concerned an examination of the role of the contemporary manager in professional football. In particular, this book examined the recruitment and appointment of managers, attitudes towards previous playing experience and formal education, the assessment and recruitment of players, the process of establishing discipline, the role of agents and the relationship between managers and directors/owners. The following sections provide a brief summary of how these objectives were attained.

## Managerial recruitment and appointment

Chapter 2 examined the recruitment and appointment of managers in professional football. Despite the professionalisation and bureaucratisation of many aspects of football clubs, the role of the manager has proved remarkably resistant to these processes. The authority of the football manager continues to be based on traditional forms of authoritarianism, which allows managers an unusually high degree of autonomy in defining their own role while placing few constraints on the appointment of their support staff. While managerial mobility is socially embedded and facilitated through personal contacts, one contribution to knowledge lies not simply in how we described the development and maintenance of such contacts but also in exploring the nature of the relationships that exist and their impact on mobility in professional football. Arguably, professional football clubs should incorporate specific appointment and selection criteria such as formal interviews and clearly defined job descriptions when appointing football managers.

## Previous playing experience and formal education

Chapter 3 identified managers' hostility towards formal education and coaching qualifications in professional football. The findings highlighted the lack of formal management training and the widespread assumption within football that previous playing experience is sufficient preparation for entry into management. A picture emerged of an industry managed largely in isolation from external management influences by those who are ill prepared, insular in outlook and drawn from a narrow segment of society. It is argued that the introduction of formal management training as compulsory for current and prospective managers in all divisions would assist them in dealing with many aspects of the manager's role. The process of learning involves the relatively permanent or enduring *change* in a person's knowledge or behaviour due to experience, or in the capacity to behave in a given fashion (Burns, 1995). Therefore, managers, like coaches, should adopt a growth mindset and consider the philosophical assumptions and practical applications of pertinent learning theory (Roberts & Potrac, 2014) that will assist them in developing expert knowledge (Jones *et al.*, 2004). For example, reflection (Schön, 1983) involves both self-awareness and self-disclosure and could assist managers develop a greater understanding and exploration of their complex, unpredictable and constantly changing working environment. One additional approach to managerial learning and development worth considering concerns 'active adaption', which involves the sharing of player and manager knowledge through conversations, group reflective practices, communities of practice and mentoring (Cassidy *et al.*, 2015; Culver & Trudel, 2008).

## The assessment and recruitment of players

Chapter 4 examined how football managers assess and evaluate current players and prospective recruits. A recurrent theme in the manager interviews concerned how they use gut feeling and instinct in the recruitment and assessment process. A key finding was the importance of a player's off-field behaviour in this process. In an attempt to attain greater objectivity, reflection with backroom staff may assist managers in overcoming subjective assessments of player attitude and ability. This is important because critical reflective practice – involving discussion and debate between managers, coaches and backroom staff – may assist in reducing confirmation bias (Tversky & Kahneman, 1973) and facilitate a more consensual decision-making process regarding player recruitment and assessment. At a more advanced level, it would be useful if managers could develop an understanding of the knowledge, skills and methods that facilitate an observation of player learning during their interactions with players in general and during coaching sessions in particular (Turnnidge et al., 2014; Jones et al., 2013). This is important because observation methods, such as those employed by Sir Alex Ferguson (Elberse, 2013), often distinguish ordinary coaches (Jones et al., 2013) and managers from superior ones. In this regard, research currently underway suggests that professional football managers' engagement in structured reflection (Gibbs, 1988) after competitive performances has a significant impact in assisting them in assessing aspects of their role in general and critical incidents relating to in-game decisions in particular. This chapter also highlighted the importance of personal contacts in the recruitment and assessment of professional football players. Of significant importance is how managers, when making such crucial decisions, consult personal contacts whom they trust.

## Maintaining discipline and control

In Chapter 5, we examined aspects of the relationship between professional football managers and their players, with particular emphasis on the ways in which managers maintain control over players at professional football clubs. More specifically, this chapter focused on the ways in which disciplinary codes are established by managers and the sanctions that are imposed on players for breaches of club discipline. The findings highlighted the arbitrary character of these codes and the central part played by intimidation and abuse, both verbal and physical, as aspects of managerial control within clubs. It was argued that these techniques of managerial control reflect the origins of professional football in late Victorian England, when professional players were the equivalent of industrial workers and, like industrial workers, were seen as requiring authoritarian regulation and control. One interesting avenue of further research, currently underway, explores how specific styles of management and leadership approaches impact on player motivation, team cohesion and success.

## Agents

Chapter 6 examined aspects of the network of interdependent relationships between professional football managers, players and agents. Central to an understanding of this relationship was an exploration of the recent shift in power from clubs to players and their agents. A key finding was that within professional football some agents have assumed significant status, which leaves them in a position in which they have considerable power over clubs, and in some cases they have become involved in unprofessional business practices. The lack of quality control over the granting of agent's licences raises questions about the commitment of the football authorities to controlling transfer dealings. One recommendation is for national football associations to adopt a more rigorous system of regulations in the granting of agent's licences and monitoring of transfer dealings.

## Directors and owners

Chapter 7 examined the relationship between managers and the owners and directors of professional football clubs. The findings identified hostility and distrust as a common feature of this relationship. More specifically, from the standpoint of managers, this hostility and distrust partially emanates from the perceived motives of directors and owners, their perceived lack of football knowledge and their interference in issues traditionally seen as falling within the manager's role. The chapter highlighted the very closed and insular world of professional football and also considered how the changing nature and status of the game has impacted upon traditional managerial roles and functions. Greater transparency is required concerning the ownership structure of clubs. One recommendation for clubs is to establish ownership and management teams incorporating specific managerial roles. Moreover, the establishment of open lines of communication between owners and managers may assist in alleviating the mutual levels of distrust and suspicion between them and facilitate the development of more trusting relationships.

## Limitations of the study and avenues for further research

In terms of the sampling methods employed, one possible criticism is that as a consequence of the absence of randomness, the results of the research cannot be generalised. In the strictest empirical sense, the first part of the criticism is accurate in that the results only apply to those interviewed. However, it is argued that the findings *can* be generalised across professional football at all levels in the UK. It is the author's view that, in the light of follow-up conversations with interviewees and key stakeholders in the game and based on his considerable experience of professional football, the issues identified in the research interviews *are* common features of professional football at all levels.

Perhaps the biggest limitation of this study concerns the lack of interviews with club directors and owners. As a result, the views expressed throughout this research are solely from players, agents and managers. While it was not the intention of this research to gain access to these key stakeholders, one interesting avenue for future research would involve an examination of the motives of these new owners in general and foreign owners in particular in relation to a number of issues identified throughout this study. This might shed some light on the motives of directors and owners whose love of football appears, from the manager's perspective at least, to spill over into the day-to-day running of the football club. While the difficulty of gaining access to club owners and directors is one possible reason for this academic neglect, research currently underway attempts to redress this imbalance.

What is certain is that the considerably underdeveloped academic literature around football management presents considerable opportunities for future research.

One emergent theme from this research that merits further study concerns the increasing number of foreign managers in the English game. It would be useful to understand how foreign managers evaluate and assess current players and prospective recruits and the role, if any, that friendship networks play in the recruitment of players. In addition, the widely held view that Western European coaches are less authoritarian is largely impressionistic and not based on any systematic data. Nor is this an area that was probed in this study. There is clearly a need for comparative studies on this issue, which would enable the exploration of similarities and differences – and the reasons for them – between British management and leadership styles and those of continental managers and coaches (Gammelsæter, 2013). More specifically, an examination of how emotional intelligence (EQ) assists in understanding manager–player relationships or how EQ may support managers in dealing with stress and conflict (Thelwell *et al.*, 2008) is warranted. Finally, one avenue for future research concerns how our individual-level values (Van Mullem & Brunner, 2013) act as guiding principles for decision making in general and in the formulation of a management philosophy in particular. This is important because a vague or uncertain philosophy quite often leads to inconsistency in management behaviours and practices.

# References

Adams, T., with Ridley, I. (1998). *Addicted*. London: Collins Willow.
Allen, K. (2004). *Max Weber: A Critical Introduction*. London: Pluto.
Allera, S. V. & Nobay, A. R. (1966). English professional football. *Political Economic Planning*, 32(496), 77–161.
Antonioni, P. & Cubbin, J. (2000). The Bosman ruling and the emergence of a single market in football talent. *European Journal of Law and Economics*, 9(2), 157–73.
Ashton, N. (2011). Top agents lift the lid on football's murky secrets. *Daily Mail*, 23 September.
Audas, R., Dobson, S. & Goddard, J. (1997). Team performance and managerial change in the English Football League. *Economic Affairs*, 13(3), 30–6.
Audas, R., Dobson, S. & Goddard, J. (1999). Organisational performance and managerial turnover. *Managerial and Decision Economics*, 20(6), 305–18.
Audas, R., Dobson, S. & Goddard, J. (2002). The impact of managerial change on team performance in professional sports. *Journal of Economics and Business*, 54(6), 633–50.
Bachmann, R. (2011). At the crossroads: future directions in trust research. *Journal of Trust Research*, 1(2), 203–13.
Bachmann, R. & Inkpen, A. C. (2011). Understanding institutional-based trust-building processes in inter-organizational relationships. *Organization Studies*, 32(2), 281–301.
Bachmann, R. & Zaheer, A. (eds) (2006). *Handbook of Trust Research*. Cheltenham: Edward Elgar.
Bale, J. & Maguire, J. (eds) (1994). *The Global Sports Arena: Athletic Talent Migration in an Interdependent World*. London: Frank Cass.
Bampouras, T. M., Cronin, C. & Miller, P. K. (2012). Performance analytic processes in elite sport practice: an exploratory investigation of the perspectives of a sport scientist, coach and athlete. *International Journal of Performance Analysis in Sport*, 12(2), 468–83.
Bandura, A. (1977). *Social Learning Theory*. Englewood Cliffs, NJ: Prentice-Hall.
Banks, S. (2002). *Going Down: Football in Crisis – How the Game Went from Boom to Bust*. London: Mainstream.
Barić, R. & Bucik, V. (2009). Motivational differences in athletes trained by coaches of different motivational and leadership profiles. *Kineziologija*, 41(2), 181–94.
Bendix, R. (1962). *Max Weber: An Intellectual Portrait*. New York: Anchor.

Besson, R., Poli, R. & Ravenel, L. (2011). *Global Player Migration Report 2011*. Neuchâtel: Centre International d'Étude du Sport, Université de Neuchâtel.

Bidart, C. & Degenne, A. (2005). Introduction: the dynamics of personal networks. *Social Networks*, 27(4), 283–7.

Biddle, S. J .H., Markland, D., Gilbourne, D., Chatzisarantis, N. L. D. & Sparkes, A. C. (2001). Research methods in sport and exercise psychology: quantitative and qualitative issues. *Journal of Sports Sciences*, 19(10), 777–809.

Blair, H. (2001). 'You're only as good as your last job': the labour process and labour market in the British film industry. *Work, Employment & Society*, 15(1), 149–69.

Bloom, G. A., Durand-Bush, N., Schinke, R. J. & Salmela, J. H. (1998). The importance of mentoring in the development of coaches and athletes. *International Journal of Sport Psychology*. 29(3), 267–81.

Bolchever, D. & Brady, C. (2004). *The 90-Minute Manager: Lessons From the Sharp End of Management*. Pearson: Glasgow.

Boon, S. D. & Holmes, J. G. (1991). The dynamics of interpersonal trust: resolving uncertainty in the face of risk. In Hinde, R. A. & Groebel, J. (eds). *Cooperation and Prosocial Behaviour*. Cambridge: Cambridge University Press, pp. 190–211.

Bourdieu, P. (1986). The forms of capital. In Richardson, J. (ed.). *Handbook of Theory and Research for the Sociology of Education*. New York: Greenwood Press, pp. 241–58.

Bourke, A. (2001). *International Mobility of Professional Football Players: A Review of the Key Issues*. Departmental Working Paper Series BA 00/01. University College Dublin.

Bourke, A. (2002). The road to fame and fortune: insights on the career paths of young Irish professional footballers in England. *Journal of Youth Studies*, 5(4), 375–89.

Bourke, A. (2003). The dream of being a professional soccer player: insights on career development options of young Irish players. *Journal of Sport and Social Issues*, 27(4), 399–419.

Bower, T. (2003). *Broken Dreams: Vanity, Greed and the Souring of Football*. London: Simon & Schuster.

Boyle, R. & Haynes, R. (1998). Modernising tradition? The changing face of British football. *Leisure Studies Association*, 62, 21–36.

Brady, C., Bolchover, D. & Sturgess, B. (2008). Managing in the talent economy: the football model for business. *California Management Review*, 50(4), 224–46.

Bray, J. N., Lee, J., Smith, L. L. & Yorks, L. (2000). *Collaborative Inquiry in Practice: Action, Reflection and Making Meaning*. London: Sage.

Brewer, M. B. (1981). Ethnocentrism and its role in interpersonal trust. In Brewer, M. B. & Collins, B. E. (eds). *Scientific Inquiry and the Social Sciences: A Volume in Honour of Donald T. Campbell*. London: Jossey-Bass, pp. 345–60.

Brewer, M. B. (1996). In-group favouritism: the subtle side of intergroup discrimination. In Messick, D. M. & Tenbrunsel, A. (eds). *Codes of Conduct: Behaviourial Research and Business Ethics*. New York: Russell Sage, pp. 160–71.

Bridgewater, S. (2006a). *Future Top Football Managers Start Here*. Press Release, June. Warwick: University of Warwick.

Bridgewater, S. (2006b). *An Analysis of Football Management Trends 1992–2005 in All Four Divisions*. Warwick: Warwick University Business School.

Bridgewater, S. (2010). *Football Management*. Basingstoke: Palgrave.
Broere, M. & van der Drift, R. (1997). *Football Africa!* Oxford: WorldView Publishing.
Brown, A. (1998). *Fanatics! Power, Identity and Fandom in Football*. London: Routledge.
Brown, G. & Potrac, P. (2009). 'You've not made the grade son': de-selection and identity disruption in elite-level youth football. *Soccer and Society*, 10(2), 143–59.
Brown, P. (2005). *Balls: Tales from Football's Nether Regions*. Edinburgh: Mainstream.
Bruinshoofd, A. & ter Weel, B. (2003). Manager to go? Performance dips reconsidered with evidence from Dutch football. *European Journal of Operational Research*, 148(2), 233–46.
Buckley, W. (2008). I get no satisfaction from my job. *Observer*, 10 February.
Buraimo, B., Simmons, R. & Szymanski, S. (2006). English football. *Journal of Sports Economics*, 7(1), 29–46.
Burns, S. (1995). Rapid changes require enhancement of adult learning. *HR Monthly*, June, 16–17.
Butler, J. K. (1991). Toward understanding and measuring conditions of trust: evolution of a conditions of trust inventory. *Journal of Management*, 17(3), 643–63.
Butler, J. K. & Cantrell, R. S. (1984). A behavioral decision theory approach to modeling dyadic trust in superiors and subordinates. *Psychological Reports*, 55(1), 19–28.
Bynner, J. & Parsons, S. (2001). Qualifications, basic skills and accelerating social exclusion. *Journal of Education and Work*, 14(3), 279–91.
Cairns, J., Jennett, N. & Sloane, P. J. (1986). The economics of professional team sports: a survey of theory and evidence. *Journal of Economic Studies*, 13(1), 3–80.
Calvin, M. (2015). *Living on the Volcano: The Secrets of Surviving as a Football Manager*. London: Century.
Camic, C., Gorski, P. S. & Trubek, D. M. (eds) (2005). *Max Weber's Economy and Society: A Critical Companion*. Stanford, CA: Stanford University Press.
Cannon, T. & Hamil, S. (2000). Reforming football's boardrooms. In Hamil, S., Michie, J., Oughton, C. & Warby, S. (eds). *Football in the Digital Age: Whose Game Is It Anyway?* Edinburgh: Mainstream, pp. 36–54.
Cantelon, H. & Ingham, A. G. (2002). Max Weber and the sociology of sport. In Maguire, J. & Young, K. (eds). *Theory, Sport and Society*. Oxford: Elsevier, pp. 293–314.
Carling, C. (2010). Analysis of physical activity profiles when running with the ball in a professional soccer team. *Journal of Sports Sciences*, 28(3), 319–26.
Carling, C., Wright, C., Nelson, L. J. & Bradley, P. S. (2014). Comment on 'Performance analysis in football: a critical review and implications for future research'. *Journal of Sports Sciences*, 32(1), 2–7.
Carlisle, C. (2013). *You Don't Know Me, But...: A Footballer's Life*. London: Simon & Schuster.
Carmichael, F., Thomas, D. & Ward, R. (2000). Team performance: the case of English Premiership football. *Managerial and Decision Economics*, 21(1), 31–45.
Carmichael, F., Thomas, D. & Ward, R. (2001). Production and efficiency in association football. *Journal of Sports Economics*, 2(3), 228–43.
Carson, M. (2013). *The Manager: Inside the Minds of Football's Leaders*. London: Bloomsbury.

Carter, A. D. & Bloom, G. A. (2009). Coaching knowledge and success: going beyond athletic experiences. *Journal of Sport Behavior*, 32(4), 419–37.

Carter, N. (1999). From gaffer to guru? An historical perspective on the football manager. In *Singer & Friedlander Review 1998–1999 Season*. London: Singer & Friedlander, pp. 50–2.

Carter, N. (2004). The pioneers: the birth of football management. *Soccer Review 2004*. Leicester: Facilitated by the Professional Footballers Association, pp. 42–5.

Carter, N. (2006). *The Football Manager: A History*. London: Routledge.

Cashmore, E. (2000). *Making Sense of Sports*. London: Routledge.

Cassidy, T. G., Jones, R. G. & Potrac, P. (2015). *Understanding Sports Coaching: The Pedagogical, Social and Cultural Foundations of Coaching Practice*. Third edition. London: Routledge.

Castanias, R. P. & Helfat, C. E. (2001). The managerial rents model: theory and empirical analysis. *Journal of Management*, 27(6), 661–78.

Christensen, M. K. (2009). 'An eye for talent': talent identification and the 'practical sense' of top-level soccer coaches. *Sociology of Sport Journal*, 26(3), 365–82.

Christensen, M. K. & Sørensen, J. K. (2009). Sport or school? Dreams and dilemmas for talented young Danish football players. *European Physical Education Review*, 15(1), 115–33.

Claridge, S., with Ridley, I. (2000). *Tales from the Boot Camps*. London: Orion.

Clifford, S. (2005). A brief stay on the South Coast: an interview with Simon Clifford, the Director of Garforth Town and the Futebol de Salao (fds) coaching schools network by Patrick Murphy. *Soccer Review 2005*. Leicester: Facilitated by the Professional Footballers Association, pp. 3–12.

Cohen, Y. & Pfeffer, J. (1986). Organizational hiring standards. *Administrative Science Quarterly*, 31(1), 1–24.

Collins, N. (2011). Football agent 'siphoned hundreds of thousands' from England star's account. *Telegraph*, 8 March.

Collins, Y. & Vamplew, W. (2000). The pub, the drinks trade and the early years of modern football. *The Sports Historian*, 20(1), 1–17.

Commission of the European Communities (2007). *White Paper on Sport*. Brussels: Commission of the European Communities.

Conn, D. (1997). *The Football Business*. Edinburgh: Mainstream.

Conn, D. (1999). The new commercialism. In Hamil, S., Michie, J. & Oughton, C. (eds). *The Business of Football: A Game of Two Halves?* Edinburgh: Mainstream, pp. 40–55.

Conn, D. (2009). Premier League clubs vote for 'homegrown' quota system from 2010. *Guardian*, 13 May.

Conn, D. (2012). Portuguese police to question Manchester United over Bébé transfer. *Guardian*, 10 May.

Conn, D. (2015). Twenty-eight English clubs are now owned overseas, increasing the risk of tax avoidance. *Guardian*, 14 April.

Cook, K. S. (2005). Networks, norms and trust: the social psychology of social capital. *Social Psychology Quarterly*, 68(1), 4–14.

Côté, J., Salmela, J. H., Baria, A. & Russell, S. (1993). Organizing and interpreting unstructured qualitative data. *The Sports Psychologist*, 7, 127–37.

Crabtree, B. F. & Miller, W. L. (eds) (1992). *Doing Qualitative Research*. Thousand Oaks, CA: Sage.

Creswell, J. W., Hanson, W. E., Plano, V. L. C. & Morales, A. (2007). Qualitative research designs selection and implementation. *The Counseling Psychologist*, 35(2), 236–64.

Critcher, C. (1979). Football since the war. In Clarke, J., Critcher, C. & Johnson, R. (eds). *Working Class Culture: Studies in History and Theory*. London: Hutchinson, pp. 161–84.

Crolley, L. & Hand, D. (2006). *Football and European Identity*. London: Routledge.

Crolley, L., Levermore, R. & Pearson, G. (2002). For business or pleasure? A discussion of the impact of European Union law on the economic and socio-cultural aspects of football. *European Sport Management Quarterly*, 2(4), 276–95.

Culver, D. & Trudel, P. (2008). Clarifying the concept of communities of practice in sport. *International Journal of Sports Science and Coaching*, 3(1), 1–10.

Cunningham, G. B. & Sagas, M. (2004). People make the difference: the influence of the coaching staff's human capital and diversity on team performance. *European Sport Management Quarterly*, 4(1), 3–21.

Curran, C. (2015). The migration of Irish-born footballers to England, 1945–2010. *Soccer & Society*, 16(2–3), 360–76.

Cushion, C. J. & Jones, R. L. (2001). A systematic observation of professional top-level youth soccer coaches. *Journal of Sport Behaviour*, 24(4), 354–76.

Cushion, C. J. & Jones, R. L. (2006). Power, discourse, and symbolic violence in professional youth soccer: the case of Albion Football Club. *Sociology of Sport Journal*, 23(2), 142–61.

Cushion, C. J., Armour, K. M. & Jones. R. L. (2003). Coach education and continuing professional development: experience and learning to coach. *Quest*, 55(3), 215–30.

Cushion, C., Ford, P. R. & Williams, M. (2012). Coach behaviours and practice structures in youth soccer: implications for talent development. *Journal of Sports Sciences*, 30(15), 1631–41.

Dabscheck, B. (1986). Beating the off-side trap: the case of the Professional Footballers Association. *Industrial Relations Journal*, 17(4), 350–61.

Dabscheck, B. (2000). Sport, human rights and industrial relations. *Australian Journal of Human Rights*, 6(2), 129–59.

Dabscheck, B. (2006). The globe at their feet: FIFA's new employment rules – II. *Sport in Society*, 9(1), 1–18.

Darby, P., Akindes, G. & Kirwin, M. (2007). Football academies and the migration of African football labor to Europe. *Journal of Sport and Social Issues*, 31(2), 143–61.

Dasgupta, P. (1988). Trust as a commodity. In Gambetta, D. (ed.). *Trust: Making and Breaking Cooperative Relations*. Oxford: Blackwell, pp. 49–72.

Dawson, P. & Dobson, B. (2002). Managerial efficiency and human capital: an application to English association football. *Managerial and Decision Economics*, 23(8), 471–86.

Dawson P. & Dobson, S. (2006). Managerial displacement and the re-employment process in professional team sports: the case of English professional football. In Jeanrenaud, C. & Kesenne, S. (eds). *Economics Applied to Sports: Five Case Studies*. Neuchâtel: Centre International d'Étude du Sport, Université de Neuchâtel, pp. 27–43.

Dawson, P., Dobson, S. & Gerrard, B. (2000). Estimating coaching efficiency in professional team sports: evidence from English association football. *Scottish Journal of Political Economy*, 47(4), 399–421.

De Vasconcellos Ribeiro, C. H. & Dimeo, P. (2009). The experience of migration for Brazilian football players. *Sport in Society*, 12(6), 725–36.

Deloitte (2015). *Deloitte Annual Review of Football Finance 2015*. Manchester: Deloitte.

Deloitte & Touche (2001). *Deloitte & Touche Annual Review of Football Finance 2001*. Manchester: Deloitte & Touche.

Demazière, D. & Jouvenet, M. (2013). The market work of football agents and the manifold valorizations of professional football players. *Economic Sociology. The European electronic newsletter*, 29.

Denscombe, M. (1998). *The Good Research Guide: For Small-Scale Social Research Projects*. Buckingham: Open University Press.

Denzin, N. K. & Lincoln, Y. S. (eds) (1998). *Strategies of Qualitative Inquiry*. London: Sage.

Deutsch, M. (1958). Trust and suspicion. *The Journal of Conflict Resolution*, 2(4), 265–79.

DiMaggio, P. J. & Powell, W. W. (1983). The iron cage revisited: institutional isomorphism and collective rationality in organizational fields. *American Sociological Review*, 48(2), 147–60.

Dixon, P. & Garnham, N. (2005). Drink and the professional footballer in 1890s England and Ireland. *Sport in History*, 25(3), 375–89.

Dobbin, F., Sutton, J. R., Meyer, J. W. & Scott, R. (1993). Equal opportunity law and the construction of internal labor markets. *The American Journal of Sociology*, 99(2), 396–427.

Doeringer, P. B. & Piore, M. J. (1971). *Internal Labor Markets and Manpower Analysis*. Lexington, MA: Heath.

Duke, V. (2002). Local tradition versus globalisation: resistance to the McDonaldisation and Disneyisation of professional football in England. *Football Studies*, 5(1), 5–23.

Dunning, E. & Waddington, I. (2003). Sport as a drug and drugs in sport: some exploratory comments. *International Review for the Sociology of Sport*, 38(3), 351–68.

Elberse, A. (2013). Ferguson's formula. *Harvard Business Review*, 91(10), 116–25.

Elias, N. (1987). The retreat of sociologists into the present, *Theory, Culture and Society*, 4(2–3), 223–47.

Elias, N. (1998). *Norbert Elias on Civilization, Power and Knowledge*. London: University of Chicago Press.

Elias, N. & Dunning, E. (1986). *Quest for Excitement: Sport and Leisure in the Civilising Process*. Oxford: Blackwell.

Elliott, R. & Maguire, J. (2008). Thinking outside of the box: exploring a conceptual synthesis for research in the area of athletic labor migration. *Sociology of Sport Journal*, 25(4), 482–97.

Emery, R. & Weed, M. (2006). Fighting for survival? The financial management of football clubs outside the 'top flight' in England. *Managing Leisure*, 11(1), 1–21.

Engels, F. (1845). *The Condition of the Working Class in England*. Oxford: Blackwell.
Evans, O. (2013). Secret agents. *Sport Business International*, 195(11), 36–7.
Ezzy, D. (2001). A simulacrum of workplace community: individualism and engineered culture. *Sociology*, 35(3), 631–50.
FA (2006). *The Football Association: Football Agent Regulations*. London: FA.
FA (2015). *FA Regulations on Working with Intermediaries*. London: FA.
Fee, C. E., Hadlock, C. J. & Pierce, J. R. (2006). Promotions in the internal and external labor market: evidence from professional football coaching careers. *The Journal of Business*, 79(2), 821–50.
Fein, S. & Hilton, J. L. (1994). Judging others in the shadow of suspicion. *Journal of Motivation and Emotion*, 18(2), 167–98.
Ferguson, A. (2013). *Alex Ferguson: My Autobiography*. London: Hodder & Stoughton.
FGRC (2006). *The State of the Game: The Corporate Governance of Football Clubs 2006*. Football Governance Research Centre Paper 2006, No. 3. Birkbeck: University of London.
FIFA (2008). *Players' Agent Regulations*. Zurich: FIFA.
FIFA (2014). *Regulations on Working with Intermediaries*. Zurich: FIFA
Fifield, D. (2009). Carlo Ancelotti aims to end Chelsea's identity crisis with a personal touch. *Guardian*, 25 July.
Fossey, E., Harvey, C., McDermott, F. & Davidson, L. (2002). Understanding and evaluating qualitative research. *Australian and New Zealand Journal of Psychiatry*, 36(6), 717–32.
Foster, K. (2001). Transfer fees: still (i1)legal after all these years? In *Singer & Friedlander Review 2000–2001 Season*. London: Singer & Friedlander, 4–7.
Fowler, R., with Maddock, D. (2005). *Robbie Fowler: My Autobiography*. London: Macmillan.
Fox, A. (1974). *Beyond Contract: Power and Trust Relations*. London: Faber & Faber.
Freeman, S. (2000). *Own Goal! How Egotism and Greed Are Destroying Football*. London: Orion.
Frick, B. (2009). Globalization and factor mobility: the impact of the 'Bosman Ruling' on player migration in professional football. *Journal of Sports Economics*, 10(1), 88–106.
Frisby, W., Reid, C. J., Millar, S. & Hoeber, L. (2005). Putting 'participatory' into participatory forms of action research. *Journal of Sport Management*, 19(4), 367–86.
Fuglsang, L. & Jagd, S. (2015). Making sense of institutional trust in organizations: bridging institutional context and trust. *Organization*, 22(1), 23–39.
Gambetta, D. (ed.) (1988). *Trust: Making and Breaking Cooperative Relationships*. Oxford: Blackwell.
Gammelsæter, H. (2013). Leader succession and effectiveness in team sport. a critical review of the coach succession literature. *Sport, Business and Management: An International Journal*, 3(4), 285–96.
Garland, J., Malcolm, D. & Rowe, M. (eds) (2000). *The Future of Football: Challenges for the Twenty-First Century*. London: Frank Cass.
Garnham, N. (2002). Professionals and professionalism in pre-Great War Irish football. *Journal of Sport History*, 29(1), 77–93.

Garnham, N. & Jackson, A. (2003). Who invested in Victorian football clubs? The case of Newcastle-upon-Tyne. *Soccer & Society*, 4(1), 57–70.
Gascoigne, P., with McKeown, J. & Davies, H. (2006). *Being Gazza: My Journey to Hell and Back*. London: Headline.
Gearing, B. (1999). Narratives of identity among former professional footballers in the United Kingdom. *Journal of Aging Studies*, 13(1), 43–58.
Geertz, C. (1973). *The Interpretation of Culture*. New York: Basic Books.
Gerrard, B. (2001). A new approach to measuring player and team quality in professional team sports. *European Sports Management Quarterly*, 1(3), 219–34.
Gerrard, B. (2005). A resource-utilisation model of organisational efficiency in professional team sports. *Journal of Sport Management*, 19(2), 143–69.
Gerrard, B. (2009). *Human Capital Formation in Elite Team Sport: Evidence from the Manchester United Soccer Academy*. Presentation at the North American Society for Sport Management Congress, Columbia, May.
Gibbs, G. (1988). *Learning by Doing: A Guide to Teaching and Learning Methods*. Oxford: Oxford Polytechnic.
Giddens, A. (1984). *The Constitution of Society: Outline of the Theory of Structuration*. Cambridge: Polity Press.
Giddens, A. (1990). *The Consequences of Modernity*. Stanford, CA: Stanford University Press.
Gilbert, W. D. & Trudel, P. (2005). Learning to coach through experience: conditions that influence reflection. *Physical Educator*, 62(1), 32–43.
Giles, T. (2008). Technical directors bad news for bosses. *Irish Independent*, 19 March.
Gilmore, S. (2001). *Life in the Frying Pan: Towards the Training and Development of English Football Managers*. Unpublished PhD thesis. University of Portsmouth.
Gilmore, S. & Gilson, C. (2007). Finding form: elite sports and the business of change. *Journal of Organizational Change Management*, 20(3), 409–28.
Giulianotti, R. (1999). *Football: A Sociology of the Global Game*. Cambridge: Polity Press.
Giulianotti, R. (2005). *Sport: A Critical Sociology*. Cambridge: Polity Press.
Glanvill, R. (2005). *Chelsea FC: The Official Biography – The Definitive Story of the First 100 Years*. London: Headline.
Gould, D., Giannini, J., Krane, V. & Hodge. K. (1990). Educational needs of elite US national team, Pan American, and Olympic coaches. *Journal of Teaching in Physical Education*, 9(4), 332–44.
Granovetter, M. S. (1973). The strength of weak ties. *The American Journal of Sociology*, 78(6), 1360–80.
Granovetter, M. S. (1974). *Getting a Job: A Study of Contacts and Careers*. Chicago: University of Chicago Press.
Granovetter, M. S. (1985). Economic action and social structure: the problem of embeddedness. *The American Journal of Sociology*, 91(3), 481–510.
Grant, M. & Robertson, R. (2011). *The Management: Scotland's Great Football Bosses*. Edinburgh: Birlinn.
Gratton, C. & Jones, I. (2010). *Research Methods for Sports Studies*. Second edition. London: Routledge.
Green, C. (2002). *The Sack Race: The Story of Football's Gaffers*. Edinburgh: Mainstream.

Groom, R., Cushion, C. & Nelson, L. (2011). The delivery of video-based performance analysis by England youth soccer coaches: towards a grounded theory. *Journal of Applied Sport Psychology*, 23(1), 16–32.

Grundy, T. (1998). Strategy, value and change in the football industry. *Strategic Change*, 7(3), 127–38.

Grundy, T. (2004). Strategy and financial management in the football industry. *Strategic Change*, 13(8), 404–22.

Gubrium, J. F. & Holstein, J. A. (eds) (2001). *Handbook of Interview Research: Context & Method*. Thousand Oaks, CA: Sage.

Gwyther, M. & Saunders, A. (2005). United they stand? *Management Today*, April, 38–43.

Hamil, S., Michie, J. & Oughton, C. (eds) (1999). *The Business of Football: A Game of Two Halves?* Edinburgh: Mainstream.

Hamil, S., Michie, J., Oughton, C. & Warby, S. (eds) (2000). *Football in the Digital Age: Whose Game Is It Anyway?* Edinburgh: Mainstream.

Harding, J. (1991). *For the Good of the Game: The Official History of the Professional Footballers Association*. London: Robson Books.

Harris, N. (2006). *The Foreign Revolution: How Overseas Footballers Changed the English Game*. London: Aurum Press.

Higgs, J. & Titchen, A. (2000). Knowledge and reasoning. In Higgs, J. & Jones, M. (eds). *Clinical Reasoning in the Health Professions*. Second edition. Oxford: Butterworth Heinemann, pp. 23–32.

Hoare, S. (2006). Chasing promotion. *People Management*, 12(4), 36–8.

Hoey, A. (2016). *The Leadership Guide*. Burton-upon-Trent: League Managers Association.

Holt, M. (2003). *A 'Fit and Proper' Test for Football? Protecting and Regulating Clubs*. Football Governance Research Centre Paper 2003, No. 2. Birkbeck: University of London.

Holt, M., Michie, J. & Oughton, C. (2006). *The Role and Regulation of Agents in Football*. London: The Sports Nexus.

Holt, N. L. (2002). A comparison of the soccer talent development systems in England and Canada. *European Physical Education Review*, 8(3), 270–85.

Holt, N. L. & Dunn, J. G. H. (2004). Toward a grounded theory of the psychosocial competencies and environmental conditions associated with soccer success. *Journal of Applied Sport Psychology*, 16(3), 199–219.

Homans, G. (1950). *The Human Group*. New York: Harcourt, Brace & World.

Hopcraft, A. (1968). *The Football Man: People and Passions in Soccer*. London: Collins.

Hope, S. (2003). *The Ownership Structure of Nationwide League Football Clubs 2002–03*. Football Governance Research Centre Paper 2003, No. 5. Birkbeck: University of London.

Horne, J., Tomlinson, A. & Whannel, G. (1999). *Understanding Sport: An Introduction to the Sociological and Cultural Analysis of Sport*. London: Spon.

Hosmer, L. T. (1995). Trust: the connecting link between organizational theory and philosophical ethics. *Academy of Management Review*, 20(2), 379–403.

Houlston, D. R. (1982). The occupational mobility of professional athletes. *International Review for the Sociology of Sport*, 17(2), 15–28.

Hycner, R. H. (1999). Some guidelines for the phenomenological analysis of interview data. In Bryman, A. & Burgess, R. G. (eds). *Qualitative Research, Volume III*. London: Sage, pp. 143–64.

Insko, C. A. & Schopler, J. (1997). Differential distrust of groups and individuals. In Sedikides, C., Schopler, J. & Insko, C. (eds). *Intergroup Cognition and Intergroup Behavior*. Hillsdale, NJ: Erlbaum, pp. 75–108.

Jaquiss, K. (2000). Football, fans and fat cats: whose football club is it anyway? In Hamil, S., Michie, J., Oughton, C. & Warby, S. (eds). *Football in the Digital Age: Whose Game Is It Anyway?* Edinburgh: Mainstream, pp. 112–17.

Jones, R. L., Armour, K. M. & Potrac, P. (2003). Constructing expert knowledge: a case study of a top-level professional soccer coach. *Sport, Education and Society*, 8(2), 213–29.

Jones, R. L., Armour, K. M. & Potrac, P. (2004). *Sports Coaching Cultures: From Practice to Theory*. London: Routledge.

Jones, R. L., Bailey, J. & Thompson, I. (2013). Ambiguity, noticing, and orchestration: further thoughts on managing the complex coaching context. In Potrac, P., Gilbert, W. & Denison, J. (eds). *The Routledge Handbook of Sports Coaching*. London: Routledge, pp. 271–83.

Jones, R. L., Harris, R. & Miles, A. (2009). Mentoring in sports coaching: a review of the literature. *Physical Education and Sport Pedagogy*, 14(3), 267–84.

Jonker, L., Elferink-Gemser, M. T., Toering, T. T., Lyons, J. & Visscher, C. (2010). Academic performance and self-regulatory skills in elite youth soccer players. *Journal of Sports Sciences*, 28(14), 1605–14.

Katz, F. E. (1958). Occupational contact networks. *Social Forces*, 37(1), 52–5.

Keane, R., with Dunphy, E. (2002). *Keane: The Autobiography*. London: Penguin.

Kelly, S. (2016). Pedagogy, game intelligence and critical thinking: the future of Irish football. *Soccer & Society*, 17(7), 1–22.

Kelso, P. (2009). Premier League wages soar as agents paid £66 million. *Daily Telegraph*, 4 June.

Kesenne, S. (2003). The salary cap proposal of the G-14 in European football. *European Sport Management Quarterly*, 3(2), 120–8.

Kimmage, P. (2005). *Full Time: The Secret Life of Tony Cascarino*. London: Scribner.

King, A. (1997). New directors, customers, and fans: the transformation of English football in the 1990s. *Sociology of Sport Journal*, 14(3), 224–40.

Koning, R. H. (2003). An econometric evaluation of the effect of firing a coach on team performance. *Applied Economics*, 35(5), 555–64.

Kramer, R. M. (1999). Trust and distrust in organisations: emerging perspectives, enduring questions. *Annual Review of Psychology*, 50(1), 569–98.

Kramer, R. M. & Tyler, T. R. (1996). *Trust in Organizations: Frontiers of Theory and Research*. Thousand Oaks, CA: Sage.

Lanfranchi, P. & Taylor, M. (2001). *Moving with the Ball: The Migration of Professional Footballers*. Oxford: Berg.

Lear, R. & Palmer, C. (2007). Is there life after playing football? Investigating the perspectives of football coaches at a club in the North West of England. *Journal of Qualitative Research in Sports Studies*, 1(1), 19–32.

Lewicki, R. J. & Bunker, B. B. (1995). Trust in relationships: a model of development and decline. In Bunker, B. B. & Rubin, J. Z. (eds). *Conflict, Cooperation, and*

*Justice: Essays Inspired by the Work of Morton Deutsch*. San Francisco, CA: Jossey-Bass, pp. 133–73.

Lewicki, R. J. & Wiethoff, C. (2006). Trust, trust development, and trust repair. In Deutsch, M., Coleman, P. T. & Marcus, E. C. (eds). *The Handbook of Conflict Resolution*. San Francisco, CA: Jossey-Bass, pp. 92–119.

Lewicki, R., Elgoibar, P. & Euwema, M. (2016). The tree of trust: building and repairing trust in organizations. In Elgoibar, P., Euwema, M. & Munduate, L. (eds). *Building Trust and Constructive Conflict Management in Organizations*. Zurich: Springer International Publishing, pp. 93–117.

Lewicki, R. J., McAllister, D. J. & Bies, R. J. (1998). Trust and distrust: new relationships and realities. *The Academy of Management Review*, 23(3), 438–58.

Lin, N. (1999). Social networks and status attainment. *Annual Review of Sociology*, 25, 467–87.

Liston, K. (2004). *Playing the Masculine/Feminine Game: A Sociological Analysis of the Social Fields of Sport and Gender in Ireland*. Unpublished PhD thesis, University College Dublin.

Littlewood, M. & Richardson, D. (2006). *Football Labour Migration: Player Acquisition Trends in Elite-Level English Professional Football, 1990/91 to 2004/05*. Presentation at the European Association for Sport Management Congress, Nicosia, September.

LMA (2009). Everton: Moyes' magic. LMA website, 1 May.

LMA (2016). Southampton FC appointment Claude Puel as first team manager. LMA website, 30 June.

Lonsdale, C. (2004). Player power: capturing value in the English football supply network. *Supply Chain Management: An International Journal*, 9(5), 383–91.

Luhmann, N. (1979). *Trust and Power*. New York: Wiley.

McArdle, D. (2000). They're playing R. Song: football and the European Union after Bosman. *Football Studies*, 2(3), 42–66.

McArdle, D. (2002). Ignoring the inevitable: reflections on the intervention of the English courts in football's contract disputes. *European Sport Management Quarterly*, 2(4), 264–75.

McCutcheon, J. P. (2002). Free movement in European sport. *European Sport Management Quarterly*, 2(4), 308–20.

McDonnell, D. (2014). We'll have a German plan in place. *Irish Independent*, 9 October.

McGarry, T., O'Donoghue, P. & Sampaio, J. (eds) (2013). *Routledge Handbook of Sports Performance Analysis*. London: Routledge.

McGillivray, D. & McIntosh, A. (2006). 'Football is my life': theorizing social practice in the Scottish professional football field. *Sport in Society*, 9(3), 371–87.

McGillivray, D., Fearn, R. & McIntosh, A. (2005). Caught up in and by the beautiful game: a case study of Scottish professional footballers. *Journal of Sport and Social Issues*, 29(1), 102–23.

McGovern, P. (2000). The Irish brawn drain: English league clubs and Irish footballers, 1946–1995. *British Journal of Sociology*, 51(3), 401–18.

McGovern, P. (2002). Globalization or internationalization? Foreign footballers in the English league, 1946–95. *Sociology*, 36(1), 23–42.

McGrath, P., with Hogan, V. (2006). *Back from the Brink: The Autobiography*. London: Century.

Mackenzie, R. & Cushion, C. (2013). Performance analysis in football: a critical review and implications for future research. *Journal of Sports Sciences*, 31(6), 639–76.

Madichie, N. (2009). Management implications of foreign players in the English Premiership League football. *Management Decision*, 47(1), 24–50.

Magee, J. (1998). *International Labour Migration in English League Football*. Unpublished PhD thesis, University of Brighton.

Magee, J. (2002). Shifting balances of power in the new football economy. In Sugden, J. & Tomlinson, A. (eds). *Power Games: Theory and Method for the Critical Sociology of Sport*. London: Routledge, pp. 216–39.

Magee, J. & Sugden, J. (2002). 'The world at their feet': professional football and international labor migration. *Journal of Sport and Social Issues*, 26(4), 421–37.

Maguire, J. (1999). *Global Sport: Identities, Societies, Civilizations*. Oxford: Polity Press.

Maguire, J. & Pearton, R. (2000). The impact of elite labour migration on the identification, selection and development of European soccer players. *Journal of Sports Sciences*, 18(9), 759–69.

Maguire, J. & Stead, D. (1998). Border crossings: soccer labour migration and the European Union. *International Review for the Sociology of Sport*, 33(1), 59–73.

Malam, C. (2004). *Clown Prince of Soccer? The Len Shackleton Story*. Newbury: Highdown.

Malcolm, D. (2000). Football business and football communities in the twenty-first century. *Football & Society*, 1(3), 102–13.

Mallinger, P. (2007). *So You Think You Want to Be a Director of a Football Club? A View from Inside the Boardrooms at Newcastle United and Kettering Town*. Milton Keynes: Authorhouse.

Marsden, P. V. (1994). The hiring process: recruitment methods. *The American Behavioral Scientist*, 37(7), 979–91.

Marsden, P. V. & Campbell, K. E. (1990). Recruitment and selection processes: the organisational side of job searches. In Breiger, R. L. (ed.). *Social Mobility and Social Structure*. New York: Cambridge University Press, pp. 59–79.

Mason, T. (1980). *Association Football and English Society 1863–1915*. Brighton: Harvester.

Mason, T. (1989). *Sport in Britain: A Social History*. Cambridge: Cambridge University Press.

Mayer, R. C., Davis, J. H. & Schoorman, F. D. (1995). An integrated model of organizational trust. *Academy of Management Review*, 20(3), 709–34.

Merson, P., with Allen, M. (2011). *How Not to Be a Professional Footballer*. London: HarperSport.

Metzler, M. W. (2005). *Instructional Models for Physical Educators*. Second edition. Scottsdale, AZ: Holcomb Hathaway.

Meyer, B. B. & Fletcher, T. B. (2007). Emotional intelligence: A theoretical overview and implications for research and professional practice in sport psychology. *Journal of Applied Sport Psychology*, 19(1), 1–15.

Meyer, J. W. & Rowan, B. (1977). Institutionalized organizations: formal structure as myth and ceremony. *The American Journal of Sociology*, 83(2), 340–63.

Miles, M. B. & Huberman, A. M. (1994). *Qualitative Data Analysis: An Expanded Sourcebook*. London: Sage.

Miles, R. E. & Creed, W. E. D. (1995). Organizational forms and managerial philosophies: a descriptive and analytical review. In Straw, B. M. & Cummings, L. L. (eds). *Research in Organizational Behavior*. Greenwich, CT: JAI Press, pp. 333–72.

Mills, J. P. & Boardley, I. D. (2016). Expert Premier League soccer managers' use of transformational leadership behaviours and attitude towards sport integrity: an intrinsic case study. *International Journal of Sports Science & Coaching*, 11(3), 382–94.

Mills, A., Butt, J. & Maynard, I. (2014). Toward an understanding of optimal development environments within elite English soccer academies. *The Sport Psychologist*, 28(2), 137–50.

Mills, A., Butt, J., Maynard, I. & Harwood, C. (2012). Identifying factors perceived to influence the development of elite youth football academy players. *Journal of Sports Sciences*, 30(15), 1593–604.

Misener, K. & Doherty, A. (2009). A case study of organizational capacity in nonprofit community sport. *Journal of Sport Management*, 23(4), 457–82.

Misener, K. & Doherty, A. (2013). Understanding capacity through the processes and outcomes of interorganizational relationships in nonprofit community sport organizations. *Sport Management Review*, 16(2), 135–47.

Mitchell, T. O., Nesti, M., Richardson, D., Midgley, A. W., Eubank, M. & Littlewood, M. (2014). Exploring athletic identity in elite-level English youth football: a cross-sectional approach. *Journal of Sports Sciences*, 32(13), 1294–9.

Mohan, G. & Mohan, J. (2002). Placing social capital. *Progress in Human Geography*, 26(2), 191–210.

Molan, C., Matthews, J. & Arnold, R. (2016). Leadership off the pitch: the role of the manager in semi-professional football. *European Sport Management Quarterly*, 16(3), 274–91.

Molm, L. D. (2010). The structure of reciprocity. *Social Psychology Quarterly*, 73(2), 119–31.

Molnar, G. & Maguire, J. (2008). Hungarian footballers on the move: issues of and observations on the first migratory phase. *Sport in Society*, 11(1), 74–89.

Monk, D. (2000). Modern apprenticeships in football: success or failure? *Industrial and Commercial Training*, 32(2), 52–9.

Monk, D. & Olsson, C. (2006). Modern apprenticeships in English professional football. *Education and Training*, 48(6), 429–39.

Monk, D. & Russell, D. (2000). Training apprentices: tradition versus modernity in the football industry. *Soccer & Society*, 1(2), 62–79.

Moorhouse, H. F. (1994). Blue bonnets over the border: Scotland and the migration of footballers. In Bale, J. & Maguire, J. (eds). *The Global Sports Arena: Athletic Talent Migration in an Interdependent World*. London: Frank Cass, pp. 78–96.

Morris, D. (1981). *The Soccer Tribe*. London: Cape.

Morris, P. E., Morrow, S. & Spink, P. M. (1996). EC law and professional football: Bosman and its implications. *The Modern Law Review*, 59(6), 893–902.

Morrow, S. (2003). *The People's Game? Football, Finance and Society*. Basingstoke: Palgrave.

Morrow, S. & Howieson, B. (2014). The new business of football: a study of current and aspirant football club managers. *Journal of Sport Management*, 28(5), 515–28.

Moustakas, C. (1994). *Phenomenological Research Methods*. Thousand Oaks, CA: Sage.
Murphy, P. (1998). Managing the managers: an interview with John Barnwell, the Chief Executive of the League Managers Association. *Singer & Friedlander Review 1997–1998 Season*. London: Singer & Friedlander, pp. 6–9.
Murphy, P. (2002). The Dutch approach to club management: three contrasting clubs with a similar ethos. *Soccer Review 2002*. Leicester: Facilitated by the Professional Footballers Association, pp. 46–52.
Nash, R. (2000a). Contestation in modern English professional football: the independent supporters' association movement. *International Review for the Sociology of Sport*, 35(4), 465–86.
Nash, R. (2000b). The sociology of English football in the 1990s: fandom, business and future research. *Football Studies*, 3(1), 49–62.
Nesti, M. (2010). *Psychology in Football: Working with Elite and Professional Players*. London: Routledge.
Nissen, R. (2014). Playing the game: how football directors make sense of dismissing the coach. *International Journal of Sport Management and Marketing*, 15(3–4), 214–31.
Nissen, R. (2016). Hired to be fired? Being a coach in Danish professional football. *International Journal of Sports Science & Coaching*, 11(2), 137–48.
Nooteboom, B. & Six, F. (eds) (2003). *The Trust Process in Organizations: Empirical Studies of the Determinants and the Process of Trust Development*. Cheltenham: Edward Elgar.
O'Leary, D. (2002). *Leeds United on Trial: The Inside Story of an Astonishing Year*. London: Little, Brown.
O'Leary, J. & Caiger, A. (2000). Shifting power and control in English football. *New Zealand Journal of Industrial Relations*, 25(3), 259–75.
Ozawa, T., Cross, J. & Henderson, S. (2004). Market orientation and financial performance of English professional clubs. *Journal of Targeting, Measurement and Analysis for Marketing*, 13(1), 78–90.
Pain, M. A. & Hardwood, C. G. (2004). Knowledge and perceptions of sport psychology within English soccer. *Journal of Sports Sciences*, 22(9), 813–26.
Park, P. (2001). Knowledge and participatory research. In Reason, P. & Bradbury, H. (eds). *Handbook of Action Research: Participative Inquiry and Practice*. London: Sage, pp. 81–90.
Parker, A. (1996). *Chasing the Big Time: Football Apprenticeships in the 1990s*. Unpublished PhD thesis, University of Warwick.
Parker, A. (2001). Training for 'glory', schooling for 'failure'? English professional football, traineeship and educational provision. *Journal of Education and Work*, 13(1), 61–76.
Parrish, R. (2002). Judicial intervention and sporting autonomy: defining the territories of European Union involvement in sport. *European Sport Management Quarterly*, 2(4), 296–307.
Parsons, T. (1935). Sociological elements in economic thought I. Historical. *Quarterly Journal of Economics*, 49, 414–53.
Partington, M. & Cushion, C. (2013). An investigation of the practice activities and coaching behaviors of professional top-level youth soccer coaches. *Scandinavian Journal of Medicine & Science in Sports*, 23(3), 374–82.

Patton, M. Q. (2002). *Qualitative Research and Evaluation Methods*. Third edition. Thousand Oaks, CA: Sage.

Pawson, T. (1973). *The Football Managers*. London: Eyre Methuen.

Peiser, B. J. & O'Franklin, M. (2000). The effects of managerial changes in English professional football, 1975–1995. *Football Studies*, 3(1), 63–72.

Penn, R. (2002). The management of a football club: a case study of Blackburn Rovers FC. *Soccer Review 2002*. Leicester: Facilitated by the Professional Footballers Association, pp. 40–45.

Perry, B. (2000a). The boss? The contemporary role of the football manager. *Singer & Friedlander Review 1999–2000 Season*. London: Singer & Friedlander, 59–62.

Perry, B. (2000b). *Football Management as a Metaphor for Corporate Entrepreneurship*. Working Paper Series 2000. Wolverhampton: University of Wolverhampton Business School.

Perry, B. & Davies, G. (1997). *The Process of Management: The Case of the Football Manager*. Working Paper Series 1997. Wolverhampton: University of Wolverhampton Business School.

Poli, R. (2006). Africans' status in the European football players' labour market. *Soccer & Society*, 7(2–3), 278–291.

Poli, R. (2010). Agents and intermediaries. In Hamil, S. & Chadwick, S. (eds). *Managing Football: An International Perspective*. Oxford: Elsevier, pp. 201–16.

Poli, R. & Rossi, G. (2012). *Football Agents in the Biggest Five European Football Markets: An Empirical Research Report*. Neuchâtel: Centre International d'Étude du Sport, Université de Neuchâtel.

Portes, A. (1995). Economic sociology and the sociology of immigration: a conceptual overview. In Portes, A. (ed.). *The Economic Sociology of Immigration*. New York: Russell Sage Foundation, pp. 1–41.

Portes, A. (1998). Social capital: its origins and applications in modern sociology. *Annual Review of Sociology*, 22, 1–24.

Potrac, P. & Jones, R. L. (2009). Micro-political workings in semi-professional soccer coaching. *Sociology of Sport Journal*, 26(4), 557–77.

Potrac, P., Jones, R. & Armour, K. (2002). 'It's all about getting respect': the coaching behaviors of an expert English soccer coach. *Sport, Education and Society*, 7(2), 183–202.

Price, L. (2015). *The Bundesliga Blueprint: How Germany Became the Home of Football*. Oakamoor: Bennion Kearney.

Putnam, R. (2000). *Bowling Alone: The Collapse and Revival of American Community*. New York: Simon & Schuster.

Quinn, M., with Harvey, O. (2003). *Who Ate All the Pies? The Life and Times of Mick Quinn*. London: Virgin.

Redhead, S. (1991). *Football with Attitude*. Manchester: Wordsmith.

Redhead, S. (1997). *Post-Football and the Millennial Blues*. London: Routledge.

Rees, A. (1966). Information networks in labor markets. *American Economic Review*, May, 559–66.

Reilly, T. & Gilbourne, D. (2003). Science and football: a review of applied research in the football codes. *Journal of Sports Sciences*, 21(9), 693–705.

Relvas, H., Littlewood, M., Nesti., M., Gilbourne, D. & Richardson, D. (2010). Organisational structures and working practices in elite European professional football clubs: understanding the relationship between youth and professional domains. *European Sport Management Quarterly*, 10(2), 165–87.

Renshaw, I., Davids, K. W., Shuttleworth, R. & Chow, J. Y. (2009). Insights from ecological psychology and dynamical systems theory can underpin a philosophy of coaching. *International Journal of Sport Psychology*, 40(4), 540–602.

Reynolds, L. T. & Herman, N. J. (1994). *Symbolic Interactionism: An Introduction to Social Psychology*. New York: General Hall.

Riach, J. (2015). Football agents fear 'wild west' as Fifa reforms seek to cap fees. *Guardian*, 31 March.

Richardson, D., Gilbourne, D. & Littlewood, M. (2004). Developing support mechanisms for elite young players in a professional soccer academy: creative reflections in action research. *European Sport Management Quarterly*, 4(4), 195–214.

Richardson, D., Littlewood, M., Nesti, M. & Benstead, L. (2012). An examination of the migratory transition of elite young European soccer players to the English Premier League. *Journal of Sports Sciences*, 30(15), 1605–18.

Ridsdale, P. (2007). *United We Fall: Boardroom Truths about the Beautiful Game*. London: Macmillan.

Riesman, D. & Benney, M. (1956). The sociology of the interview. *Midwestern Sociologist*, 18(1), 3–15.

Ristock, J. L. & Pennell, J. (1996). *Community Research as Empowerment: Feminist Links, Postmodern Interruptions*. Toronto, ON: Oxford University Press.

Roach, K. & Dixon, M. A. (2006). Hiring internal employees: a view from the field. *Journal of Sport Management*, 20(2), 137–58.

Roberts, S. J. & Potrac, P. (2014). Behaviourism, constructivism and sports coaching pedagogy: a conversational narrative in the facilitation of player learning. *International Sport Coaching Journal*, 1(3), 180–7.

Robson, B., with Allsop, D. (2006). *Robbo: My Autobiography*. London: Hodder & Stoughton.

Roderick, M. (2001). The role of agents in professional football. In *Singer & Friedlander Review 2000–2001 Season*. London: Singer & Friedlander, pp. 13–16.

Roderick, M. (2003). *A Labour of Love: Careers in Professional Football*. Unpublished PhD thesis, University of Leicester.

Roderick, M. (2006). *The Work of Professional Football: A Labour of Love*. London: Routledge.

Rogan, J. (1989). *The Football Managers*. London: McDonald Queen Anne Press.

Ronay, B. (2010). *The Manager: The Absurd Ascent of the Most Important Man in Football*. London: Sphere.

Rossi, G., Semens, A. & Brocard, J. F. (2016). *Sports Agents and Labour Markets: Evidence from World Football*. London: Routledge.

Roth, G. & Schluchter, W. (1979). *Max Weber's Vision of History Ethics and Methods*. London: University of California Press.

Rotter, J. (1971). Generalized expectancies for interpersonal trust. *American Psychologist*, 26(5), 443–52.

Rotter, J. (1980). Interpersonal trust, trustworthiness, and gullibility. *American Psychologist*, 35(1), 1–7.

Rousseau, D. M., Sitkin, S. B., Burt, R. S. & Camerer. C. (1998). Not so different after all: a cross-cultural discipline view of trust. *Academy of Management Review*, 23(8), 393–404.

Russell, D. (1997). *Football and the English: A Social History of Association Football in England, 1863–1995*. Preston: Carnegie.

Schön, D. A. (1983). *The Reflective Practitioner: How Professionals Think in Action*. New York: Basic Books.

Schoorman, F. D., Mayer, R. C. & Davis, J. H. (2007). An integrative model of organizational trust: past, present, and future. *Academy of Management Review*, 32(2), 344–54.

Scott, M. (2007). Stevens bung inquiry reports 'serious breaches'. *Guardian*, 8 June.

Scott, M. (2009). Fifa to give up regulating player agents. *Guardian*, 13 November.

Scott, M. (2010). Football coach shortage. *Guardian*, 1 June.

Scully, G. W. (1994). Managerial efficiency and survivability in professional team sports. *Managerial and Decision Economics*, 15(5), 403–11.

Seippel, O. (2006). Sport and social capital. *Acta Sociologica*, 49(2), 169–83.

Shapiro, S. P. (1987). The social control of impersonal trust. *The American Journal of Sociology*, 3(3), 623–58.

Shulman, L. (1986). Those who understand: knowledge growth in teaching. *Educational Researcher*, 15(2), 4–14.

Siekmann, R., Parrish, R., Martins, R. B. & Soek, J. (2007). *Players' Agents Worldwide*. Cambridge: Cambridge University Press.

Silverman, D. (2011). *Interpreting Qualitative Data: A Guide to the Principles of Qualitative Research*. London: Sage.

Simmons, R. (1997). Implications of the Bosman ruling for football transfer markets. *Economic Affairs*, 17(3), 13–18.

Simmons, R. (2001). Making sense of the FIFA/UEFA proposals to reform the football transfer system. In *Singer & Friedlander Review 2000–2001 Season*. London: Singer & Friedlander, pp. 8–12.

Sinnott, J. (2011). Standard Liege's Bruyninckx leads way in developing mental capacity. *Sports Illustrated*, 23 December.

Sitkin, S. B. &. Roth, N. L. (1993). Explaining the limited effectiveness of legalistic 'remedies' for trust/distrust. *Organizational Science*, 4(3), 367–92.

Sloane, P. J. (1969). The labour market in professional football. *British Journal of Industrial Relations*, 7(2), 181–99.

Smith, B. & Sparkes, A. C. (2009). Narrative analysis and sport and exercise psychology: understanding lives in diverse ways. *Psychology of Sport and Exercise*, 10(2), 279–88.

Solomon, L. (1960). The influence of some types of power relationships and game strategies upon the development of interpersonal trust. *Journal of Abnormal Social Psychology*, 61(2), 223–30.

Southgate, G. (2006). Southgate demands coaching change. BBC Sport website, 1 December.

Southgate, G. (2010). We are breeding players that are looking for an excuse. *Sunday Times*, 4 July.

Speight, A. E. H. & Thomas, D. A. (1997). Conventional arbitration in the professional footballers' labour market: an assessment of the FLAC experience. *Industrial Relations Journal*, 28(3), 221–35.

Spencer, N. (2001). UEFA threaten to ban clubs with unqualified coaches. *Telegraph*, 8 May.

Stam, J., with Butler, J. (2001). *Jaap Stam: Head to Head*. London: Collins Willow.

Stead, D. (1999). The 'Bosman legacy': some reflections on the Bosman case's impact on English football. In *Singer & Friedlander Review 1998–1999 Season*. London: Singer & Friedlander, pp. 23–6.

Stead, D. & Maguire, J. (2000). 'Rite de passage' or passage to riches? The motivation and objectives of Nordic/Scandinavian players in English league soccer. *Journal of Sport & Social Issues*, 24(1), 36–60.

Stevens, J. (2006). *The Quest Inquiry: Inquiry Recommendations*. London: Quest.

Stewart, G. (1986). The retain and transfer system: an alternate perspective. *Managerial Finance*, 12(1), 25–9.

Stewart, G. & Sutherland, J. (1996). The trainee system in professional football in England and Wales. *Education & Training*, 38(1), 24–9.

Stivers, R. (1994). *The Culture of Cynicism*. Oxford: Blackwell.

Sugden, J. & Tomlinson, A. (eds) (2002). *Power Games: A Critical Sociology of Sport*. London: Routledge.

Sutherland, R. J. (1986). Hiring as an investment decision: the recruitment policies of the professional football club. *Managerial Finance*, 12(1), 20–4.

Szczepanik, N. (2009). Players the winners as football bucks trend. *Times*, 4 June.

Sztompka, P. (1998). Trust, distrust and two paradoxes of democracy. *European Journal of Social Theory*, 1(1), 19–32.

Sztompka, P. (1999). *Trust: A Sociological Theory*. Cambridge: Cambridge University Press.

Szymanski, S. & Kuypers, T. (1999). *Winners and Losers: The Business Strategy of Football*. London: Viking.

Taylor, D. (2003). Leeds alerted by O'Leary's Villa misery. *Guardian*, 13 November.

Taylor, D. (2008). Hughes insists City owners let him choose new signings. *Guardian*, 5 September.

Taylor, L. (2009). Bruce makes his local more cosmopolitan. *Observer*, 6 December.

Taylor, M. (1999). No big deal. *When Saturday Comes*, November (153), 28–9.

Taylor, M. (2001). Beyond the maximum wage: the earnings of football professionals in England, 1900–39. *Soccer and Society*, 2(3), 101–18.

Taylor, M. (2006). Global players? Football migration and globalization, 1930–2000. *Historical Social Research*, 31(1), 7–30.

Taylor, M. (2008). *The Association Game: A History of British Football*. Harlow: Pearson.

Taylor, M. (2010). Football's engineers? British football coaches, migration and intercultural transfer, c.1910–c.1950s. *Sport in History*, 30(1), 138–63.

Taylor, R. & Ward, A. (1995). *Kicking and Screaming: An Oral History of Football in England*. London: Robson Books.

Taylor, R., Ward, A. & Thatcher, M. (1997). The people's game. *People Management*, 3(16), 22–7.

Tesch, R. (1990). *Qualitative Analysis: Analysis Types and Software Tools*. London: Falmer Press.

Thelwell, R. C., Lane, A. M., Weston, N. J. & Greenlees, I. A. (2008). Examining relationships between emotional intelligence and coaching efficacy. *International Journal of Sport and Exercise Psychology*, 6(2), 224–35.

Thomas, K. T. & Thomas, J. R. (1999). What squirrels in the trees predict about expert athletes. *International Journal of Sport Psychology*, 30(2), 221–34.

Tilly, C. & Tilly, C. (1998). *Work under Capitalism*. Boulder, CO: Westview Press.

Tischler, S. (1981). *Footballers and Businessmen: The Origins of Professional Football in England*. London: Holmes & Meier.

Tomas, T. (1996). *Soccer Czars*. London: Mainstream.

Turnnidge, J., Côté, J., Hollenstein, T. & Deakin, J. (2014). A direct observation of the dynamic content and structure of coach–athlete interactions in a model sport program. *Journal of Applied Sport Psychology*, 26 (2), 225–40.

Tversky, A. & Kahneman, D. (1973). Availability: a heuristic for judging frequency and probability. *Cognitive Psychology*, 5(2), 207–32.

Uslaner, E. (2002). *The Moral Foundations of Trust*. Cambridge: Cambridge University Press.

Vamplew, W. (1988). *Pay Up and Play the Game: Professional Sport in Britain 1875–1914*. Cambridge: Cambridge University Press.

Van Mullem, P. & Brunner, D. (2013). Developing a successful coaching philosophy: a step-by-step approach. *Strategies*, 26(3), 29–34.

Waddington, I. (2000). *Sport, Health and Drugs: A Critical Sociological Perspective*. London: Spon.

Waddington, I. (2001). The soccer schools. In *Singer & Friedlander Review 2000–2001 Season*. London: Singer & Friedlander, 29–33.

Waddington, I. (2002). Jobs for the boys? A study of the employment of club doctors and physiotherapists in English professional football. *Soccer and Society*, 3(3), 51–64.

Waddington, I. & Roderick, M. (2002). The management of medical confidentiality in English professional football clubs: some ethical problems and issues. *British Journal of Sports Medicine*, 36(2), 118–23.

Waddington, I., Roderick, M. & Parker, G. (1999). *Managing Injuries in Professional Football: The Roles of the Club Doctor and Physiotherapist*. Report prepared for the Professional Footballers Association. Leicester: Centre for Research into Sport and Society, University of Leicester.

Wagg, S. (1984). *The Football World: A Contemporary Social History*. Brighton: Harvester.

Wagg, S. (1998). Sack the board, sack the board, sack the board: accountancy and accountability in contemporary English professional football culture. *Leisure Studies Association*, 62, 37–53.

Wagg, S. (2007). Angels of us all? Football management, globalization and the politics of celebrity. *Soccer & Society*, 8(4), 440–58.

Walters, G. & Rossi, G. (2009). *Labour Market Migration in European Football: Key Issues and Challenges*. Birkbeck Sports Business Centre Research Paper Series 2(2). Birkbeck: University of London.

Walvin, J. (1986). *Football and the Decline of Britain*. London: Macmillan.

Wang, L. & Gordon, P. (2011). Trust and institutions: a multilevel analysis. *The Journal of Socio-Economics*, 40(5), 583–93.

Weber, M. (1948). *From Max Weber: Essays in Sociology*. London: Routledge.

Weber, M. (1949). *The Methodology of the Social Sciences*. New York: The Free Press.

Weber, M. (1962). *Basic Concepts in Sociology*. London: P. Owen.

Weber, M. (1964). *The Theory of Social and Economic Organization*. Toronto, ON: The Free Press.

Weber, M. (1968). *Economy and Society: An Outline of Interpretive Sociology*. New York: Bedminster Press.

Weedon, G. (2011). 'Glocal boys': exploring experiences of acculturation amongst migrant youth footballers in Premier League academies. *International Review for the Sociology of Sport*, 47(2), 200–16.

Whitehead, M. (1998). Bosmania! Player power gone mad? *Sports Law Administration & Practice*, 5(6), 1–6.

Wilders, M. G. (1976). The football club manager: a precarious occupation. *Journal of Management Studies*, 13(2), 152–63.

Williams, A. M. (2013). *Science and Soccer: Developing Elite Performers*. London: Routledge.

Williams, A. M. & Reilly, T. (2000). Talent identification and development in soccer. *Journal of Sports Sciences*, 18(9), 657–67.

Wilson, J. (2011). *Brian Clough: Nobody Ever Says Thank You*. London: Orion.

Winter, H. (2007). Keane aims for coaching heights. *Telegraph*, 4 July.

Wylie, I. (2004). Football's most effective manager. *Management Today*, March.

Young, P. M. (1968). *A History of British Football*. London: Stanley Paul.

Zucker, L. G. (1986). Production of trust: institutional sources of economic structure, 1840–1920. In Straw, B. M. & Cummings, L. L. (eds). *Research in Organizational Behavior*. Greenwich, CT: JAI Press, pp. 53–111.

# Index

Page numbers with a n indicates an endnote.

agents: central role 118; client trust 123; FIFA regulation 118, 121, 136; Football League ban 28; hostility towards 121–3; increased numbers, factors leading to 119–21; information sources, valued access 130–1; licensing system 121; negotiating power 132–5, 154; negotiations and manager tactics 123–5; payment regulations 136; player's contract negotiator 128–30; post-Bosman hire surge 32, 119; recruitment role (early 1900's) 17, 119; types of 118, 136n; unethical and illegal practices 125–7
alcohol consumption 17, 93, 98, 106–7
Allardyce, Sam 76, 77, 85–6, 87
Ancelotti, Carlo 143
Arsenal: backroom support 54; business orientated 34; foreign players 82; Mee's appointment 24; Wenger's appointment 33, 45; Wenger's management 116
assistant managers/coaches 54–7
Aston Villa 17, 19, 33
*Athletic News* 18

backroom staff: competence issues 59–60; first appointments 20; function and qualities 54–5; promotion from within 44; scientific approach endorsed 35; trusted support 55–8, 153; unfamiliarity and trust 60–1
Barnwell, John 61, 63

Beck, John 108
Benitez, Rafael 42, 77
Bentley, J.J. 18
Best, George 28
Bevan, Richard 77
Blackburn Rovers 21, 34, 37, 53
Boothroyd, Aidy 77
'Bosman II' ruling 35–6
Bosman, Jean-Marc 31, 120
Bosman ruling 31–3, 120
Bourdieu, Pierre 74
Brady, Chris 87–8
Brewer, Marilynn B. 42–3, 141
Bridgewater, Susan 77
Bruce, Steve 69, 82, 87
Buckley, Frank, Major 19–20, 27
Busby, Matt, Sir 25, 27, 29

Caiger, Andrew 134
Cameron, John 16, 18
Carter, Neil 1, 51–2, 72, 73, 112
category-based trust 141
Chapman, Herbert 19–20, 21, 22, 64
Charles, John 26
Charlton, Jack 33
Chelsea: agents' fees 120; all-foreign starting XI, first 31; director responsibilities 35; foreign managers 33; Mourinho's appointment 132–3; Mourinho's reign 38, 116–17
Chester Report 1966 26
Christensen, Mette K. 79, 91
Claridge, Steve 108, 109
Clarke, Steve 116–17
Clough, Brian 24, 27, 54, 69, 108, 109, 142

club owners and directors: financial mismanagement 38, 140; interference in manager's role 145–9, 154; lack of football knowledge 141–2, 154; manager/boardroom relations 142–4; manager distrust 140–1, 146–7, 149, 154; overseas involvement, impact of 139, 140, 145, 150n; PRO Licence dispensations 37, 71–2; recruitment interference 52, 60–1; strategic contacts for recruitment 41, 43–4, 46–7; success-related expectations 51
club owners and directors (1885–1940): early attitude to professionalism 14–15; Football League, early years 15–16; managerial scapegoating 18–19; managing style, hostility towards 21; player behaviour, dealing with 17–18
club owners and directors (1940–70): cost-effective management 26–7; expectations, media fuelled 25; management appointments 23, 24, 28–9
club owners and directors (1970–2000): director payment permitted 33–4; entrepreneurial owners and flotation culture 33–4; manager licenses, resistance to 29–30
club owners and directors (2000–2015) 37–8, 140
club secretaries 14–15, 16
club trainer (pre-1940) 18, 19
coaching: FA's slow introduction 22; formal education, mixed attitudes 71–3; LMA programmes 70; PRO Licence mandatory 37, 71; qualifications, original objections 22–3
Computer Coach 86
Conn, David 38, 140
Critcher, Charles 73, 101
Crompton, Bob 21
Curbishley, Alan 90, 145
Curtis, Harry 20
Cushion, Christopher 86–7, 91, 102

Davies, Gron 50, 65–6
Dawson, Peter 47
Dein, David 34
Dennis, Richard 24
Derby County 16, 27

Dobson, Stephen 47
Docherty, Tommy 142–3
domination (Weber) 7–8, 113
Downing, Stewart 127
Dunning, Eric 106
Dunn, John 91

Eastman, George 26, 39n
Edwards, Martin 34, 142
embeddedness and trust 9–10, 138–9
England team (pre-1970) 22–3, 25
English Football Association *see* Football Association (FA)
English Premier League: agents' fees 120; Bosman ruling, effects on 31–3; broadcasting rights auction 30; commercialisation 1–2; managerial pressures 2; manager's role narrowly defined 51–2; manager turnover 36–7; PRO Licence mandatory 71; wage increases 120
Eriksson, Sven-Goran 33
European Court of Justice 31, 120
European football: Bosman ruling, effects on 31–3; club competitions, qualification pressure 25; coaching qualifications, endorsement of 23, 29, 37; formal education 74; transfer market, EU ruling 2001 35–6

FA Cup competition 15
Ferguson, Alex, Sir: backroom support 54; managerial pressures 2; managerial responsibilities 35; media celebrity 38; mentor role 69, 76; observation methods 77, 153; openness to change 76; owner/director conflict 142; peer support and trust 44; player assessment 87; player discipline and control 95, 98, 106; recruitment success 79
FIFA: agent licensing 118, 121; Players' Agent Regulations 136; Working with Intermediaries 136
Finney, Tom 25
Football Association (FA): agent licensing system 121, 136n, 154; agent practices, breach of 132–3; agents, arguments against 122; appointment procedure, resistance to 51, 152; coaching, original objections 22–3; coaching, slow acceptance 22;

formation and responsibilities 15; management qualifications, resistance to 29, 70; manager licensing system 29–30; manager's responsibilities (1961) 28; maximum wage rule 15, 17; player registration 80; retain and transfer system 15, 26, 39n; Working with Intermediaries guidance 136, 137n

Football Association of Ireland (FAI) 15

Football Association of Wales 15

Football League: agent payment regulation 136; agents ban 28; Bosman ruling, effects on 31–2; formation 15; management qualifications 29; original club structure 15–16; player registration 80; Premier League split 30; transfer compensation scheme 31; wage and contract disputes 17, 26

football managers: advocacy for qualifications 76–7; agents, dismissive hostility 122; appointment and turnover (post-1940) 28, 36–7; backroom staff, competence issues 59–60; backroom staff, trusted support 54–8, 153; baggage and problem players 94–7; boardroom/manager relations 142–4; club organisation, vague position within 53, 114; coaching qualifications, initial rejection 23–4; conduct rules, club variations 100–1, 105–6, 114–15, 153; cost-effective man-management 26–7; financial mismanagement 38, 140; first appointment, unpreparedness 69–70; football knowledge in boardroom 141–2; foreign managers, 1990's influx 33; foreign managers' style 116–17, 117n, 139; formal education, mixed attitudes 71–3; illegal payments 126–7, 140; individual style, assessment challenges 75–6; intimidation and abusive conduct 102–4, 107–10; job candidacy 41, 45; job description, no standardisation 50, 114–15, 152; job insecurity 47, 147; knowledge of the game and instruction 66–8; learning and development 152, 153; learning from observation 68–9, 77, 153; licensing system, resistance to 29–30, 71–2; manager's defined role 51–2; media scrutiny and expectations 25; negotiating power 134–5; owner/director interference 145–9, 154; owner/director mistrust 140–1, 146–8, 149, 154; personal contacts and recruitment 43–7, 49–50, 60–1, 82–5, 152; personal contacts and support networks 41–3, 45–6, 76; pioneers and new approaches 19–21; player attitudes, on/off field 91–4; playing experience, key quality 63–6, 152; recruitment and negotiation tactics 123–5, 128–31, 134; role creation 19; role refinement 34–5; statistical data, increased use 86–7; success-related expectations 51; surveillance practices 97–8; talent identification methods 87–90; 'tapping up' practices 41, 47–9, 84–5, 131; team matters, total control of 52–3; 'tracksuit manager' 20, 24; young players, treatment of 102–5, 110–11, 115–16

formal education: advocacy for qualifications 76–7; anti-intellectualism widespread 73–5; European football 74; hostility to, class related 73; LMA programmes 70; manager style, assessment challenge 75–6; mixed attitudes to coaching 71–3

Freeman, Simon 145

friendship networks 41, 46, 56

Fulham 33

Gearing, B. 73–4
German Football Association 29
Giddens, Anthony 9
Giles, Johnny 138
Gradi, Dario 79
Graham, George 92
Granovetter, Mark: embeddedness and trust 9–10, 54; malfeasance, opportunity for 49; networks, strength of weak ties 8–9
Greaves, Jimmy 26
Guardiola, Pep 38
Guillou, Jean-Marc 82

Hauser, Peter 39n
Hewison, Bob 20
Hibbitt, Kenny 63
Hill, Jimmy 26
Hodgson, Roy 55
Holt, Nicholas 91
Hopcraft, Arthur 142
Howe, Eddie 77
Hughton, Chris 76

Ince, Paul 37
Independent Transfer Tribunal 26
international managers: backroom staff appointments 55; foreign appointments 33
Italian Football Federation 23

Jones, R.L. 91, 102

Keane, Roy: culture of distrust 138; learning from observation 69; manager abuse 109, 110; peer support 42; PRO Licence, value of 76–7
Keegan, Kevin 34, 52, 145
Kelly, Mike 55
Kramer, Roderick M. 141

Lanfranchi, Pierre 32–3
Law, Denis 26
League Managers Association (LMA): boardroom relations 143; employment contracts 50–1; formation 30; management qualifications 37, 70, 77; management recruitment flawed 61; support services 42
Leeds United 17, 27
legal-rational authority (Weber) 7–8, 113–14
Lewington, Ray 55
Liverpool: director interference 29; foreign managers 33; management teams 149; role refinement 35, 52
Lloyd, Larry 108
Luhmann, Niklas 57

Mackenzie, Robert 86–7
Magee, Jonathan 107, 132, 134
Maguire, Joseph 91–2, 121
managerial recruitment and appointment: backroom staff, competence issues 59–60; backroom staff, trusted support 54–8; candidate short-lists 41, 45; club organisation and culture 62–3; Dutch approach 53–4, 63; owner/director interference 60–1; peer support and trust 42–3, 45–6; recommendation disadvantages 47, 60–1; role definitions and team matters 50–4; social capital and strategic contacts 43–7, 49–50; 'tapping up' practice 47–9
managerial scapegoating 18–19, 28
Manchester City 17, 95
Manchester United: agents' fees 120; backroom support 54; business orientated 34; David Moyes's appointment 47; director interference 29; player stockpiling 32; *see also* Ferguson, Alex, Sir
Mancini, Roberto 95
masculinity, appropriate value 20, 73, 74, 101, 107–8, 112, 115
Matthews, Stanley 22
maximum wage rule 15, 17, 25–6
McGillivray, David 74
McGuire, Mick 125
McIntosh, Aaron 74
McNenemy, Lawrie 24
media (post-1940) 23, 25, 30
media (pre-1940) 18–19, 21
Mee, Bertie 24
Mendes, Jorge 133
Middlesbrough: agents as recruiters 17; backroom staff 55; player dissatisfaction 24; PRO Licence dispensation 37, 71–2
Mourinho, José: appointment 132–3; coaching qualifications 37; foreign managers' style 116–17; managerial pressures 2; media celebrity 38; problem players 95
Moyes, David 47, 51, 68, 143, 145

national quotas, abolition of 31
Neville, Gary 55
Newcastle United: entrepreneurial owner 34; foreign manager 33; George Eastman court case 39n; owner/director interference 34, 52, 145; PRO Licence dispensation 37
newspapers 18–19

O'Leary, John 134
O'Neill, Martin 35
on/off field behaviour: alcohol consumption monitoring 17, 93, 98; baggage and problem players 94–7; off-field excess and media attention 28, 91; player attitudes 92–4, 115–16, 153; surveillance practices 97–8

Parker, Andrew 101, 107, 111, 115–16
participatory action research 3–4
Patton, Michael 87
Pearce, Stuart 76
Pearson, Nigel 55
Penn, Roger 53, 112–13
performance analysis (PA) 86–7
Perry, Bob 44, 50, 65–6, 111
personal contact networks: access to job opportunities 40–1, 43–6, 60–1, 152; agent and player trust 123; friendship networks 41, 46, 56; player recruitment 28, 82–5; reciprocity 46; support and knowledge-based trust 42–3, 45–6, 56–8, 76; trust, multi-level approaches 9–10
Platt, David 37
player assessment: baggage and problem players 94–7; desirable characteristics 91–2, 104; financial value 90; instinct and gut feeling 79, 87, 88, 152–3; multi-faceted approach 85; performance analysis (PA) 86–7; player attitudes, on/off field 92–4, 115–16, 153; sport science techniques 85–6; talent identification methods 87–90
player discipline and control: alcohol consumption issues 17, 93, 98, 106–7; authoritarian management, player acceptance 110–11, 115–16; bomb squad and number reallocation 104–5; conduct rules, club variations 99–101, 153; fines or docked wages 17–18, 100–1, 111; intimidation and abuse towards 102–4, 107–10; man management 20, 153; youth arrogance 104
player recruitment: agent collaboration 81, 120–1; agents' negotiating power 132–4; Bosman ruling, effects on 31–3, 120; contract reform of 1970's 26–7, 31; director responsibility, increase in 35, 140; financial factors 90; financial incentives 17; foreign players, readjustment problems 80–1; illegal payments 17, 26, 126–7; informal contact networks 43–4, 82–5, 153; management pressures 79; manager's control of 52–3; negotiations and manager tactics 123–5, 128–31, 134; on/off field behaviour considered 17, 28, 91–8; overseas academies and scouting networks 81–2, 120; overseas players, influx of 32–3; owner/director interference 52, 147–8; player's bargaining powers 133–5, 137n; pre-1920 16–17; recommendation and agents 17, 28; scholarship system 80; strategies 80–1; talent identification methods 88–90; 'tapping up' practices 84–5, 131
Players Union 15, 25–6
playing experience: first manager post, unpreparedness 69–70; football career, key quality 63–6, 152; knowledge of the game and instruction 66–8; management skills through observation 68–9
Premier League *see* English Premier League
professional football: anti-intellectualism widespread 73–5; core values, class related 73, 107; culture of distrust 138; manager's defined role 51–2; results-based industry 51, 151; shop-floor culture, persistence of 111–12; traditional authoritarianism 112–16
professional football (1885–1920): class-defined origins 14–15, 112; club ownership 15–16; FA's original employment rules 15; media attention 18–19; player discipline and control 17–18; recruitment of players 16–17; training needs 18
professional football (1920–40): coaching 22; managerial roles and duties 19–21; media attention 21; player hostility 21

professional football (1940–70):
coaching qualifications, mixed
reaction 22–4; manager appointments
and turnover 28–9; media, growing
involvement 25; player management
27–8; player recruitment 28; wages
and contracts restructure 25–7
professional football (1970–2000):
Bosman ruling, effects on 31–3;
broadcasting rights auction 30; club
owners and flotation culture 33–4;
coaching and management
qualifications 29–30;
commercialisation 30; managerial
responsibilities 34–5; overseas players
and managers, influx of 32–3
professional football (2000–2015):
coaching qualifications 37; financial
mismanagement 37–8; manager
appointments and turnover 36–7;
media celebrities 38; transfer market,
EU ruling 2001 35–6
Professional Footballers' Association
(PFA): FA recommended 122;
management qualifications 29, 37,
76, 77; maximum wage abolition 26;
overseas player ban lifted 32; transfer
compensation 31
public relations 21, 44
Puel, Claude 65

Queiroz, Carlos 54
Quinn, Mick 108

Ramsey, Alf 23, 25
Ramsey, George 19
Redknapp, Harry 52, 92, 95, 145
Reed, Les 62, 65
research methodology: balanced
involvement 13; data analysis and
presentation 4, 5; interviewee
selection 4–5; interviews 2–3;
limitations of study 154–5;
participatory action workshops 3–4
retain and transfer system 15, 25–6, 39n
Revie, Don 25, 27
Rice, Pat 54
Richardson, D. 94
Robinson, Peter 35
Robson, Bryan 46, 55, 68–9
Roderick, Martin 102, 115, 116, 122, 130, 134

Rodgers, Brendan 52, 77
Roeder, Glenn 37
Rotter, Julien 10, 144
Rous, Stanley 22

Sanchez, Lawrie 90
Scholar, Irving 34
Scottish Football Association 15, 143
Scott, Matt 136
Secretaries and Managers' Association 19
secretary-managers (pre-1940):
directors, hostility towards 21; media
links and raised profile 18–19, 21;
player behaviour, dealing with
17–18; public relations 21;
recruitment and training 18;
responsibilities 16, 19; role creation 16
Seed, Jimmy 20
Shackleton, Len 141–2
Shankly, Bill 25, 29
Shapiro, Susan P. 144
social capital 43–7, 49–50
Southampton 61, 62
Southgate, Gareth 37, 72, 104
specialist staff *see* backroom staff
Stam, Japp 65, 87
Stead, David 91–2, 121, 132
Sunderland 87
Sztompka, Piotr 138

talent identification 87–9
'tapping up' practices 41, 47–9, 84–5, 131
Taylor, Daniel 145
Taylor, Gordon 77
Taylor, Louise 87
Taylor, Matthew 27, 32–3, 38
Taylor, Peter 24, 54
theoretical frameworks: Granovetter's
contribution 8, 9–10; Weber's
contribution 5–8
Tottenham Hotspur: club flotation and
business orientation 33–4;
entrepreneurial owner 34; first
secretary-manager 16; Redknapp's
appointment 52, 145
Touré, Kolo 82
'tracksuit manager' 20, 24
traditional authority 53, 59, 75, 112–16

transfers: agents involvement 121, 130–1; Bosman ruling and player movement 31–3; EU ruling 2001 35–6; fee increases (1970's) 26; fees introduced 17; financial mismanagement 38, 140; player's bargaining powers 133; registration and contract system 80; retain and transfer system 15, 26, 39n

trust: agent and player trust 123; category-based 141; distrust, evolving process 141, 146, 148–9; embeddedness and trust 9–10, 138–9; interpersonal, building of 10–11, 42–3, 57–8, 144; knowledge-based 42–3, 143–4; loyalty and trust, value of 56–8, 83–4; multi-level approaches 9–11

UEFA: PRO Licence mandatory 37, 71; PRO Licence, value of 76–7; transfers and employment regulations 31, 36

Venglos, Jozef 33
Vogts, Berti 33

Waddington, Ivan 106
Walker, Jack 34
Watson, Tom 19
Weber, Max: charisma, aspects of 8, 60, 113, 117n; domination 7–8, 113; ideal types concept 6–7; legitimate authority 7–8; motivation and actions 5–6; traditional authority 53, 59, 75

Wenger, Arsène: Arsenal appointment 33, 45; backroom support 54; managerial pressures 2; managerial responsibilities 35; media celebrity 38; overseas networks 82; peer support 42; player control 116; recruitment success 79

West Ham 17, 145
Whittaker, Tom 20
Winterbottom, Walter 22
Wolverhampton Wanderers 104
Woodward, Clive 61
Wright, Ian 116

young professionals: African players' treatment 126; arrogance and celebrity seekers 104; intimidation and abuse towards 102–4; negotiations and manager tactics 128–9; socialisation into club culture 101–2, 110–11, 115

youth development schemes: Buckley's success 20; conformity and toleration 110–11, 115; contract reform of 1970's 26–7; player behaviour problems 94, 104; relegated by overseas influx 32; restrictions on transfers 36; scholarship system and recruitment 80